*BAD COMPANY*

# JOSEPH HENRY JACKSON

# BAD COMPANY

## THE STORY OF CALIFORNIA'S LEGENDARY AND ACTUAL STAGE-ROBBERS, BANDITS, HIGHWAYMEN AND OUTLAWS FROM THE FIFTIES TO THE EIGHTIES.

University of Nebraska Press
Lincoln and London

*Publishers on the Plains*

**UNP**

Some of the material in the "Joaquin Murieta" section first appeared in *The Pacific Spectator*, by whose permission it is used here.

*First Bison Book printing: 1977*
Most recent printing indicated by first digit below:
    2    3    4    5    6    7    8    9    10

**Library of Congress Cataloging in Publication Data**

Jackson, Joseph Henry, 1894–1955.
  Bad company.
  Reprint of the 1st ed. published by Harcourt, Brace, New York.
  Four of the chapters were published in 1939 under the title: Tintypes in gold.
  "Notes on sources": p. 327
  Includes index.
  1. Outlaws—California—Biography.
2. California—Biography. 3. California—History—1850–1950. I. Title.
F866.J24    1977    979.4'04'0922    [B]    77–7300
ISBN 0–8032–0930–4
ISBN 0–8032–5866–6 pbk.

Bison Book edition published by arrangement with Charlotte C. Jackson.

Manufactured in the United States of America

*TO CHARLOTTE*

# CONTENTS

INTRODUCTION

N THE FIRST YEAR OF THE CAL-
ifornia gold rush there grew up a concept which found its
way into songs and skits, into news stories, into comic books
of the day, and finally into the public mind. Though a
stereotype, it was essentially a stereotype with reason behind it. This was the character of the "Honest Miner," unfortunate perhaps in his pursuit of riches, scrabble-bearded
and ragged, reckless with his money, yet a man in whose
eye a letter from home might start a tear, a rough and
hardy frontiersman but one who would always stand by his
"pard," who would impulsively adopt a baby in some
"Roaring Camp," defend the rights of others, and trust
implicitly in the honesty of his neighbor. This "Honest
Miner" was to some extent the creation of the romantic
fictioneer of a later time, but there was truth behind the
highly colored portrait. In its first year, the gold rush was
largely a fine and exciting game organized, so to put it, by
a crowd of good friends. A miner could and did leave his
tools at his claim as sole evidence that this square of ground
or that river frontage was taken up; he could walk away

confident that other miners would respect his claim. A miner could and did carry gold dust in quantity on his person without being molested. Whether or not the "Honest Miner" was quite as emotional, as solidly heart-of-gold as the storytellers made him, he was a miner and he was honest, or at any rate ninety-nine times out of a hundred.

But in the second year of the rush the picture underwent a startling change. An observant Scot named Hugo Reid who had long been a rancher in California put it plainly in a letter to a friend. "Do not go to the mines on any account," he wrote. "They are loaded to the muzzle with vagabonds from every quarter of the globe, scoundrels from nowhere . . . assassins manufactured in Hell for the express purpose of converting highways and byways into theaters of blood!"

Hugo Reid knew what he was talking about. The California gold mines were filling up with bad characters, sometimes from the East or from Sydney prisons, who had come to the mines to pick up fortunes by their wits, sometimes from California itself, men who had begun honestly enough but had been forced more or less by circumstances into evil ways. The winter of 1849-50 was exceptionally hard; supplies could not get through to the mines, and thousands had to leave the placers for the new, mushrooming towns and cities which could not absorb them. Too, there was the harsh treatment given the "foreigner" by the American miner who resented the Mexican and the *Californio* especially and set up fantastic taxes to keep them out of the mines. Nor did it stop at taxes; Mexicans, Peruvians, and Chileños were beaten, driven off their claims, robbed, and often enough killed on the slightest pretext or none at all. It was natural that many of these should take to the road in revenge, or, in the case of the unemployed American, simply to make a living.

By 1850, then, rascals were common in the gold region. No man's property or life could be called safe. The easygoing days of the "Honest Miner" were gone. And the gold-seeker found that he had to do something about it or leave the whole foothill country to the "scoundrels from nowhere."

He did something about it. An Englishman, Frank Marryat, noted the change when he observed that practically everybody in the mines now carried a gun, "generally a Colt's revolver, buckled behind, with no attempt at concealment." He wrote, too, that in the mines "it is prudent to look on every man as a rogue until you know him to be honest." After he had a chance to see how the Colt's-revolver method worked, however, he came to a further conclusion: "From the fact of all men being armed, robberies are less frequent in the mines than would be expected."

This was true. In a very short time robbery in the gold-mining country once more became relatively rare, this time simply because it did not pay. A few tried it, as the reader will discover in this book. Tom Bell and Rattlesnake Dick were among those who thought themselves clever enough. But Bell was unceremoniously strung up to a tree, and Dick was shot to death in a running gunfight with officers of the law. The lesson was not long in making itself felt. Outlawry of the planned and organized kind did not thrive in the mines. Though the five "Joaquins," of whom Murieta was one, began their careers of robbery and violence in the gold region, they soon left it; when they were run to earth in 1853 it was in the unexplored fastnesses of the Coast Range, several hundred miles away, that they had set up headquarters. The brutal Tiburcio Vasquez, bandit of a few years later, chose the same spot for his stronghold. Even Black Bart, the greatest—and mildest— of the lone stage-robbers, held up most of his stages on the extreme outer fringe of the mining region and often in parts of the State wholly remote from the gold fields.

It is clear, in view of this, why H. H. Bancroft, California's first great historian, chose to introduce his chapter on bandits and banditry with this heavily ironic paragraph: "There seems to be a prejudice in some quarters against the profession of highwayman. It has become the custom of our refined and discriminating civilization, when such a person is caught, to kill him; for which reason many good men have been kept out of the profession, and have in consequence fallen into evil ways." Bancroft may have been reading De Quincey; his approach here is more than a little reminiscent of that essayist's remark that he deplored the act of murder because it so often led to "robbery, drinking and Sabbath-breaking, and from that to incivility and procrastination." But there is no doubt that Bancroft was quite right. There had developed in California, and most strongly in the mines where a man had to act quickly and harshly in his own interest, a profound and actively expressed prejudice against the profession of highwayman. It was not long either before the prejudice became general, and all Californians determined upon a concerted effort to clean out the nests of cattle-and-horse-thieving robbers and the daring lone holdup men who were making the roads so dangerous for an honest citizen and his money. The effort, prolonged and persistent, was made, though it was the middle Seventies before the last of the outlaw gangs was dispersed, and the early Eighties when the last of the great lone bandits, Black Bart, was caught. And, as the reader will see, it became less and less a question of Judge Lynch and Colt's revolvers buckled behind, and more a matter of duly appointed sheriffs and deputies doing their jobs.

In this book the reader will find a little of the story, not told as straightaway history but rather in the form of sketches of some colorful individuals engaged in the bandit trade, especially those who were among the sharpest thorns in the side of a California which was trying hard to grow up. None of these sketches is, or pretends to be, a detailed biography of its subject, nor have I set out to develop fully the character of any of these bandits, outlaws, stage-robbers, and stickup men. I have selected certain notables out of a notably bad company of men who, in one way or another, preyed upon Californians in the State's earliest days. These are here caught, by an imperfect camera, at certain highlighted moments in their careers. As far as I could, I have made the portraits accurate, but shapes and lines thin out and are distorted by time; when one examines even the brightest and clearest of the contemporary likenesses-in-print—and many reporters of that day wrote with fine clarity and vigor—one finds areas that are weakly illuminated, false shadows, the subjects too obviously posed in stiff, unnatural positions. The sketches in this book are therefore tintypes, no more, which is what I meant to suggest when four of them were published ten years ago under the title *Tintypes in Gold*. Yet I believe that in some cases a true and reasonably three-dimensional portrait has been accomplished, though often it varies widely from the picture to which readers, particularly Cali-

fornians, have become accustomed. Also, while my bandit-
subjects obligingly permitted me to try to bring them into
focus, I was aware that something else appeared, though
less sharply as was proper, on the ground-glass finder. This
was the background—the struggle for order in the new
community on the newest American frontier. It began with
the gold rush, lasted three decades, more or less, and eventually attained its goal in spite of two common miscon-
ceptions described by Josiah Royce when he wrote: "One
was that on the whole there was no struggle, the other
that on the whole there was no order." As Royce added,
there were both, and the careers here described are evidence
in their way that Royce saw the truth. That there was a
struggle, and that order finally came of it, appears too in
what the reader may see reflected—obliquely, since this is
a book primarily about bandits and not about their captors
—in the glimpses he will get of the peace officers of the
time as they went about their business. Such men as James
B. Hume, first sheriff of Hangtown and then Wells,
Fargo's chief of detectives; Harry N. Morse, long sheriff
of Alameda County across the great Bay from San Francisco; and many more performed their tasks with the careful, methodical persistence of the first-rate policeman, and
their contribution, often made in the face of a niggling,
carping, and hostile press, was of the highest importance in
California's long shaking-down process. Some day a writer
with an eye for their admirable though less picturesque
traits of character, will give them their due. Meantime our
concern is their quarry.

One more point may be made. It is the habit, when a
law-breaker is finally put out of the way, to romanticize
him. His defiance of the rules by which other men find it

expedient to regulate their conduct touches a sympathetic chord in certain hearts and, in spite of all evidence to the contrary, by the time an outlaw may properly be mentioned in the past tense he has become, nine times out of ten, a daring, gallant, rip-snorting sort of fellow who has done no more than take from society what was rightfully his, and therefore deserves to be remembered only for his courage, his expert horsemanship, his unvarying politeness to the ladies. Such matters as any small murders he may have committed, his robberies, and his general brutality may be no more than barely mentioned, and then with a deprecating smile. It is doubtful whether the victims of such banditti would hold to this view, but by the time the sentimentalizers get to their work (each so industriously rewriting those who have preceded him, and each adding his own tidbits according to his fancy), it is likely to be too late for the victim to put forward his first-hand opinion.

For these and other reasons I have tried here to stick to the facts as these are available in the files of old newspapers, in prison records, in the voluminous account-books and reports of Wells, Fargo & Company, and similar sources, and when these run counter to the legend I have attempted to weigh the evidence and come to a conclusion. I am aware that such image-breaking is not always enthusiastically received. There are many who prefer to cherish the romantic legend, however much it may be shown to be pure fantasy; and I suppose there is no good reason why they should not do so. Nevertheless it has seemed to me worth while to assemble the facts as far as they may be determined, and to set them down in some sort of order for the sake of the reader or student who may prefer his history—and his bandits—that way. Because it is also a fact, as many know, that frequently the truth is by all odds more interesting than the fiction. To my mind, at least, that final fact is demonstrated more than once in this book.

Working on a book of this kind, involving as it does constant reference to early-day records, the author incurs first of all an honest obligation to the long-gone, anonymous editors and reporters for the early-day newspapers in whose columns the digger-after-facts, if he is patient and persistent, can find something about almost anything, but especially about such disturbers of the peace as those with whose careers this book concerns itself. Though they often wrote floridly, in the style of their time, those newsmen were careful about details; even better, the custom of the press then encouraged the expression of opinion, and in the stories written for the early papers about the bandits and robbers whose activities were news, the student today may find bits of color, anecdote, and personal opinion which are invaluable in building up a just and reasonable portrait of the individual in whose likeness he is interested. To these early editors and reporters, then, this acknowledgment of indebtedness.

Hundreds of others were helpful in varying degrees during the task of running down the details of robberies, pursuits, prison-terms, and the like. I should like to thank especially Mabel Gillis, Librarian of the California State Library, and Caroline Wenzel, head of the California Room there, whose broad knowledge of the early California scene has aided so many writers in that field; George P. Hammond, Director of the Bancroft Library at the

University of California in Berkeley, and his Assistant
Director, Eleanor Bancroft, and especially Librarian Frank
Brezee who found for me the clue that led to the story of
Sheet-Iron Jack; Guy J. Giffen, specialist in Far Western
bandits and their history, and Mrs. Guy J. Giffen, Secre-
tary of the Society of California Pioneers; Mrs. Edna
Martin Parratt, Managing Director of the California Historical Society; Douglas C. Rigg, Assistant Warden of
the California State Prison at San Quentin, whose patient
checking of old records enabled me to be sure of dates
sometimes badly scrambled in early accounts; G. W.
Wickland and George Dawson, of the Wells, Fargo Bank
& Union Trust Company of San Francisco, and Miss
Catherine Harroun and Miss Irene Simpson of that bank's
History Room for their help in making available to me
the early records of Wells, Fargo & Company, particularly
those concerning Detective James B. Hume and his work
as bandit-catcher for the Company; Samuel J. Hume, son
of Detective Hume, who allowed me to examine many of
his father's letters and scrapbooks; Thomas W. Streeter of
Morristown, New Jersey, who gave me permission to make
photostats of his unique copy of John Rollin Ridge's
*Murieta;* Savoie Lottinville of the University of Okla-
homa Press, who found for me Ridge's letter to his Cherokee cousin, Stand Watie, which cleared up for the first
time the mystery of that original *Murieta's* scarcity; Ed
Grabhorn of The Grabhorn Press in San Francisco, who
let me photograph two interesting early paintings in which
the artist had put on canvas his idea of Joaquin Murieta;
Franklin Walker of Mills College, pioneer in tracing the
ramifications of the Murieta legend from the original
Ridge semi-fiction, and Francis P. Farquhar who elabo-

rated on the same theme; Mrs. Ethel de la Montanya Newell, granddaughter of Sheriff, later Detective, Harry N. Morse, for very useful information about her grandfather; George Fields of San Francisco, who gave me a copy of the Beadle Dime Library's thriller of 1884, *The Gold-Dragon*, in which, though its author purported to write of *Black Bart, the PO-8*, there is little likeness to any bandit living or dead; John J. Newbegin, San Francisco bookseller, whose encyclopedic memory for odds and ends of relevant fact and whose willingness to run down a reference often helped me to be sure of a name or a place; Tom Harbinson who put me in the way of one or two enormously useful clues by the gift of a book I badly needed; Ben Macomber of the San Francisco *Chronicle*, who completed for me one elusive but greatly needed historical verification that contributed to the Vasquez story; Eric Cochrane of Berkeley, a most helpful sideline observer on all matters pertaining to Murieta; and Marjorie Brown, Librarian of the San Francisco *Chronicle*, and her staff, for helping to check details too numerous to mention.

JOSEPH HENRY JACKSON

*Berkeley, California*

# JOAQUIN MURIETA

**F**ROM THE BEGINNING OF TIME men have needed heroes. Invariably, too, men have found that if no true hero comes handy they must invent him. The observation is not new; it has often been made, and of gods as well as heroes.

Moreover, a hero is peculiarly necessary where men are engaged in some especially difficult task. In America the legends of Davy Crockett, Mike Fink, Paul Bunyan, John Henry, and many others testify to this. The new, expanding West required such men and they sprang into being. The process is a familiar one; the layman, as well as the folklorist, recognizes it for what it is and though he may choose to believe uncritically, almost always makes allowances at the back of his mind.

In the 1850s the gold-mining region of California was the newest West. The trouble was that while fighting Injuns and alligators, conquering the Mississippi with flatboat fleets, logging off the great north woods, or laying ten thousand miles of steel rail were achievements that called for giants and were therefore celebrated by the emergence of gigantic heroes, the search for gold was another matter.

Digging and washing the river gravels was hard labor, but it was not dramatic hard labor; a hero hip-deep in an icy mountain torrent is a chilly hero at best; there is pertinacity, perhaps, but no proper greatness merely in subsisting on moldy pork and soggy biscuit in order to get rich. A dyspeptic shaking with ague is not the stuff of which men build a legend.

California's folk-hero, then, if there was to be one at all, had to be some figure other than the patiently grubbing, usually unlucky, ragged and fever-ridden "honest miner."

Such a figure had long existed in men's folk-memories. He was the hero who had sprung spontaneously to life whenever and wherever some people had much and others had nothing. He was, in every land, the man who took from the rich and gave to the poor. He was the Dashing Outlaw, in whose person all might find recklessly displayed their own hidden defiances, their private longings to be something both worse and better than they had it in them to be. In California, in the fantastic early 1850s when he was needed, no such heroic figure existed, but that did not matter. The Forty-niners invented him, and called him by the name of a marauding cattle-thief who did exist—Joaquin Murieta.

Here the reader may wonder exactly how the legend was crystallized. If, as one of the State's soundest historians has said, Murieta was "Never anything but a vicious and abandoned character, low, brutal, and cruel, intrinsically and at heart a thief and a cut-throat," how did the popular picture of Murieta as a gay and daring Robin Hood take shape? If, as is the fact, the romantic story of Joaquin Murieta has become a firm fixture in California's mythology—so firm that it is considered historical truth by most Californians—how did it get there? At what point did Murieta begin to move out of the realm of fable and become in fact a flesh-and-blood hero with all the trimmings? Or, if one prefers, the other way round? Fortunately it is possible for the student to put his finger precisely upon the source. A best-selling pamphlet began the whole thing.

Part of the purpose of this essay is to trace the Murieta story in some of its more curious aspects as it took on the form in which it has been repeated and believed down the years, rewritten into solemn "biographical studies," made into plays, poems, and motion pictures, becoming finally an accepted part of a softly lighted, rosy panorama of California's early days in which giants walked the land, fabulous nuggets of gold turned up on every claim, and the bearded miner wept gentle tears as he wrote his letters home in such odd moments as he could spare from prying fortunes out of the rocks with his knife and throwing his poke of dust on the faro table. The gold rush was not very much like that. Nor was Murieta anything at all like the gallant outlaw legend has made him. Perhaps it will be instructive to examine, first, the facts about Murieta, up to the point when an unsuccessful journalist in San Francisco decided he might pay his more urgent debts by writing a little book about a bandit.

In 1848 and 1849, the California foothills, in which there seemed to be hidden an endless supply of gold, were not yet overcrowded. When the site of one discovery mushroomed into a thriving camp it was always possible to strike off into the hills, locate another creek or river-fork, and take your chance on what you might find. In another year or two this was no longer the case. The rush had funneled its tens of thousands into the gold region, and it was becoming clear that the area was limited; beyond certain fairly well defined bounds there was no gold, and the business of mining became fiercely competitive.

One of the ways to get rid of competition is to eliminate competitors, and this is what happened in the mines. Logic had nothing to do with it, wherefore no one saw anything strange about defining Mexicans, along with Chinese and Chileans and others, as "foreigners." California had been a Mexican province, to be sure; it had been conquered and taken from Mexico a scant three years or so earlier. But it was American country now, and the Pike County Missourians, the Yankees who had come venturing around the Horn and across the plains, even the "Sydney ducks" who had made their way from Britain's penal colony in Australia, suddenly grew very righteous indeed about just who would be permitted to mine gold. They began by imposing heavy taxes and went on to plain violence, publicly whipping, and even sometimes hanging, such "foreigners" as failed to obey the harsh regulations designed to force them out of the mines. The Chinese suffered least; accustomed to bending before authority, they industriously washed the tailings in camps which American miners had deserted for newer strikes, kept to themselves, paid their tax, and prospered in their way. But the Mexican miners were a different breed. Few of them found it easy to play the part of a lesser race; it seemed to them that if a German or a Frenchman or an Italian could come to California and freely dig for gold, they could and should be allowed to do the same. The "American" miner, therefore, selected the Mexican as his chief target when he wanted to get competition out of the way. The Mexicans had lost the war, hadn't they? A Mexican was just a Mexican, wasn't he? Besides, there were more of him.

By the early Fifties, California realized that several Mexicans, presumably miners who had been dispossessed by Americans, had made up their minds to prey upon those who had refused them the right to look for gold. Some of these thieves made a regular business of it, running off cattle, stealing horses, holding up lonely travelers and relieving them of their purses, sticking up saloons and stores. Some of the more successful at the business had even begun to build up full-sized gangs. Doubtless many of these bad characters kept bad company because they preferred it; certainly not all of them had turned bandit because of unfair treatment at the Yankees' hands. But at the time it was generally admitted that, in many cases, otherwise decent Mexicans had taken to robbery and the like after rough warnings to leave a good claim or suffer the consequences. There were enough of them, at all events, so that Californians grew seriously concerned about the depredations these outlaw bands were committing. Newspapers, after their fashion, called upon the authorities to protect the citizenry, stating in ringing editorials that something must be done.

For a year or two little was accomplished beyond the discovery that the most notable among these banditti all seemed to be named "Joaquin." By putting various reports together, it was found that there were at least five such Joaquins, surnamed Carrillo, Valenzuela, Ocomorenia, Botellier (or "Botilleras"), and Murieta. Whether these headed separate bands or were members of one group no one could be certain. All that was known was that "Joaquin" seemed to be extraordinarily ubiquitous; he could steal fifty head of cattle far down the great Valley, and at the same hour on the same day relieve a wayfarer of his gold dust two hundred miles to the north on the outskirts of Murphy's Diggings. It was confusing, to say the least. It was also sufficiently annoying so that the press kept urging the State legislature to do something about it.

In the spring of 1853, the legislature finally did. The first proposal was that the State of California offer a reward of five thousand dollars for "Joaquin," dead or alive. Mr. J. M. Covarrubias, of the Committee on Military Affairs, demurred. Very sensibly he pointed out that to set a price upon the head of an individual who had neither been examined nor convicted of any crime was to proceed upon the assumption of his guilt—a method of approach to the problem not exactly in keeping with the dignity of a great state. Further, said Mr. Covarrubias, the offer of so large a reward might lead individuals eager for the cash to bring in any Mexican they might be able to bushwhack; since no one was quite sure what "Joaquin" looked like, it would be difficult to know just how to pay a reward. Over and above this, he added, one of the many "Joaquins" was called Carrillo, and there were several perfectly respectable citizens of the State, including a judge, who bore that name. The legislature listened to him, but the pressures were great and something had to be done. The matter of the reward was officially forgotten. Instead, the legislators passed an act authorizing a transplanted Texan named Harry Love to raise a company of mounted rangers, not to exceed twenty men, to muster these into the service of the State for three months unless sooner discharged by the Governor, and to lead them in an attempt to capture the "party or gang of robbers commanded by the five Joaquins," naming these separately. It is clear enough from this that Californians knew no more about Murieta than about Valenzuela or the other Joaquins. The Governor approved the act on May 11, 1853, and Captain Harry Love and his rangers went out to see what they could find. Their keenness may have been whetted by the fact that Governor Bigler, on his own responsibility, had posted a reward of one thousand dollars for any Joaquin captured or killed.

Captain Love and his men rode up and down the valleys and into the hills of the coast range where one Joaquin or another had been reported. Some of the rangers were solid enough citizens, but others were notorious in different ways. One, named Harvey, had killed Major Savage, locally famous as leader of the battalion that had found Yosemite Valley. Another named Herbert afterward distinguished himself by shooting a waiter in a hotel dining room in Washington. Captain Harry Love himself eventually lost his reason and came to his end barricaded in his home and shooting it out with a posse which, in his madness, he conceived to be an army of enemies who had long plotted his destruction. At any rate, the captain and his rangers, good and bad, rode up and down California for two months without results. It was beginning to look as though maybe the ninety-day enlistment would run out before they found even one Joaquin. In that case no one would collect the Governor's thousand dollars.

Then, on July 25, the rangers found some Mexicans. Piecing together the stories of Harry Love and various members of his group, it is possible to get at least an approximate idea of what happened.

Some of the rangers, riding in the general region of the Panoche Pass, to the west of Tulare Lake, came upon a party of men, evidently Mexicans, sitting on the ground around a fire with their horses some distance away. Harry Love may or may not have been with his men at this moment; there has been long and heated argument on the point. As was natural, the rangers asked questions. The questions were resented, chiefly by one Mexican who is said to have remarked that he was the leader and that the rangers had better talk to him if they wanted to know anything. Suddenly both groups were shooting. In the melee the man who had claimed to be the leader was killed. Another was badly wounded but led the rangers a long chase before he fell dead; this one was later identified as Manuel Garcia, called "Three-Fingered Jack," a known thief and murderer for whom the law had been searching for some years. Several of the band got to their horses and escaped. Two were captured alive; of these one succeeded in drowning himself while being taken to the jail in Mariposa, and the other, safely delivered there by the rangers, was seized by a mob and hanged, the rumor at the time being that the lynching was committed not by enraged citizens but by a group of fellow-Mexicans who feared he might tell too much. As for the two dead men, Garcia's head had been so badly damaged by a pistol ball that there was no use trying to keep it; instead, his mutilated hand was cut off and preserved in spirits. The head of the other, the one who had said he was leader of the band though no ranger ever testified that he had declared his name, was cut off and similarly preserved in a jar of alcohol. With these tangible

proofs that they had at least captured and killed somebody, the rangers rode northward, losing one of their
prisoners at a river crossing, as has been noted, and de-
livering the other to the sheriff in Mariposa, then heading
for Sacramento where a severed head, not to mention a
three-fingered hand, would entitle them to their pay and
to the reward so generously offered by the Governor himself.

It is interesting to observe here that when the news got
into print a few days later, the newspaper stories mentioned no surname; all of them noted the capture and
death of "Joaquin" but that was all. Which Joaquin? No
one said anything about that. The Quartzburg correspondent of the San Francisco *Alta*, more alert than most, wrote
his letter to the paper on July 27, briefly describing the
killing of "the notorious murderer and robber, Joaquin,"
and adding that Captain Love was on his way to the
capital with "the head of Joaquin preserved in spirits."
The San Francisco *Herald* had a similar story; its reporter
wrote that Captain Love had captured and killed "The
famous bandit, Joaquin, whose name is associated with a
hundred deeds of blood." The reader will observe that
nowhere was there any discussion of an outlaw called
Murieta. It was not that anyone was concerned to hide his
name or any name. Joaquin was Joaquin, that was all. No
one knew which of the lot had been captured and no one
cared much, so long as the cattle-stealing was stopped and
the sovereign State of California had shown it could protect its citizens.

There was still the matter of the reward, and to the
student today it looks very much as though there must have
been skulduggery somewhere. Only Harry Love and his

band were authorized to go out and capture Joaquin-Whatever-His-Name-Was. Only Harry Love and his company could collect the Governor's reward. By an act of the legislature, the rangers' task was set as the capture of Joaquin—Murieta, Carrillo, or anyway some Joaquin. What more natural than that Captain Love and his men should do what they were by law authorized to do? They rode out, and they rode about, and they rode back again with a head preserved in a bottle. You don't collect a reward on an unnamed head; so much is obvious. Therefore the head was duly "recognized" as belonging to one of the Joaquins, namely Murieta. The reward was collected and so were ninety days' wages for twenty rangers and their captain. Still better, a short time later a generous legislature, stimulated thereto by someone unspecified, decided that one thousand dollars was nowhere near enough for such an achievement, and voted an additional five thousand dollars to Captain Harry Love and his men.

It is not surprising that the whisper of shenanigans got about. Indeed, less than a month after the capture and beheading were announced, the editor of the San Francisco *Alta* was voicing openly what so many were hinting. On August 23, 1853, he printed his story:

> It affords amusement to our citizens (he wrote) to read the various accounts of the capture and decapitation of "the notorious Joaquin Murieta." The humbug is so transparent that it is surprising any sensible person can be imposed upon by the statements of the affair which have appeared in the prints. A few weeks ago a party of native Californians and Sonorians started for the Tulare Valley for the expressed and avowed purpose of running mustangs. Three of the party have returned and report that they were attacked by a party of Americans, and that the balance of their party, four in number, had

been killed; that Joaquin Valenzuela, one of them, was killed
as he was endeavoring to escape, and that his head was cut
off by his captors and held as a trophy. It is too well known
that Joaquin Murieta was not the person killed by Captain
Harry Love's party at the Panoche Pass. The head recently
exhibited in Stockton bears no resemblance to that individual,
and this is positively asserted by those who have seen the real
Murieta and the spurious head.

But the *Alta's* editor was not content with this. He had
his own ideas about Captain Love and his crowd, and he
was willing to express those too. He continued, testily:

All the accounts wind up by recommending the continuing
of Love's company in service. All right. The term of service
was about expiring, and although I will not say that interested
parties have gotten up this Joaquin expedition, yet such ex-
peditions can generally be traced to have an origin with a few
speculators.

In conclusion, the *Alta* had its word also on this whole
situation of too many Joaquins:

At the time of the murder of General Bean at Mission San
Gabriel, Murieta was strongly suspected of the crime and efforts were made to arrest him but he managed to escape. Since
then, every murder and robbery in the country has been attributed to "Joaquin." Sometimes it is Joaquin Carrillo that
has committed all these crimes; then it is Joaquin Murieta,
then Joaquin something else, but always *Joaquin!* The very
act of the Legislature authorizing a Company to capture "the
five Joaquins" was in itself a farce, and these names were
inserted in order to kill the bill.

Clearly the *Alta's* view was that the whole affair was
a humbug, and that Captain Love and his men had got
themselves a Mexican head—Valenzuela's, perhaps, or
another's—had arranged for affidavits that it was Muri-

eta's head, since he was wanted for the specific crime of murdering General Bean and his capture would reflect the greatest credit on them, collected their reward and their pay, and called it a day.

In the light of later knowledge—the legislature's subsequent authorization of another five thousand dollars to Captain Love—it looks as though the *Alta* might have been on the right track. The so-called "Head of Murieta" was shown in different museums for many years, though it was never completely accepted as Murieta's and was constantly the subject of debate. There were arguments also as to Joaquin himself, where he had come from in the first place, what crimes he had actually committed, whether he had gone back to Mexico if the head-in-spirits was really not his. For many years the debate raged, off and on, in the newspapers. Once a story turned up that William Henderson, the ranger who was said to have performed the decapitation, was dogged at night by the ghost of "Joaquin," demanding in sepulchral tones that his head be returned forthwith; the haunting visitation was said to be driving that hitherto respectable man to drink. But no one had good proof of anything; that was what it came to. For every affidavit there was a denial. The first printed poster advertising the exhibition of the grisly preserved head (and the hand of Three-Fingered Jack) further confused the issue by spelling the name "Muriatta." The *Alta* contributed a final tidbit by stating categorically that " 'Joaquin' is a fabulous character only, and this is widely known." As for the public, it believed what it chose to believe. Before long the entire story had begun to grow into a legend.

2

Just what form the Murieta legend might have taken if left to itself is a matter for speculation now. For something happened to give it definite shape. This was a little paper-covered book, *The Life and Adventures of Joaquin Murieta, Celebrated California Bandit*, by John Rollin Ridge, a part-Cherokee journalist and poet known by his Indian pen name, "Yellow Bird," who wrote and published it in San Francisco in 1854 to make his fortune. The fortune got away from Ridge, even though his book caught on splendidly, was pirated and reprinted in several languages, was poetized, dramatized, remade three-quarters of a century later into a "biography" and even brought to the screen. But the highly colored yarn accomplished something, nine-tenths pure invention though it was. It is not too much to say that Ridge, in his preposterous little book, actually created both the man, Murieta, and the Murieta legend as these stand today.

John Rollin Ridge, however dubious he may have been as a historian and biographer, understood his public's relish for good strong storytelling. His *Joaquin Murieta*, now an excessively rare volume in its first edition, admirably fitted the pattern of the time. Here at last was the hero the public had been looking for. And though Ridge's narrative, masquerading as fact, was a palpable fiction, abounding in "conversations" between Murieta and his men in secret caves and the like, it was nobly decorated with rhetorical flourishes, built frankly to Robin Hood specifications, and altogether exactly what Californians wanted to hear. Consider for a moment Ridge's picture of the Joaquin nobody really knew.

Murieta, as Ridge depicts him (and as the legend to this day devoutly insists he was), is a young man of excellent reputation, "gracefully built and active as a young tiger." He has turned outlaw because a party of American miners (*a*) raped his lovely young wife, Rosita, before his eyes, (*b*) hanged his brother in his presence on a trumped-up charge of horse-stealing, and (*c*) tied Joaquin himself to a tree and whipped him—a series of events which might well have soured the sweetest character. It was no more than natural, Ridge feels, that Joaquin should swear "an oath of the most awful solemnity, that his soul should nevermore know peace until his hands were dyed deep in the blood of his enemies!" Adds Ridge, plainly aware of the exigencies of chapter-to-chapter suspense, "Fearfully did he keep his oath, as the following pages will show!"

Ridge's narrative lives up to this promise. With his beautiful Rosita, Joaquin takes to the hills, gathers about him a group of satellites including Rosita's brother and the fearsome Three-Fingered Jack, and proceeds to rob and kill at a pace any flesh-and-blood bandit would have been hard pressed to maintain. Ridge himself grants that "the scenes of murder and robbery shifted with the rapidity of lightning." Yet, with all this slaughter, theft, and hairbreadth escaping, Joaquin finds time to succor maidens whom others of his gang would despoil ("Young woman, you've heard of Joaquin Murieta. I am the man. When you hear people abusing me hereafter, perhaps you'll think I'm not quite so big a scoundrel as they say I am, after all!"), to reward humble men who aid him, to punish those who would betray him to the law, all the while keeping his hot-headed subordinates firmly in hand. Even the ruffianly Three-Fingered Jack quails before his young chieftain, though he is the sort who can (and does) growl, after a day of hanging up Chinese miners by their queues and slitting their throats, "Ah, Murieta, this has been a great day! Damn 'em! How my knife lapped up their blood!" Yet for all his firmness of character, Ridge's Joaquin has his sentimental moments too, as when he encounters a one-time friend, the only American who has really been decent to him. Murieta, writes Ridge, embraced his old acquaintance. Then, " 'Joe,' said he, as he brushed a tear from his eye, 'I am not the man that I was. I am a deep-dyed scoundrel, but so help me God! I was driven to it by oppression and wrong!' " After sufficient adventures, Ridge concludes his tale with a summary of the newspaper accounts which record Joaquin's death and decapitation at the hands of Captain Love and his rangers, hinting by way of climax that this taking-off came only just in time, since Murieta was about ready to execute his grand plan for a full-dress revolution against the hated "Yankees."

It is a question, of course, how much of this yarn was accepted as fact when it was first published. Californians may have relished such well-spiced reading, but they had known the truth after all; they must have been aware that Ridge was telling a tall tale. Moreover, the many readers of *The Pioneer* must have noted the odd similarity between an incident in one of the *Shirley Letters* which had appeared in that magazine—in whose editor's office Ridge was a familiar visitor—and Ridge's story of the indignity which finally drove Joaquin to banditry. Dame Shirley's account of a Mexican tied to a tree and whipped, and her scornful comments upon American miners who would commit such an act, are, to say the least, curiously like Ridge's story about Joaquin, published so soon afterward, not to mention his heavily ironic remarks about "these *very* superior specimens of the much-vaunted Anglo-Saxon race!"

At all events the little book was headed for success because it was good, gory adventure, and the Robin Hood formula is always sure-fire. And this might have been the sum of it but for a bit of bad luck. Collectors in the field have long wondered why copies of Ridge's original story were so scarce. Other pamphlets as slim (Ridge's is a ninety-page affair, covered in yellow paper) have survived well enough. The answer turned up a few years ago in a volume, *Cherokee Cavaliers*, in which appears a letter written by Ridge from Marysville, California, on October 9, 1854, to his Cherokee cousin, Stand Watie. Ridge's purpose in the letter is to ask Watie to finance him in a newspaper, to be published "somewhere in Arkansas or some place where it will be safe from the commotion of Cherokee affairs," and "devoted to the interest of the Indian race." In the letter Ridge also says that he has not done too well in California, and continues "I expected to have made a great deal of money off of my book, my life of Joaquin Murieta (a copy of which I have sent you) and my publishers, after selling 7,000 copies and putting the money in their pockets, fled, bursted up, *tee totally* smashed, and left me, with a hundred others, to whistle for our money!" He adds that he hopes to have the book published next in the "Atlantic states," but there is no evidence that anything came of that plan. Thus the door was left open for what happened next.

Five years went by; just enough time for the Murieta

story to make its way into the folklore of California, for the detailed and circumstantial fiction to become confused with the original slim body of fact. Then the editor of the California *Police Gazette* decided, in the autumn of 1859, that his public would enjoy the "true" story of Joaquin Murieta as a serial. For his paper, an anonymous writer reworked Ridge's yarn, changing names here and there, but following Ridge in all essentials, even to some of the dialogue. The *Gazette* published it in ten issues as *The Life of Joaquin Murieta, Brigand Chief of California*, with illustrations by a well-known artist of the time, Charles Christian Nahl. This "revised" version was followed by the *Life* in the form of a paper-bound book under the same imprint. Now, whether Ridge liked it or not, his story of the bandit was really launched. There were some differences in this pirated version; the *Gazette's* rewrite man called Murieta's wife "Carmela" instead of Rosita, allowing the American miners to kill as well as ravish her, and inventing a second mistress, "Clarina." It is this twist that enables the student to trace the many re-piratings and re-publishings which began at once; almost all of them are "Carmela-Clarina" versions, probably not from the serial publication but from the *Gazette's* paper-back, which enjoyed an even wider sale than Ridge's own book.

These stolen editions appeared first in Spain and Mexico, and Joaquin became in those countries almost as great a legend as in California—always, now, as "Murieta," the head-in-alcohol and Ridge's story having established the name. From Spain, the story traveled to France and thence to Chile, where a Roberto Hyenne was the "author," publishing his work in Santiago as a translation from the French. In this printing, the Mexican Mu-

rieta naturally becomes *El Bandido Chileño*. Mexico
picked up that edition (the bibliographical story here is
as fascinating to the specialist as a detective tale) and re-
issued it with minor changes, of course moving Murieta
back into Mexico for his birth. Curiously, Spain re-pirated
Hyenne's version under a Barcelona imprint, as *El Cabal-
lero Chileño*, by a "Profesor" Acigar.

As this juggling of editions began to get fairly under
way, one Charles E. B. Howe of San Francisco made the
Ridge, or "Rosita," version into a five-act play, *Joaquin
Murieta de Castillo*. In this considerably overblown drama,
Joaquin's wife is called Belloro, which the author obligingly "translates" as Golden Bell, and one lesser character
is rather charmingly spelled as though he were an adjective
—"Ignacious." There is no record that Mr. Howe's play
was ever performed, in spite of the properly moral conclusion expressed in the final speech, which was given to
Captain Harry Love to declaim as the dying bandit sank
to the ground: "Crime brings its own reward, and the
stern hand of justice deals out the weight of punishment!"
(Mr. Howe evidently felt that the stage was no place
for such bloody affairs as decapitation or manuscission.)
This drama may have helped give circulation to the story
that Joaquin, on seeing a poster in which the State of
California offered five thousand dollars for him, dead or
alive, scrawled beneath the offer "I will give $10,000"
and signed it. As the reader has already seen, the State was
prevented from making any such offer by the good common
sense of Legislator Covarrubias. True, in the play, as in
the Ridge story and in the *Police Gazette* pirating, the
offer is said to have been made not by the State but by San
Joaquin County, but as the yarn soon began to be told—

and as it is repeated today—the State itself is sponsor, wherefore it is as well to note the origin of the story here. It should be added, however, that there is no official record that the county ever made such an offer either.

At any rate, Mr. Howe's play, neatly printed and published if never actually staged, seems to have helped Ridge to interest a new and financially sounder publisher in his own narrative. Unhappily he did not live to see it issued. The enterprise was delayed and it was in 1871, after Ridge had died of "softening of the brain," that a San Francisco firm brought out the new edition with a preface in which the author was excusably bitter about the theft and rewriting of his work, complaining sharply of the "spurious edition" that had been put out (the *Police Gazette* version) and the "crude interpolations" that had been made in his story, to the "damage of the author's literary credit." As a matter of fact, the *Police Gazette* story, though obviously rewritten from Ridge, is far better done, its anonymous author having cut many of the flowery philosophical passages, modified some of the more outrageous speeches of Three-Fingered Jack, and in other ways edited the narrative to its advantage. Whether because he was extra careful or because there was actually a second edition of the Ridge narrative which has never turned up, the publisher called this 1871 printing the "Third Edition."

It did very nicely, too, for while South American and European countries were learning about Murieta from translations, Americans had been kept informed as well. In fact both England and the United States got a fresh angle on Joaquin from the swaggering Cincinnatus Hiner Miller, who composed a long and very bad poem, published in England as *California* and in Oregon as *Joaquin*, in which he suggests that the bandit's inamorata was a lineal descendant, no less, of Mexico's royal Montezuma. Perhaps it was this poem which misled a later writer to describe Murieta as having a "deep, ragged knife-scar" across his forehead, Miller's hero having

> *"A brow cut deep as with a knife*
> *With many a dubious deed in life."*

Even in his old age Miller remained illogically fond of this early work, as indicated by a footnote in his Author's Edition, forty years afterward, in which he wrote, "It was from this that I was in derision, called 'Joaquin.' I kept the name and the poem too, till both of them were later respected." He adds, "My elder brother, who had better judgment and finer taste than I, thought it too wild and bloody; and so, by degrees, it has been allowed to disappear, except this fragment." The fragment in the Author's Edition is, mercifully, brief.

Joaquin Miller, however, had become a kind of literary cult by the early 1880s, and with his poem to stimulate new interest, the Murieta legend was given fresh life, now beginning to find a large eastern audience.

The Beadle Dime Library contributed its bit by bringing out a 32-page, triple-column issue titled *Joaquin, the Saddle King*, by Joseph E. Badger who had already a large following among boys and men with his *Equinox Tom*, *Captain Cool-Blade*, and *Alabama Joe*. Mr. Badger said frankly—or the Beadles did for him—that this story was "A Romance." The DeWitt 15-cent Library, which picked up the tale and called it *Joaquin: The Claude Duval of California*, was not quite as honest, describing it as "A Romance Founded on Truth." This version was

later re-done in the Echo Series at twenty-five cents, with
a new title, *Joaquin: Or The Marauder of the Mines*. No
author signs either of these, which are Carmela-Clarina
versions. But it may have been one of these paper-backs
which led someone named Marcus A. Stewart to try his
hand at a long poem called *Rosita: A California Tale*. In
a prefatory note, Mr. Stewart writes that the head of
Joaquin Murieta is currently on exhibition at Jordan's
Museum in San Francisco, adding "Whether it be the
veritable *cabeza de Joaquin* or not, I do not pretend to
say." In any event, in Mr. Stewart's poem Rosita is not
the wife of Joaquin, whose bride is called Marie, but of
one of his lieutenants named Ramon, and the author goes
to the length of identifying her with a stage-driver of the
period named Charley Parkhurst who was found after
death to be a woman—this last incident a matter of actual
record. The *Rosita* poem is chiefly of interest because of
its hint that Joaquin Murieta was not killed but went back
to enjoy a long and happy life in Mexico, Mr. Stewart in-
forming his readers that Joaquin and his Marie lived out
their days

> "... *in a land*
> *Far south of California's strand*"

but remaining carefully vague as to just what country this
was. Since there did spring up a popular story that Murieta
had escaped the rangers, and had gone back to his native
Mexico, it is possible at least to speculate on Mr. Stewart's
part in giving currency to the tale. Worth noting is the
fact that a *History of Nevada County*, published at about
the same time, says that Murieta had "a sister living in
Marysville," that this sister went to see the bottled head

and was overheard to remark to a companion, "That is not my brother!" The author of the volume goes on to say that many people at the time believed Murieta safe in Mexico, "where he was seen and recognized by many who knew him, years after his supposed death." No evidence is furnished, just the bare statement.

By this time, as the reader will perceive, the Murieta story was doing very well indeed. Joaquin had grown far beyond his original, purely local stature. Now he had become a famous figure in the United States, in Europe, and in Latin-America, all the while becoming less a fiction and more a fact, a folk-hero entirely divorced from the meagerly substantiated figure of the actual Joaquin. All that was needed to give this Murieta the final stamp of authenticity was acceptance by a recognized historian.

Two men stepped forward to perform this office. They were Hubert Howe Bancroft and Theodore Hittell, whose histories of California have been reference works ever since they were published.

Both of these men took their Murieta from Ridge's fiction. Bancroft used the Ridge "Third Edition" straight, embroidered his account with further fanciful dialogue, and added some quotations from various newspaper reports published at the time Captain Harry Love produced the pickled head said to belong to Murieta. Hittell, writing somewhat more carefully, admitted that the sources on Murieta were "to a great extent unreliable," but nevertheless quoted Ridge as his authority, crediting him throughout with exact page references to the "Third Edition" of the story. That did it. In spite of Hittell's cautionary remarks, people saw only that Murieta had got into the history books and the legend was confirmed. A

few of those who wrote the county histories which were
now beginning to appear in numbers, tried to call a halt.
Charles E. Upton, author of the volume on El Dorado
County, wrote conscientiously that Murieta's story "is
not a part of El Dorado's history, none of his depredations
having been committed here, nor any record being found
of his ever having visited the county." But Mr. Upton
and one or two more were exceptions. While Calaveras
County's people were vying with those of Tuolumne
County on the question of Murieta's first Californian habi-
tation, the historian of Amador County was writing, "This
renowned bandit commenced his career in this county,"
though he had the grace to add, "His exploits . . . have
been multiplied and exaggerated until the clearest sight
can no longer distinguish them from the fabulous." But
authors as careful were few. By this time anyone who
wrote anything about the early days of the gold rush tried
somehow to squeeze Murieta into his story. California's
magazines—*The Overland Monthly* and *The Argonaut*
among them—printed pioneers' "recollections" of Joaquin
Murieta, one of the most fantastic being a story by a doctor
who said he had attended Murieta's sister (this was clearly
another sister, since she lived in San Andreas and not in
Marysville) and had been guided to her hideaway (why
should the sister be in hiding?) by a woman who suddenly
shed dresses and revealed that she was Murieta himself.
So pleased was *The Argonaut* with this "memoir," signed
only with initials, that it reprinted the whole piece forty-
five years later, this time omitting even the initials. (It
is this piece which refers to the "deep, ragged scar" on the
bandit's forehead, the author evidently having taken liter-
ally Miller's poetic reference to the "scars of a dubious

life.") *The Overland*, by the way, has the honor of being the first to refer to the five-thousand-dollar-reward story as an offer "by the State of California," and must also be credited with being the first to suggest that Murieta was identical with one of the other Joaquins named by the Act of the Legislature appointing Love's rangers; the magazine's feature writer says "Joaquin Carrillo, better known as Joaquin Murieta," though he stops short of suggesting that all the rest of the five Joaquins were mere pseudonyms too.

While all this had been going on, "likenesses" of Murieta had begun to make their appearance. The pioneer of all pictures was the work of a Mr. Thomas Armstrong, staff artist on the Sacramento *Union*, whose handsomely done engraving, though neither he nor the paper used the name "Murieta" in connection with it, became the Murieta prototype. It appeared in that paper's Steamer Edition for April 22, 1853, labeled merely "Joaquin, the Mountain Robber." It is particularly interesting to observe that the text described a man wholly different from the Murieta later accepted as truth; this Joaquin is "about 35 years old," had been "a guerrilla for some years in Mexico during the war," was "over six feet tall and strong as a bull," and was "in disposition cruel and sanguinary." Despite this, those who choose to believe the Murieta legend as Ridge developed it—the romantic tale of the young, chivalrous boy who turned bandit only when American miners mistreated him—have always been willing to accept the Armstrong engraving as an actual portrait of their "Murieta." What someone called "the shining will to believe" is nowhere more delightfully demonstrated in the whole Murieta saga.

This picture, to be sure, was made before the capture and before there was a head to look at. Ridge's first edition had a full length portrait. Yet a second "likeness," this one by Charles Nahl, seems quite obviously taken from Armstrong, and the Nahl picture, redrawn by one Butler for the *Police Gazette* serial version of the story in 1859, is just as obviously derived from the Armstrong "original." Nahl later painted a picture of Murieta mounted on a spirited horse, flashing defiance from his dark eyes as he dashes across an undefined background; that painting hangs now in San Francisco's Union League Club. In at least two volumes of California memoirs there is reproduced a painting said to have been made by "a young priest" (unidentified), and the great printer, Edwin Grabhorn, owns a canvas which by the most generous interpretation could be called a "primitive" and which looks as though perhaps it is intended as a picture of Murieta, though it bears neither date nor any direct identification of its subject. None of these "portraits," of course, is likely to have been anything but the artist's private conception of how Murieta might have looked, or adaptations of the "Joaquin" that Armstrong engraved (quite clearly *not* Murieta unless one denies all the other Murieta stories), or perhaps drawings made, as at least one is said to have been, from the head preserved in spirits. It would have been useful to the latter-day historian if someone had thought to photograph that bottled head, but apparently no one did, though it was reported as available for inspection in one sideshow or another up to the time of the San Francisco earthquake and fire in 1906.

But the portraits were the least of it. In one adaptation after another, with error added to error and invention piled upon invention, the story of Joaquin Murieta was now both a fable and a fact. For forty-odd years the tale had grown, had been told and retold, to the point where the teller who had been a part of the early gold rush—and there were some of these left, though they were getting along in years—could and did recall what he had heard and what he had read and what he had really known as all very much the same thing. After all, in the case of Murieta, the two men who had written California's most authentic histories had put Joaquin into their books, hadn't they? And history books are truth; anybody knows that. As the century ended, the Celebrated California Bandit, as John Rollin Ridge had created him, was solidly embedded in the romantic story of the Days of Gold.

## 3

If editors in search of a sensation and feature writers with a yarn to sell had left the Murieta legend alone for a while, perhaps it might have settled into some more or less definite shape. After all, the story now carried the weight of almost fifty years; most of those who had been adults at the time were dead and gone; the whole thing was hearsay anyway. Here was California's folk-hero complete, including the traditional proportion of inconsistencies, unlikely happenings, and outright impossibilities. He was almost entirely a figment of men's imaginations, but there was no harm in that. So are all folk-heroes, and the better for being such creations. One takes them or one leaves them alone, but if one does take them then due allowances are made and everybody is happy. In the case of Murieta it might have fallen out like that.

But as the first two decades of the twentieth century wore along Californians began to become conscious of their past. Moves were made to restore more of the old Franciscan Missions. There was a World's Fair. The citrus industry turned out to be something really big, and the movies found a quiet Methodistical suburb named Hollywood, focused their first coast camera and took the shot heard round the world. There were land booms and railroad promotions, and the tourist trade burgeoned. Suddenly Californians were hunting eagerly for every hint of romance and pseudo-romance in their past. Without doubt, Murieta was a part of that past. And the Murieta that Ridge had invented was as romantic a figure as the most demanding Californian could ask. Now began the refurbishing and dusting-off which, in the second half-century of the legend's existence, has pulled and hauled Joaquin Murieta into a position where the thoughtful student cannot, with all the will in the world, consider the thoroughly doctored story anything but plain fantasy. Gigantism in a hero is all very well, but there is a limit to what the imagination will take in. Paul Bunyan might have performed mighty tasks, but even that giant of achievement was content to be Paul Bunyan, and to stick to his logging. The new writers who dug up what had been slowly built into the Murieta story and then sat down and embroidered it in their own fashion, using the techniques of modern reporting to hint that they had done original research without ever quite making the claim, did no good service to the old tale they were trying to improve. Instead, they succeeded in blowing it up beyond credibility—beyond even the credibility that attaches to any legend old

enough to have attained a measure of respectability, pure
folk-tale though it may be.

The process began slowly. During the early 1900s not
much got into print about Murieta. Thomas S. Duke, an
ex-captain of police in San Francisco, spent his latter years
compiling a fat volume of famous criminal cases, chiefly
of the West, which he published in 1910. He has a chapter
on Murieta as a matter of course, in which he is careful
to say that he takes his account from Ridge's book, though
he injects a few oddments that he picked up somewhere
else—the notion that "Murieta" was really "Carrillo,"
a confusion started by an earlier writer in *The Overland*,
as the reader will recall, and a brand-new addition of his
own, to the effect that the bandit's "Rosita" was really
named "Mariana Higuera." How he came into possession
of this 65-year-old tidbit, Captain Duke doesn't say. Besides this, the only publication on Murieta of any importance was by Charles Caldwell Park who wrote, under
the pen name of "Carl Gray," a fearfully bad novel called
*A Plaything of the Gods*, which is based on the pirated
"Carmela" version; in it the author brings something new
to the legend by having Murieta meet sudden death when
a boat in which he is peacefully punting about some unspecified lake suddenly capsizes and drowns him out of
hand. In Los Angeles, where the Spanish-speaking population was large enough to make it profitable, a *Life and
Adventures of the Celebrated Sonorian Bandit, Joaquin
Murieta* had been steadily in print for some years; the
fifth edition bears the date 1919. As the reader will guess,
this was a "Carmela" version, derived from the old *Police
Gazette* issue. Then, in the fall of that year, the new spate
of Murieta yarns began.

It led off with a *Saturday Evening Post* piece by Frederick R. Bechdolt. What Mr. Bechdolt had got hold of, not too surprisingly, was a story based on the "Rosita" version, and he told it fairly straight out of Ridge, though with a few supplementary touches from previous writers on the subject. In his account, for example, the story of the five-thousand-dollar reward offered by the State of California is repeated, with its postscript of Murieta's daring act in writing "I will give $10,000" beneath it; most of the romanticizers have liked that one since Howe first gave it circulation. Perhaps Mr. Bechdolt knew his *Post* readers well enough to be fairly sure that the decapitation scene would carry too much grue for their stomachs; perhaps he simply knew his editor. At any rate, he carefully omits all references to that episode, concluding his story with the expiring Murieta crying, as the rangers' bullets thudded into his body, "No more! Your work is done!" But his story, in that widely read medium, was enough to start a whole new cycle of Murieta writing, in which some really daring imaginations got a chance to embroider the legend. The story of Murieta's coat of chain mail, made for him by a "skilled Frenchman," had already been circulated, together with the tale that only after he had dressed the unhappy artisan in his own armor, emptied his pistol at his breast and found him intact, did Joaquin pay the price agreed upon. So had the tale that a Mexican boy whom Fremont and Kit Carson had once befriended grew up to be, no less, the veritable Murieta. Fremont himself, in his memoirs, is responsible for that one, the difficulty with the yarn being that if you accept Fremont then you must reject the classic Murieta myth, since the boy's age just won't fit. These tales were already part of the story. Now some new and interesting accretions began to attach themselves to the original legend.

Some of them, set down in a prose style which in all kindness can be described only as deplorable, may be found by the curious in the files of the San Francisco *Call*, where a girl reporter published a series on Murieta, from December, 1923, to February, 1924.

What this young woman did was to use the Murieta story as a framework on which to drape whatever odds and ends about California's past she could find. Written in the stridently sentimental tone that the paper's editor and its readers seemed to like at the time, the narrative is a frantic rehash of previous stories about Murieta, chiefly the "Rosita" version, larded with fragments of California's history having nothing whatever to do with the bandit, though the old story is violently twisted in all sorts of directions so that the author may place Murieta in whatever spot she happens to be writing about at the moment. Here Murieta is named "The Napoleon of banditry." "Four hundred men called him captain!" writes the author; how she arrived at the figure she doesn't explain. "Around his saddle horn," she declares, "were strings of human ears!" These, one must suppose, were sliced from victims' heads by hard-working squads of the "four hundred," since the lady reporter says, only four lines later, "Joaquin himself did not mutilate fiendishly." (Perhaps "fiendishly" is used here in the special newspaper sense of that time, when a "fiend" was just one particular sort of criminal. In that case, the lady may have meant that bandits, when cutting, did not bother with mere ears.) As for descriptive passages, Ridge's purplest paragraphs fade to a pale lavender beside this young woman's way with words. His account of the youthful Joaquin's beating, at the hands of American miners, is as the effort of a schoolboy amateur compared with her proudly professional "He lay insensible at last, from head to foot one mass of blood!" And when it comes to Three-Fingered Jack who, the reader will remember, loved to slit Chinese throats, our young woman writer scornfully rejects such relatively gentle pastimes. In her story, "Three-Fingered Jack, the outlaw's unholy lieutenant, bit the hearts of his victims, tore off their heads!" However, it is in her handling of Rosita's ravishment that the author really shows what she can do. Here is the young Joaquin when he regains his senses after the miners' beating: "He struggled painfully to his feet like one who had long been sick, and saw the trampled rose, his lovely Rosita, his beautiful one, outraged to the death, dying in agony beside him. It was at this moment, beside the Stanislaus, that the blackness of Hell passed forever into the soul of Joaquin Murieta!" She continues, evidently loth to drop a good thing once she's into it, "He buried her in the valley of the Calaveras—the Place of Skulls—the tears of shame not yet dried on her rounded cheeks." Perhaps the middle-aged lady readers of the *Call*, who could remember back as far as their youthful days when they pored at night over the pink pages of *The Family Journal*, wiped a furtive tear now and then from their own less-rounded cheeks as they read. At the very least, the paper's feature editor must have assumed they did; it would be going entirely too far to suggest that he could have liked this sort of thing himself.

To be sure, aside from doing its bit to corrupt taste, the series is not significant. What is important is that the *Call* chose to use every familiar trick of the trade to suggest to the never-analytical reader that the material of the story was authentic. In a note preceding the first instalment, the interested student may find a neat example of the smooth way in which an unsuspecting reader may be led to believe that fiction is fact. Worded very carefully, this "precede" describes the author's travels through "every corner of California known to '49," and concludes "In such ways the life of Joaquin gradually came together. It may not all be true. But it comes direct from the lips of his friends." Since Murieta was killed in 1853, even if he had been accustomed to consort on a friendly basis with ten-year-olds, those tots would have been eighty in 1923. Of course, the editor's note did not state that "direct" meant directly from those friends to his lady feature writer. But in such cases the unwillingness of the newspaper reader to do even the simplest arithmetic in his head is a well-known phenomenon in the trade. As for the writer's "travels," perhaps they took place, though the most casual investigator would have had no trouble finding all her details, barring such delightful imaginative touches as strings of human ears and the tearing-off of heads, at no farther touring distance than any fair-sized California library.

This was only the beginning. Within a year, the Los Angeles fifth edition of the *Life* in Spanish had been "discovered," translated into English by someone named Francis P. Belle, and published in Chicago as a fresh contribution to the Murieta saga. Almost immediately a small California press got hold of the Ridge "Third Edition" and reprinted it together with the *Life* of another bandit, Tiburcio Vasquez. Then Joseph Gollomb brought out a volume called *Master Highwaymen*, among whom he included Murieta. This contribution has the distinction of casting new light on the subject of Joaquin's intellectual capacity. Mr. Gollomb finds in Murieta a hitherto unsuspected taste for the classics, writing that "Even in later days when he lay by the campfire in mountain fastnesses where his outlaw bands retired between raids, Joaquin had Cervantes and Racine for company." The reader may well wonder how this bit of gossip about the bandit's reading habits came Mr. Gollomb's way; hardly, one imagines, "direct from the lips of friends," though one can only speculate on who else could possibly know. By way of lagniappe, too, Mr. Gollomb has his Murieta serving "as personal bodyguard" to Mexico's Santa Anna. Since this could have been no later than 1846, and since this particular retelling of the tale is based on the "Carmela" version in which Murieta was just fifteen at that date, the student is left to the conjecture that Santa Anna could not have felt himself in any great danger.

After this, Murieta tales came thick and fast. One, in *Sunset Magazine* the following year, involves a treasure hidden in the Tejon Pass region and discovered by Indians who were cheated out of their find by the arrival of Murieta's ghost on horseback—with, of course, saddlebags solid enough to carry the treasure away. An Englishwoman named Jill Cossley-Batt did a book, *The Last of the California Rangers*, in which, ascribing the story obliquely to William James Howard (who had actually been with Harry Love's posse), she involves Murieta in an episode with the first woman hanged in California, Juanita of Downieville. The lady reporter of the *Call* was ahead of her on that one; very likely Miss Cossley-Batt included the files of that paper in her "research."

The stories kept coming. One Ernest Klette produced

something titled *The Crimson Trail of Joaquin Murieta*, described by the publisher as "a biography in story form." Frankness demands that it be set down as neither biography nor story: In another novel, *The Sheriff of Chispa Loma*, by Charles H. Snow, Murieta figures thinly disguised as "Juan Moreno" and his girl is called "Rosalia." Published the same year was *On the Old West Coast*, being further gatherings among the papers of Horace Bell, the ranger of Southern California who had written *Reminiscences of a Ranger*. In these memoirs, Bell writes that he once owned the supposed likeness of Murieta said to have been painted by "a young priest." He says further that it was made in the early summer of 1853 "by a young padre at Mission Carmel" on an occasion when Joaquin sought sanctuary there. A look at the roster of "Resident and Other Fathers" at the mission at that time shows only two, a Fr. Vilarrasa, and the Right Reverend J. S. Alemany. Since Bishop Alemany was hardly "a young padre," Fr. Vilarrasa, age unknown, is the only possibility. It is unfortunate that Major Bell did not see fit to print the letter he said he had from the padre, nor to mention his name.

All of this, if the industrious embroiderers of Ridge's original fiction had only known it, was merely preparatory. For now came the book which did more than any writing about Murieta since Ridge himself to fix the picture of the bandit in the minds of Americans. It was called *The Robin Hood of El Dorado*, and the author was Walter Noble Burns who brought out his opus in 1932.

As the reader will agree, the title had everything. Murieta was no Robin Hood—if Robert the Heud of Lincolnshire had ever been—but Ridge had made him one, and most of the writers since had fallen in with the natural pattern. Even the more cautious historian, Hittell, who had set him down for a "vicious and abandoned character, low, brutal, and cruel, intrinsically and at heart a thief and a cut-throat," had done his bit by quoting the highlights of the Ridge fiction. And it was the obvious thing for the public at large, which obstinately wanted a hero, however imaginary, to accept this estimate. To combine the idea of a Robin Hood with the ever-magical words "El Dorado" was an admirable stroke of promotional genius. It could hardly have been bettered. Evidently Hollywood thought so, at any rate, for Mr. Burns's book sold to the motion-picture people almost as soon as it was published. And the book also sold to the public; it went into several printings and was then taken up by a reprint house which issued it successfully in a lower-priced edition.

Mr. Burns's publishers were careful about flat statements, but they suggested that this *Robin Hood of El Dorado* was actually a "biography." It is, of course, since it could be nothing else, written eighty-odd years after Murieta's demise, a kind of collection and rewriting of whatever else had been said about the bandit—and the reader has just seen how this body of material was derived. Mr. Burns made a good story of it; his experience in other books of the kind had taught him the techniques, and he makes his tale a fast-moving narrative, well adjusted to the readers and the period for which it was written. It seems clear that he must have read both the "Rosita" and "Carmela-Clarina" versions, for it is possible to trace both through his text. Little needs to be said about the book beyond this except, perhaps, to note Mr. Burns's method of reconciling the two earliest stories and sorting out the confusions which, since it would appear that he did not know one was pirated from the other, must have puzzled him some. He does it very simply; unwilling to give preference to either yarn, he simply calls the heroine "Rosita Carmen."

It was about this time that a copy of the Ridge first edition turned up and, since it antedated the *Police Gazette* story by some five years, gave students a chance to compare. The result was that San Francisco's Grabhorn Press brought out, not the first Ridge, but the *Police Gazette* story, with a scholarly preface by Francis P. Farquhar in which the early piratings were painstakingly traced and in which he made it clear that this version was chosen for republication simply because the *Gazette's* anonymous rewrite man had done the job better. Here, for the first time, someone had applied the apparatus of scholarship to the Murieta legend, and students had a chance to get an inkling of what had been going on.

But it was too late, of course. In 1936, Hollywood got around to making its movie, with Warner Baxter as Joaquin, and a story which differed from the Burns book in approximately the degree in which Hollywood stories usually do differ from their book-sources. In what appears to have been a promotional stunt for the picture, Peter B. Kyne wrote a *Robin Hood of El Dorado* series for the San Francisco *Chronicle*, beginning February 23, 1936, and concluding, not too strangely, during the week that the movie was announced. And in the summer of 1949 appeared a novel, *The Dream Ends in Fury*, by Samuel Anthony Peeples, based more or less on the Murieta legend. The author very sensibly notes that it is "imaginative."

This, then, is pretty nearly the story so far, or at least the highlights of it. It would be too much to suggest that the Murieta saga ends here, or that any effort to wrench the legend back to its basis of fact will have any effect to speak of. Joaquin Murieta, the dashing, gallant outlaw, with his romantically lovely sweetheart (or sweethearts?), his fearful henchman who so loved to slit Chinese throats, his reckless rides and daring narrow escapes, his chivalrous treatment of the weak, and his bitter revenge upon any who betrayed him, is too firmly rooted in California's story; the official and semi-official sanctions given the legend by those who should have known better saw to that, and the embroidering of the myth by those merely out to retell a story put the finishing touches to the job.

Moreover, there is no reason why Murieta should not be fictionized, made into as black a villain or as shining a hero as happens to suit the temperament of the fictioneer or the temper of the time. To be embalmed in novels, poems, plays, and pictures is the ultimate fate of all folk-heroes, and good swashbuckling material they make too. But perhaps it is as well to have the facts as far as they may be ascertained, and to know at least where these end and the fictions begin; and in the case of Murieta, as this brief study has shown, the known facts are few and the inventions many. It may seem an unhappy thing to remind the good citizens of Hornitos and Angels Camp, of Columbia and Sonora and Murphy's and a hundred other towns remaining from gold-rush days that the tunnels and caves, the cellars and stone ruins and box-canyons to which they point so proudly as Murieta's hideaways may never have seen Murieta or any Joaquin. Indeed, to some readers such captiousness with a first-class legend may appear no more than wilful contrariness, a deliberate destruction of a pretty dream to no purpose.

But the chances are no harm is done. There is no record that fairy tales commonly dissolve when faced with a mere truth. The beds that George Washington slept in, the writing-desks at which the Marquis de Lafayette carried on his interminable correspondence—the law of probabilities has never operated to lessen their number. Nor will any amount of truth ever destroy or even damage the Murieta Legend. His eyes flashing, his knife ever ready for a *gringo's* ribs, his gallantry unquestioned, his horsemanship superb, and his aim unerring, Joaquin Murieta will ride down the years as California's most romantic bandit. His cattle-thievery forgotten, his cold-blooded murders (if in fact he committed them) conveniently ignored, he remains the perfect gold-rush manifestation of man's compulsion to make a hero out of the best materials available, because The Hero is a creature men need.

Nevertheless it is pleasant, at least, to give credit where it is due, to John Rollin Ridge who manufactured, practically out of whole cloth, a bandit-hero for a new, raw region which wanted a Robin Hood in its background. Californians will continue to cherish their legend, as why should they not? For the record, however, it is probably as well to append to California's history this footnote on what the right fiction, at the right moment and in the right place, can do when it meets a simple need. It is Ridge's justification that, since there wasn't a Murieta—at any rate not much of a Murieta—it was necessary to create one.

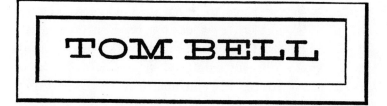

**E**VEN IN CRIME THERE MUST be pioneers.

The curious thing is that in California's early gold-rush days one particular kind of crime took so long to develop. There were brawls, stabbings, and shootings in the mines, to be sure, even in the halcyon days of '48, before the tide of forty-niners began to wash into the foothills. There were hard characters among the miners, plenty of them. Yet, no matter what else they did, there was one point at which they stopped, one line over which they refused to step. They did not steal gold. By common consent, honesty was the best policy. Men hung together when it came to safeguarding the treasure in which all had a share.

With the skyrocketing of population in the 1850s, the crime curve jumped. Gamblers and thieves found their way into the diggings. Sometimes men turned outlaw. The old decencies were breaking down under pressure. Yet, odd as it seems, the gold shipments were pretty generally left alone. The record is clear. Individual travelers might be robbed, beaten, even on occasion done to death. Joaquin Murieta and his men might play fast and loose with cattle and purses, and Three-Fingered Jack freely indulge his charming taste for hanging Chinamen in rows by their queues and then slitting their throats, one by one. Nevertheless, in the larger sense, the gold was safe. No one knows now how many thousands of miles the stages covered in those first years, nor how much treasure they carried. But stages and gold got through. Before the end of 1853, Murieta was dead, his head in a bottle in a sideshow—if it was his head. But neither he nor anybody else had attempted to hold up a stage. It simply wasn't done.

As a matter of fact, no one tried that trick until the summer of 1856. In July of that year, a one-time physician turned bad man came to the conclusion that he was tired of the second-rate cattle-stealing and stick-up business he and his associates had been operating along the forks of the Yuba River. It was time he tried something really big. So deciding, he made himself a pioneer, though he did not know that nor care. He laid his plans carefully. On August 12 the shocking headlines spread the news throughout the State. The unheard-of had happened. Tom Bell and his gang had stopped the Camptonville-Marysville stage with Langton's express messenger aboard, in his care a chest containing $100,000 in gold. California had seen its first organized stage holdup.

Californians had already heard a good deal about Tom Bell.

Most of what they heard, however, was both contradictory and confusing. Tom Bell, one report had it, was a strapping, ferocious fellow, ready to shoot on sight, showing his victims no mercy. The Sacramento *Union's* Grass Valley reporter lent color to this story by writing, "Tom Bell carries six revolvers and several bowie knives, and wears a breast-plate of thin boiler-iron around his body." To this exciting description, the correspondent appended the prophecy that Bell would one day find himself at the end of a rope. As it turned out he was a better seer than newspaperman.

But no sooner did the citizen of California get this swashbuckling Tom Bell firmly fixed in his mind's eye than someone else, speaking with equal authority, would come along with an entirely different story. Tom Bell was no fierce fellow encased in armor and bristling with weapons. Indeed, if he possessed one notable characteristic it was his gentleness, his pity for his victim, his innate kindness of heart. It was well known that on one occasion, when a companion in crime had found it necessary to wound a traveler who had shown a disposition to protect his moneybelt, Tom had tenderly bound up the bullet hole, halted a teamster and commanded him to take the injured man to the nearest doctor. Further, he had shouted a parting admonition to the driver to proceed carefully so that the patient might not be jolted. The storyteller did not always remember to add that while they were at it Tom Bell and his fellow-road-agent had also taken pains to relieve the teamster of his cash. Just the same, this tale was held to show that Tom Bell was a man like other men, ever ready to help a sufferer, in short, a true knight of the road.

It was pleasant to know these things about the notorious highwayman, of course, and perhaps the plain citizen might have stretched a point to reconcile the conflicting stories. But when yet other men appeared and pooh-poohed both these painstaking word-pictures of Tom Bell, it was, to say the least, disconcerting. Such men did appear, and in numbers. They said they had known Tom Bell for years, and that he was neither a tin-armored fiend, sprouting pistols and knives, nor yet a sympathetic nurse to wounded travelers. He was, they said, a smallish, inoffensive kind of man who had once mined near Rough and Ready and, being unsuccessful, had taken to such crimes as robbery and horse-stealing. If he had ever shot a man it was news to them. Bullets were not in his line. Nor did he have any "gang." In the opinion of these positive gentlemen, the pother about Tom Bell was all nonsense, and the chances were that there had been some extensive legpulling.

There was an answer to this puzzle, though the newspapers never got it straight until after Tom Bell, cattle-rustler and killer, gang-leader, highwayman and stage-robber, was finally caught. The simple explanation was that there were two Tom Bells. And the second one, the Tom Bell with whom this narrative concerns itself, knew all about the other. In fact, it was because there was already a Tom Bell known to be engaged in odds and ends of crime in the neighborhood of the Placer and Yuba County diggings that our man chose his pseudonym. If there was any way in which he might help to confuse the law, he was in favor of it. For by the time he took to the road in earnest, he had had his brush with the authorities and wanted no more of them or their jails.

In his home town of Rome, Tennessee, Dr. Thomas J. Hodges was well thought of. He was a trifle young for the doctoring trade perhaps but respectable enough. When Colonel Cheatham organized his regiment of Tennessee Volunteers to help the United States Government realize its manifest destiny in Mexico, Dr. Hodges was accepted as a medical attaché. He was not made an officer. A man did not need rank to bandage wounds and prescribe salts. Moreover, this Dr. Hodges was a fine upstanding specimen, an inch over six feet tall and broad-shouldered, though there was little flesh on his bones. If necessary, he could handle a rifle and bayonet as well as the next man.

There is no record of how Dr. Hodges acquitted himself in Mexico, nor is there any evidence to show how or where he acquired the badly broken nose, "dented in at the bridge, level with his face," which a historian of the time mildly admits must have given him a "somewhat repulsive appearance." We know he came to California, like many another soldier who had been given a taste for adventure by the war. He may or may not have practiced medicine after he arrived in the gold-diggings; some newspaper writers have said so but do not explain how they knew it. We may be fairly certain, however, that he tried mining and gambling—here the Doctor is the authority on himself—and that since neither of these pursuits seemed to get him anywhere, he took to grand larceny. What he stole does not appear in the record. But in May, 1855, Dr. Thomas J. Hodges found himself in the toils of the law. San Quentin Prison was yet to be built, wherefore he was sent to Angel Island, in San Francisco Bay. On Warden Jack Hayes' books, however, there was no Dr. Hodges. When the county peace officers had come down on him, the Doctor had remembered a fellow he had heard about, a criminal in a small way in and around the mines near Auburn. Under the circumstances, any name would be better than his own, and the Auburn cattle-thief was in no position to complain if his was borrowed. "Tom Bell," said the Doctor when they asked him his name. As Tom Bell he was taken to the Island to serve his time.

He did not stay there long. The first thing he did was to fall sick, very sick indeed. He was so badly off, in fact, that the authorities were worried. There was no doctor on Angel Island, and Warden Hayes didn't want prisoners dying on his hands if he could help it. But there was a doctor over in San Francisco at the county jail. Thither Tom Bell was sent, so that the medico might have a look at him.

The facts were that Tom Bell-Hodges was not sick at all. His knowledge of medicine, so the old account runs, enabled him to sham illness well enough to deceive all concerned, even San Francisco's prison doctor. What symptoms he developed, why the city physician failed to see through them—these details do not appear. The contemporary newspaper account notes merely that he was so ill that he was "granted the privilege of exercise with extended liberties." This, of course, was what he was after, though as it fell out he might as well have saved himself the trouble. For there were schemes brewing that Tom knew nothing about.

The story of how Tom Bell and half a dozen others actually escaped comes from one Bill Gristy, *alias* "Bill White," who had been sent to Angel Island for ten years for stealing three horses from the Girard House up in Placer County. Gristy became Tom's right-hand man after they got away together, but a year later he was caught and made a full confession of his crimes, in which he gave details of the escape. If he told the truth, the affair was no bold adventure, but a frame-up from start to finish, arranged in advance, the guards firing blank cartridges, the whole hullabaloo arising from the fact that General Estell, who had the prison-mess contract with the State, had found out he was losing money. What the General wanted, Gristy explained, was to get out of his contract, and the easiest means of doing this was to work toward a complete overhaul of the prison system. One of the simplest ways of bringing this about was to arrange a few escapes. There had been one or two, and the news-papers had commented acidly on the management. A good, wholesale prison-break would bring matters to a head. For this reason, Gristy said, he and several others, including Tom Bell, were given their chance to run, and took it.

The student may believe Gristy's story, or he may choose to follow those who say merely that Tom's make-believe illness enabled him to steal silently away. Which-ever story one selects, the facts are that Tom Bell and Bill Gristy knew each other in prison, that both got away, and that Bell thought enough of Gristy's hardihood and gen-eral talent for crime to make him his constant associate thereafter. As later events showed, Tom's judgment was bad. For, in the end, it was Gristy who was responsible for bringing Tom Bell, a sheriff's posse, and a stout rope together under a convenient tree.

2

Two experienced criminals, both of a mind to continue their careers in crime, are the makings of a gang.

Tom Bell and Bill Gristy lost no time in getting together as choice a collection of tough characters as had ever been organized in the mines. Two of the first to join up were Ned Connor and Jim Smith, who had been in on the escape from the San Francisco jail. Somewhere Tom picked up one Montague Lyon, better known as "Monte Jack," an accomplished horse-thief, who brought with him a Mexican named Juan Fernandez. To this group was added a seventh, Bob Carr, generally called "English Bob." These seven were the nucleus of the organization Tom Bell began to build up. Splitting into twos and threes, they worked the foothills from Auburn north, robbing travelers, stealing cattle, breaking and entering stores and saloons, and generally making themselves obnoxious. No matter which of them committed a crime, he made sure that the victim believed it was "Tom Bell" who had robbed him. That was part of Tom's plan.

For a time it worked. Californians were completely mystified by this "Tom Bell" who could appear in two places at the same time, rob a store in Placer County one afternoon and be two hundred miles away sticking up a late traveler the same night. No sooner did a sheriff get his men out and on the trail of Tom Bell up in Nevada County than the word came that Bell and two friends had just been seen at the Mountaineer House, between Folsom and Auburn. The Mountaineer House was known to be in disreputable hands; its owner, Jack Phillips, a "Sydney duck," was suspected of working with various shady characters. But by the time the peace officers called at his inn to make inquiries, Mr. Phillips would be sitting respectably at his desk checking over bills, with no one else near the premises but the stage-driver and his pas-

sengers who had stopped for a breather before tackling
the hills on the way to Nevada City. There was simply
no tracking down a man who could strike so fast and so
often in so short a time.

Nevertheless, in spite of Tom Bell's careful organization, reports on him began to filter through. Sheriffs
exchanged letters, each adding a bit here and a bit there.
Slowly a picture of the wanted man began to take shape.

The first authenticated bit of information was Tom's
broken nose, certainly a mark that a robber could not conceal. They learned that he was a tall man, broad-shouldered, and wiry in build. They discovered that he was
vain of his whiskers, and that he kept them trimmed so
that the long, sandy moustache circled his mouth and
joined with the goatee of the same sandy hue; they found
out that his hair was thick and blond and that he wore
it long, hanging to his shoulders. He was of a quick and
restless temperament, fearless in a fight, a regular cata-
mount of a man. All this helped. Particularly it aided
the officers in distinguishing the various "Tom Bells."
When the right man committed a crime they'd know it
thereafter.

Yet the right man, and the wrong ones too, went on
with the usual depredations. Teamsters were stopped,
robbed, and told to roll along. Apparently any victim
would do, rich or poor, for early in the spring of 1856
a vegetable peddler was held up near Rabbit Creek. The
day after that a driver named Dutch John, who was haul-
ing a cargo of lager beer from Volcano to (it is almost
incredibly apropos) Drytown, was stopped by five men
who told him they were "taking contributions." They did
not say for what cause they were requesting tribute, but

one of them did vouchsafe the information that this was Tom Bell's gang and the driver had better be quick about paying up. Dutch John passed over all he had—thirty dollars and a quarter. The robbers gave him back the two bits and told him to buy himself a drink with it.

All this was duly reported in the newspapers, whose editors became more and more sarcastic about the inability of the peace officers to run Tom Bell down. "What," inquired the editor of the Sacramento *Union*, "is the result of this failure to catch one who is, after all, only an ordinary man? He is now, doubtless, emulous of the reputation of Joaquin; is striving for the character of the dashing highwayman, and hopes that his life may be written, as Jack Shepard's was, after he shall have expiated his crimes upon the gallows." The editor added automatically that it was about time something was done, or as he largely put it, "It is incumbent upon our State authorities to take immediate steps in the premises." For good measure, he hinted that there was talk of organizing a ranger company.

The State, however, had an answer. Governor Johnson informed the *Union* that in spite of its hint about rangers the State had no arms at its disposal, no power to authorize the fitting-out and maintaining of such a company, and that a special act of the Legislature was necessary before anything could be obtained to start such an enterprise. The editor of the *Union* replied rather sourly that he knew all that in the first place; but that, after all, if a group of bold plunderers had brought the State's roads to the point where even the vegetable peddlers and lager-beer merchants were no longer safe, what security had the immigrants from the plains who were coming in the fall?

The Governor, the *Union* suggested, might not be able to equip ranger companies and pay them without benefit of Legislature, but at least he was empowered to offer rewards for the capture of desperados who had committed such heinous crimes against the State. That being the case, the editor said, why didn't the Governor get after it? "Although," he hastened to add, "what should be done is not for us to say; we repeat that our object is merely to direct attention to this matter."

Attention being duly directed as the *Union* desired, its editor said nothing further. Less than a week later, Mr. Woods, toll-gatherer at the bridge near the mouth of the Yuba's south fork, was informed by three horsemen that times were hard and that, anyway, members of Tom Bell's gang did not pay toll. "Mr. Woods," said the San Francisco *Bulletin* which reported the occurrence, "is not the man to take this kind of thing lying down. He rushed back to his house, got his rifle, fired several shots at the three and pursued them as far as French Corral. A company started in pursuit and pressed the men so hard that one was forced to dismount and take to the scrub. The pursuers secured his horse and took it to San Juan where it was recognized and sent back to its owner near Grass Valley. The horse had been stolen only a few days earlier. The course of the robbers was seen to be up the ridge, but the trail grew cold and they were not caught."

It was shortly after this that Mr. Farmer of the Mountain Springs House near Amador City had the biggest adventure of his life. Just before he locked up for the night he was made very suspicious by three men who asked him detailed questions about the road. One of them was tall, blond, and bewhiskered, with a repulsively broken nose,

and Mr. Farmer did not like his looks. The men had not
bothered him further; they had finished their drink and
gone on. But Mr. Farmer was convinced that he had had
a narrow escape. He made doubly certain that all locks
were secure, readied his pistol, and retired. Later that
night he was awakened by the sound of horses in front
of the house and a loud knocking at his door. Prudently
he put his head out of the window and inquired what was
wanted. There were four mounted men below, one of
whom explained that they had lost the road and wanted
to know how to get to Ione. Mr. Farmer was not to be
fooled. "The road," he said, "is not far off. I reckon you
can find it!" Not at all dismayed by his coolness, the
leader then asked Mr. Farmer if he kept a bar. No, said
Mr. Farmer, he didn't. Wouldn't he please let them in
and give them something to eat, then? Mr. Farmer's
reply, as reported by the Amador *Sentinel*, is classic in its
brevity and firmness. "No," he replied, "rather think I
won't!" and shut the window. It was not until he got his
copy of the *Sentinel* the next Saturday that the worthy
keeper of the Mountain Springs House found out what
he had done. He had turned away four members of the
Mokelumne Hill delegation to the Democratic Conven-
tion, lost on their way to Sacramento.

The spring and early summer of 1856 saw more and
more trouble on the highway, but it also contributed to
the gradually growing dossier on Tom Bell.

Officers had learned, for example, why it was that so
many travelers who paused for refreshment at the Western
Exchange Hotel, on the Sacramento-Nevada City road,
were robbed soon after they left. The proprietress, red-

haired and buxom Mrs. Elizabeth Hood, who was sometimes called "Mrs. Cole" and occasionally (perhaps for
the sake of variety) "Mrs. Cullers," had been admirably
discreet in most of her affairs, but somewhere she had
slipped—someone found cause to suspect that she was in
the pay of Tom Bell. More, this anonymous investigator
(who promptly reported to the Sacramento police) had
observed the manner in which members of the gang made
themselves known to Mrs. Hood and to the bartenders.
It was a very simple little signal—a bullet bored through
and hung on a knotted string. Anyone might have such an
oddity in his pocket. But when a customer pulled it out
with his money and swung it idly as he paid for his drink
or his dinner, then the man behind the bar or the woman
behind the desk knew him for one of Bell's men and obligingly "spotted" for him the travelers who carried large
amounts of cash. It had been discovered, too, that Tom
Bell had two favorite mounts, a fine blooded mare whose
name does not appear, and a magnificent horse he called
"Buckskin." Full descriptions of both were put on file
in the sheriff's office in Sacramento.

Finally, the police had learned of the association between Bell and Bill Gristy. Once indeed they nearly
caught Gristy. A messenger from Judge Sewell at Nigger
Hill brought word that Gristy was hiding in the neighborhood, and that if the Sacramento officers wanted him
they'd better come and get him. Deputy-sheriffs Taylor
and White left posthaste. But they were too late. In the
cabin where Gristy had been hiding was a man unknown
to them who gave his name as John Woodruff. He might
have remained forever unknown to the officers and undisturbed by them if he had not gone into a rage, demanding

to know who had "blowed on him." No one had, nor did Deputies Taylor and White have any idea of the crime for which he might be wanted; but since he had kindly announced himself a criminal of some sort they took him along back to Sacramento with them. There he was examined by men who knew Gristy. The *Union* reported that these said they had never seen the man before and that he was most certainly not Bill Gristy, but that the authorities had locked him up on general principles.

Placer County officers were keeping an eye on the Mountaineer House, too, and on its unsavory proprietor. Sooner or later, if their suspicions were correct, Bell or one of his crowd would stop in to see Jack Phillips and there would be a good excuse to close up his place. Then there would be one less hole where Bell could go to earth. The net to which police so often and so mysteriously refer was being tightened. It would be merely a matter of time now, they were quite sure.

Whether it was his knowledge that pursuit was growing closer, or merely his natural love for the dramatic that moved him is hard to say. Whichever it was, Tom Bell now laid plans for the most spectacular robbery he and his gang had ever tried. No teamsters, random vegetable peddlers, or lager-beer merchants this time. Bell was out for something big, nothing less than a stage and its treasure-box. That it was a new type of crime in the mines did not deter him. Like many another successful bad man, before and after his time, Tom Bell was beginning to believe he was invincible. If anybody could tackle a stage he could. At any rate, he was going to try.

The gang began by making itself less conspicuous. As the summer of 1856 wore along there were fewer outrages ascribed to Bell and his men. True, a Mr. Argrave who owned the Grizzly Store near Nevada City was severely beaten about the head one night by three men who had waked him, saying that they were miners on their way to the Middle Yuba and were desperately in need of food. Not as shrewd as Mr. Farmer who had so tartly declared that he "rather thought he wouldn't" and shut his window, Mr. Argrave was moved to pity, got out of bed, and foolishly opened his door. The three men disposed of him with their gun-butts, took seventy dollars from the till, presented pistols at the heads of two genuine miners who were sleeping in the store, and backed out of the door, advising all concerned to start no trouble with "members of Tom Bell's gang." They may have been Bell's men and they may not. But aside from this incident, things were uncommonly quiet in the northern mines. It was even supposed by some that Tom Bell had moved to another part of the country, perhaps even out of the State altogether.

### 3

On the morning of August 11, the regularly scheduled stage pulled out of Camptonville on the long Marysville road.

There was a full complement of passengers, and John Gear was driving as usual. Beside him sat the Langton Express Company's messenger, one Dobson, his rifle across his knees. He was there for a reason. Stage transportation was considered safe enough, but this time he was responsible for a very special item. In the strong-box stowed beneath the seat was one of the largest shipments of gold Langton's had carried for months, amounting to almost

$100,000. A good part of this treasure belonged to Mr. Rideout, gold-dust dealer of Camptonville, who was accompanying his shipment to Marysville. Because he did not like the swaying stage, however, Mr. Rideout had decided to go by horseback. His decision was to be the means of saving his gold for him, but he did not know that. All he knew, as he eased his horse down the steep slope just outside town, was that it was good practice to keep a few minutes ahead of the stage. That way he wouldn't be bothered by the powdery dry-season dust.

At Dry Creek, not far out of Marysville, the Camptonville road forked, one spur taking the higher side of the little ravine made by the stream, the other following the lower side.

Mr. Rideout came to the fork at about half-past four in the afternoon, and he was very glad to get there. It had been a hot trip, and the trees and brush hereabouts suggested a grateful coolness. The journey was almost over; in a short half hour he would be in town, his gold checked in at Langton's office and locked tightly in the safe. There was no hurry now, and at the fork he chose the longer and slower trail, the tree-shaded old road that branched away from the dusty stage-route. It wouldn't mean more than a few minutes' difference, and he might as well be comfortable. He had not ridden more than a hundred yards along the upper road when three men spurred their horses out from behind a clump of brush, pointed pistols at his head, and commanded him to dismount.

Mr. Rideout was not armed and, as he afterward said, he had no notion of resisting. But the surprise attack left him for the moment without power to move. He simply sat there, looking at the masked men, too startled even to raise his hands. The order was harshly repeated and Mr. Rideout, still feeling like a man in a nightmare, automatically obeyed. Since the robbers seemed only to want his horse, he struck out through the brush toward the edge of the little ravine, his confused purpose being to clamber down, cross Dry Creek, and make his way up to the other road where he knew the stage would appear at any moment. He had not taken a dozen steps before one of the masked men called him back, hinted that he had better reach high, and went through his pockets. He was carrying no money; all his treasure was in the Langton box. Disgusted at their failure to gain anything from their victim, the robbers then ordered him to cross over the ravine to the other road, as he had first intended. As he slid down the bank, he realized that they had not moved. They were still there on the old road, watching him go.

Mr. Rideout must have felt both angry and embarrassed. He could hear the stage coming, and he knew that in a moment he would have to step out, looking like a fool, stop John Gear, confess that his horse had been taken away from him, and ride on into town, an object of pity, which no man likes to be. He could not know that the accident of his unexpected appearance had interfered with as good a plan as a smart bandit ever devised. Ten minutes earlier, Mr. Rideout's decision to take the old fork of the road would have made no difference to Tom Bell and his men. The three who cut across to intercept him would have had ample time to dispose of his horse, turn its rider loose where he could do no harm, rejoin their companions, and carry out their scheme. Six mounted and masked men, three on each side of the road, would have stopped the Marysville stage and six gun-muzzles in such a case are almost as good as six hundred. But Mr. Rideout hadn't been ten minutes earlier. And as he scrambled awkwardly up the far bank to reach the road ahead of the coming stage, it was three men, not six, that rode out into the main route ahead of him, pistols drawn. As he paused to take in this new development, two sounds came simultaneously to his ears. One was the snarling voice of the leader in front, ordering Gear to stop the stage. The other was the crashing in the brush, as the three robbers behind him rode desperately down through the undergrowth to join their companions.

There is no way to tell what might have happened if there had been no Mr. Rideout at the forks of the Marysville road at the wrong moment; if the robbers had deployed according to Tom Bell's original scheme, three on a side; if they had ridden out together, guns leveled, a grim sextette determined to have the treasure-chest, no matter what. It is not pleasant to know one's self surrounded, and though the courage of Dobson, Langton's messenger, was never in question, it is still true that a man cannot shoot in two directions at once. But Mr. Rideout had come along. The band had split, even though only for a minute or two, and the attack could be made from one side of the stage only. In the circumstances, Dobson didn't think twice. He raised his rifle and fired, tumbling one of the bandits from his horse at the first shot.

In any such running gun-fight, the surprising thing always is the rapidity with which the affair takes place. By time time Mr. Rideout got up the bank and to the stage, the skirmish was over. Some forty shots had been exchanged, several of the passengers who were armed having fired from inside the coach. The two leaders of the gang had withdrawn into the thicket, pulling their wounded companion with them, and at their retreat Dobson had shouted to Gear to drive on. As the stage started, the trio of reinforcements gained the road, the gold-dust dealer's horse with them, and one of the three—a Mexican, Mr. Rideout said later—fired again. Dobson, though he was wounded in the right arm, turned in his seat for a last shot. His bullet sent the Mexican spinning into the brush. Mr. Rideout then acted with admirable presence of mind. Finding his own mount beside him again, he swung into the saddle and raced after the stage. As he drew abreast, John Gear shouted to him to ride ahead. This was no place to stop and take stock. Dobson was wounded, and others might be. Would Mr. Rideout get on into Marysville and spread the news as fast as possible? Mr. Rideout was happy to oblige.

The official historian of Nevada County, reporting the fight more than two decades later, solemnly wrote that by the time the stage entered town a procession had formed and ridden out to meet it, headed by a brass band. If there is any truth in the story, the band can have played only on the outward journey. For by the time the escort—if indeed there was one—met the stage, the frightened travelers had had time to check up. There was no cause for music. Dobson was not the only casualty. John Campbell, a passenger, had been wounded in the forehead, creased by a glancing shot that had just missed his eye. Another man had been shot in both legs. The stage was riddled with holes. And a woman, Mrs. Tilghman, wife of a Marysville barber, had been killed instantly by a bullet through her head. The treasure was saved, but there could have been no point in triumphal tootlings merely for the sweet sake of Langton's honor.

Next day the Marysville *Express* printed a full account of the attempted holdup. Music was not mentioned, and the editor uttered the proper sentiments in the matter of the dead and wounded. Tragedy or not, though, he was unable to resist one small whipcrack of humor at the end of his story, the kind of hardy jest that was the breath of life to those early-day rough-and-ready journalists. He closed his account with a quote from one of the passengers who, so he said, told him that at the first shot one white man and four Chinese had left the stage abruptly, headed back toward Camptonville. The editor assured his readers that they had not been seen since.

The Marysville editor had had his little joke, but the newspapers of the region, indeed of the entire northern part of the State, were not inclined to see anything funny about this latest and greatest outrage. From descriptive details supplied by the observant Mr. Rideout and John Gear, there was no doubt in anybody's mind. It was Tom Bell again. And the papers demanded with one voice that something be done about it. This time they got action. Captain William King of the Marysville police started out with his own posse. Up in Sacramento, Detectives Robert Harrison and Daniel Gay were detailed "to capture or destroy the band"; their further instructions were to occupy themselves with nothing else until Tom Bell was brought to justice. Throughout the mines men thought only of one thing. This vicious bandit must be caught and no nonsense about it. In the whole history of

California's early days there was never a more united effort to run a criminal down.

It was not very long before the people of California had evidence that this organized search was beginning to have its effect. It came from an unimpeachable source, in the form of a letter from Tom Bell himself, his first direct communication with the law since the days when he had been a prisoner with a strangely baffling illness. It was sent to Captain King of Marysville who promptly made it public in the Marysville *Express*.

"My dear Captain King," it read, "I think you could make more by not being quite so officious, for I have had opportunities to put several hundred dollars in your pocket. There was the matter of the Walker and the Martin mares, for which there was $400 reward offered. I could have told you where you might find them, but your vigilant search after me keeps me from putting you on to a great many good things. But don't think for a moment that your vigilance causes me any uneasiness, or that I seek for an armistice. No, far from it, for I have unfurled my banner to the breeze, and my motto is 'Catch me if you can!'"

What Captain King thought of this attempt to bribe, combined with its defiant boast, is not recorded. But there was more. Tom had some further bragging to do, and a complaint to make. He continued: "Captain, I know you are pretty smart, but I think if you would only travel with me a short time I would teach you some tricks that you have never thought of. Probably you hear a great many things, but you must know I am not guilty of every accusation that is alleged against me. For instance, some malicious scoundrel tried to saddle the murder at Frenchman's Bar on me, but he could not do it, and although I am looked upon as a desperado and know that I could expect no leniency at the hands of the people should they ever catch me, still I am too proud to commit such an atrocious and cowardly murder as that was. Truly yours, Tom Bell."

A search of the files may some day disclose the facts of the murder to which Tom referred. In the meantime, it is interesting to speculate upon just what he was trying to accomplish by his letter. There is no reason to believe in the genuineness of his pious horror concerning the murder, whatever the circumstances. There was nothing brave about shooting Mrs. Tilghman to death, nor is there any evidence that Bell was other than a cold-blooded, vicious gunman and thief. There is, to be sure, the legend already referred to, in which Bell is said to have bound up a leg wound for one of his victims. But even if this really happened—and the story takes so many forms that the student is bound to doubt its authenticity—the incident is still no more than an expression of the rough humor of the time. The reader will remember that the teamster who was told to take the victim into town was also robbed for his pains, which obviously made the joke much better. And this is the only story that so much as hints at any streak of pity in Tom Bell. It is much more likely that Tom wrote his letter to Captain King partly in the spirit of bravado, partly perhaps on the slim off-chance that the officer might respond to the hint of a bribe (after all, there was no harm in trying), and partly in the desire to establish in the record a denial of a crime which would certainly mean the noose for him if he should be caught. For Tom Bell must have sensed the earnestness of the pursuit. He must have known that half a state was out to get him this time, determined that he would pay the penalty for his past crimes as well as his latest shocking attempt to rob a stagecoach.

Having published the outlaw's letter, Captain King went on with his methodical labors, scouring the area about Marysville in ever-widening circles. He turned up no clues, but he and his men kept at it. At least their activities would keep Bell away from that part of the country, maybe flush the gang for some other officer's quick shot.

There is no proof that King's quiet thoroughness was responsible, but early in September Detective Harrison of Sacramento had a piece of luck. His partner, Gay, had been taken off the case and replaced by a Marysville man, J. M. Anderson, and one fine day a member of Bell's gang fell into their hands. He was not one of the leaders, merely an associate of the outlaws who called himself Tom Brown. Still, he was likely to know about their movements. Detectives Harrison and Anderson supply no details; their report notes only that they "induced" Tom Brown to confess his complicity in various crimes of the gang and to tell what he knew of their whereabouts. They got nothing out of him about Tom Bell; perhaps he knew nothing. But he said he could show them exactly where five of the gang were in hiding, among them Bill Gristy and another Bell lieutenant named Walker. They were camped in a tent above Folsom, and not far from the Mountaineer House whose proprietor kept them supplied with food. The detectives agreed that this information was valuable. All that was necessary now was for Brown to take them to the place. He demurred, but eventually gave in. Having told so much, there was little else he could do. The detectives swore in two deputies whom they knew to be good men in a fight, Captain A. J. Barclay and a Marysville butcher whose name does not appear. With Brown as their guide, the four proceeded to Folsom and the Mountaineer House.

The fact that it was dark when they arrived did not worry the officers. When the iron was hot—that was the time to strike. Rapidly they outlined a plan of attack. Harrison and Anderson each had a double-barreled shotgun loaded with buckshot; the other two had rifles. The scheme—it was Harrison's, and he deserves full marks for courage—was for Brown to pull open the tent flap and greet his fellow-outlaws. Harrison and Anderson were then to spring in and cover the inmates with their guns. If a single shot was fired, so Harrison's instructions ran, the two outside were to riddle the tent with bullets; the officers would take their chances. The details thoroughly understood, Harrison and Anderson walked toward the lighted tent, nudging Brown ahead of them with the muzzles of their shotguns.

The first move went exactly as it had been laid out. Brown hailed his friends and entered the tent, holding back the flap while the two detectives rushed in and demanded surrender. If the five outlaws had all been seated, as four were, perhaps that would have been the end of it. But one was on his feet. In the center of the tent was a small table on which lay several pistols, and on the far side of it stood Walker, bending over a piece of mirror arranging his necktie. When the officers called to him to surrender he snatched one of the pistols from the table, shouted, "No! Never!" and fired, the ball passing between the two men. Harrison pulled the trigger of his shotgun and Walker dropped, the full charge of buckshot in his chest. Then both officers fell flat to avoid the bullets as the men outside fired through the canvas, according to plan.

But the detectives had made one mistake. It had not occurred to them to surround the tent. And the omission of that detail gave Bill Gristy his opportunity. Anderson, both barrels of his gun still loaded, covered the other three men who were glad enough to keep their hands above their heads and sit where they were. But Gristy knew that the sidewall near him was slack enough to allow a man to slide under it. He took his chance and dived for that wall, firing his pistol over his shoulder as he went. As Captain Barclay and the butcher rushed in, they saw him slipping away and yelled to Harrison, who swung round in time to let go the other barrel in Gristy's direction. He was just too late. They found out later that Gristy had sustained a severe scalp wound, but that was not enough to stop him. By the time the officers got out of the tent, he had vanished. There was one more shot fired; this time at Anara, one of the three that Anderson was covering, who made a desperate effort to follow Gristy. Anderson's aim was good; Anara fell with a charge of buckshot in the thigh. And that was that. Gristy had got away, but Walker was dead; the man Brown and three others were prisoners. None of the officers was injured. It was a good night's work.

The pursuit went on. From Camptonville came word that a small posse had run down Monte Jack, hiding on the premises of a Mexican named Ramirez. When they went to get him, Ramirez resisted the search and was promptly shot. The bandit got away, though the officers brought in three horses, one of which wore a bridle positively identified as Monte Jack's. Two days later the sheriff of Yuba County received a message from the Oregon House requesting him to come out immediately and pick up some members of Bell's gang who had been caught and held there. None of the men was Bell, nor were any of his sub-lieutenants represented, but there was evidence to connect three of them with Bell and they were jailed. Next day Marshal Nightingale, assisted by Captain Calloway of Marysville, arrested five more of Bell's men. The Sacramento *Union* reported the incident, adding the comment, "Well done thus far!" Shortly afterward the Calaveras *Chronicle* noted that Deputy-sheriff Shuler had brought in Jack Phillips of the Mountaineer House on the charge of having harbored members of Bell's gang and having "gathered information for their special benefit." Once they were very close to capturing Bell himself, when Sheriff Henson of Placer County and a posse had word that some of the gang were at the Franklin House near Auburn. Henson and his men got there just as Bell, Ned Connor (one of those who had broken prison with Tom and Bill Gristy a year and a half before), and a man known only as "Texas" were settling themselves in their saddles. In the fracas Connor was killed, but "Texas" and Bell made their escape.

All this was well enough, but the officers were out to get Tom Bell, and they were not going to relinquish the search until they found him. Sooner or later they would pick up his trail. Meantime they would continue making the mines too hot to hold him. When he or any of his close associates made the first slip, there would be somebody close at hand to follow it up.

4

If Tom Bell had been satisfied with a smaller gang in the first place, or if he had been able to keep all his men under his sharp eye, perhaps he would never have been caught. He was not a stupid man, cold-blooded and vicious though he had become, and he might have seen that his only course lay in leaving this part of the State, perhaps in adopting a less risky mode of life altogether. Many another robber and bandit of early-day California saw the light and either mended his ways or moved into some other section. Beginning over again in this new country was a relatively simple matter, provided only you went far enough away for your commencement.

But Bell's gang was large, and now its members were scattered. After the fight at the Franklin House, Tom and "Texas" had to lie low. His men might be conducting themselves wisely or they might not; there was no way he could control them. If his lieutenants exercised reasonably good judgment, all might yet be well. The commotion would die down sooner or later; winter was only a few weeks off and pursuit would be more difficult during the heavy rains and the cold. He had established a base camp, in a district where none of the officers would ever think to look for him. Now if he could only round up his men, or at least the most important among them, and give them his instructions it would be an easy matter to stay hidden until spring. By that time anything might happen. He sent out word by his grapevine that Bill

Gristy was to join him in the new hideout for special orders.

Bill got the word and took the trail southward into an area of the Mother Lode that Tom Bell had never worked. So far, all the gang's crimes had been committed in the Northern Mines up on the Yuba River and the American, where the pickings had seemed the best. Now Gristy and his companion, a Mexican, rode down the foothills toward the Stanislaus, the forks of the Tuolumne and the Merced.

As they came in sight of the flat lava spur of Table Mountain, Gristy had an idea. Since they were far out of their old territory, where no one could know them, why not ride on into Knight's Ferry and have a decent meal? It was perfectly safe. This far down the Lode, people were unlikely to be actively interested in Tom Bell, much less in his companions in banditry.

The trouble was that Gristy overestimated the quality of his own judgment and woefully underestimated the peace officers. It is a little habit criminals have; indeed it is part and parcel of their criminality. Knight's Ferry very likely seemed a dull country town to Gristy, a village of quiet farmer folk, with none of the sparkle and life of Nevada City, for instance, or Auburn. Yet it contained perhaps the one man in all the Southern Mines that Gristy should have avoided. He was Major T. W. Lane, owner of the Madison Mine at Angel's and proprietor of the Knight's Ferry hotel. It was neither of these activities that made him dangerous to Gristy, but the fact that he was a good friend of Captain Jack Hayes, Warden at the Angel Island prison. In fact, he knew Captain Hayes well enough to go over and visit him on the Island whenever he was down in San Francisco. During his last call, a year or two earlier, the Captain had given him a tour of his domain. And Major Lane had a quick eye for faces and an exceptionally retentive memory.

In a modest letter he wrote two weeks later to the San Joaquin *Republican* to straighten out a few of the facts for the editor, Major Lane said only that when the pair rode into town that evening "the white man was recognized by me as an escaped convict, known by the name of 'Bill White.' He was an accomplice of Tom Bell and a distinguished member of the band." He explained later that he had seen Gristy, *alias* White, on his visit to the prison, though he never made it clear how he knew Gristy to have been the same man who was associated with Bell. Perhaps the Major had talked with sheriffs who had come through town; maybe he was merely interested in following the doings of bandits anywhere. Whatever it was, as soon as he saw Gristy he got hold of the local under-sheriff and told him what he knew. Gristy and his Mexican friend were arrested before they so much as sat down to the dinner for which they had risked their liberty. Both were informed that their captors knew them to have been concerned in the Camptonville stage holdup, and both were thrown into the stone jail. A night's meditation on the pickle they were in might soften them up.

It softened them both, Gristy to the extent of breaking down completely, confessing all his crimes and revealing the location of Tom Bell's present secret camp, the Mexican far enough so that when he was told to direct a posse to the hideout he agreed. This was all anyone wanted to know. The law in its regular course could take care of these small fry. In the meantime, Bell was the man to go after.

Word was sent up and down the mines. Sheriffs and deputies arrived in town and rode out again; men gathered on street corners. Gristy was taken away to stand his trial in the north, where his crimes had been committed. The Mexican was held as a guide. It took time, but within three or four days plans were perfected, and the Knight's Ferry group, led by Judge Belt and a Mr. Armstrong, set the Mexican on a horse and told him to lead the way. Bell would be their prisoner or they would know the reason why.

South of Knight's Ferry the Tulare Lakes once connected with the San Joaquin River by a long slough. Near that junction, about six miles above Firebaugh's Ferry, was the small ranch to which the Mexican led Judge Belt and his posse. Bell, he told them, had found the place and taken it over, brought down from the north his old co-worker Mrs. Elizabeth Hood and her three daughters, aged eight, nine, and eleven, to keep house for him and his men. Somewhere he had got hold of two brothers named Farnsworth, elderly men of little use at the bandit's trade but able to cut wood, care for the horses, and do chores around the place. That was the story as far as he knew it. For the rest, they would soon be there and could see for themselves.

Judge Belt and his little group of determined citizens must have been sadly disappointed when they came through the willows into the little clearing to which the Mexican guided them. When they first saw the sentry posted at the edge of the flat, they may have been mo-

mentarily excited by the prospect of a battle. But almost
at once they recognized him. He was none of Tom Bell's
gang but a deputy from San Joaquin County named
McNish. As they rode up to the camp, his boss, Sheriff
Mulford himself, hailed them. Yes, he had arrived the
day before. He and his man had "borrowed" Bill Gristy
from the officers who were taking him north for trial, and
he had guided them. But they had not found Bell. They
had caught the two Farnsworth brothers, secured the
stock and horses that Bell had left in camp, and sent
Mrs. Hood and her children down to Stockton. A guard
had been posted to arrest any new arrivals, but so far
they had seen no Bell men. Judge Belt and his posse did
the only thing they could do. They put a good face on it,
joined forces with Sheriff Mulford and his crowd, and
took their turns standing guard.

This was on Monday, September 29. By Wednesday
they were growing bored with their vigil; no bandits had
turned up and there was no sign that any ever would.
Doubtless someone had warned Bell and his gang. They
might be anywhere by this time—half way to Mexico
probably. Sheriff Mulford, however, was of the bulldog
breed. Having got this much of a grip on the situation he
was not going to let go, at any rate not quite yet. Wednesday and Thursday went by quietly, sentries posted and
changed at proper intervals, meals eaten, the misdeeds of
Tom Bell discussed and rehashed until everyone was sick
of the topic. On Friday Sheriff Mulford gave in. If Bell
did not put in an appearance by the next morning they
would strike camp and disperse.

The sheriff kept his word. On Saturday morning there
was the bustle of packing and departure. The sheriff and

his group, all Stockton men, headed down river, starting before the Knight's Ferry party. Judge Belt and his posse were on their way within half an hour, following the road to Firebaugh's where they intended to make the crossing. One man was left behind—Robert Price of Sonora—who was going to ford the river a little higher up and take the road north and east for home. As the last of the Judge's men rode out of the clearing, Price waved good-bye and turned his horse toward the hills.

Once more Tom Bell's chances turned on the accidental appearance of a lone rider on an unexpected road. For as Mr. Price crossed the river, spurring his horse up the far bank, he caught a glimpse of a mounted man in the willows. For a split second he thought of hailing him, just out of friendliness, but something made him pause. Plainly the man did not realize he had been seen. He sat his horse silently, not moving; Price could see him out of the tail of his eye as he gained the road, still there among the trees, watching him out of sight.

Afterward Mr. Price admitted that he could not tell exactly why he had been suspicious. He had not seen enough of the man to identify him; it was only that in so lonely a spot a stranger had been so plainly anxious to avoid observation. At any rate, the incident was enough to make him turn south and west again as soon as he was out of sight of the river. There was another ford a little way down, and he could recross and communicate what he had seen to Judge Belt.

The Judge was very interested. Perhaps the stranger would turn out to be an innocent traveler. If so, no harm was done; the most the posse could lose would be half an hour's time. His men agreed that they should at least go back and have a look. The Judge shrewdly distributed his forces so as to make sure the area was at least fairly well covered. He and Mr. Price and one other would ride back to where that oddly silent mounted man had hidden himself. The rest of the company would deploy in a loose skirmish line on the plains, where they could see and follow if any rider broke out of the trees.

As they rode, the Judge questioned Mr. Price further. Had he been able to get any impression of the man? No, Mr. Price couldn't say that he had, excepting that he was sure the horseman was trying hard to keep concealed. Had he seen his face? No, he hadn't got a decent look at him at all; he was there in the woods, that was all Mr. Price knew. Was anyone with him? Mr. Price didn't think so; at any rate, he had seen no others.

It is difficult now to understand why Tom Bell's sharp ears did not detect the sound of three horses coming down the trail. Perhaps he heard them, but, knowing that the sheriff's men had gone, believed them to be ordinary travelers. However that may have been, Bell made no move to escape when the three rode up. Sitting relaxed in his saddle, he was talking to a mounted Mexican who was evidently paying close attention. And by the time he looked up, sensing something wrong, there were two mounted men with rifles leveled at him. A third—it was Judge Belt himself—had dismounted and was standing a little closer, his double-barreled shotgun cocked and aimed. Bell made no move excepting to drop his rifle to the ground as he was told, and then to raise his hands slowly above his head. The first word was spoken, fittingly, by Judge Belt. "I believe," said the Judge, "that you are the man we have been looking for." Bell looked at him coolly for a moment, and answered, "Very probably." That was enough for the Judge. "Tie him up!" he said.

Mr. Price rode closer, covering Bell from one side, while the Judge continued to keep his shotgun aimed at Bell's head. The third member of the party removed a Navy revolver and a bowie knife from the bandit's belt and tied his wrists securely, ordering him to dismount, which he did without a murmur. His arms were lashed behind him, the Mexican was made fast, and the little party turned down the river toward Firebaugh's, six miles away. It was as tame as that. There had been plenty of color in Bell's eighteen months as a road-agent; his act in attempting to hold up the Camptonville stage was in itself as dramatic a crime as the mines had seen in the half-dozen years since the gold rush began. But now the drama had somehow gone out of it. His gang dispersed, his right-hand man turned informer, Tom Bell, the terror of the mines, trudged along the hot road, trussed elbow to elbow with his Mexican companion like any common cattle-thief. There could not have been any doubt in his mind. He knew he was never going to walk down a road again anywhere.

At Firebaugh's they asked Bell a few desultory questions. He admitted he was Tom Bell, didn't he? Yes, he was Tom Bell. Where had he been hiding? In the camp that his captors had found the Monday before. He had done no robbing in that time, though he had been in a fight a week earlier, up near Auburn. Yes, Judge Belt and his posse had heard about it; Ned Connor had been killed, did Bell know that? He had heard so, he said. Had he anything else to say for himself? Well, Bell said, he would like to make a complete confession; he would feel better if they would allow him to tell the whole story before they hanged him.

Judge Belt talked it over with his aides but decided against permitting this. The afternoon was getting on, and a rider had been sent hurrying after Sheriff Mulford to tell him of the capture; now it occurred to them that the sheriff would insist on taking the prisoner to jail and giving him the benefit of due process of law. That did not suit them. Bell's band had not thought about due process of law when they raked the Camptonville stage with their fire. Mrs. Tilghman, the barber's wife, had been given no chance; a bullet from someone's gun—it might just as well have been Bell's—had killed her in that battle. And how about Mr. Argrave, mercilessly beaten about the head while his store was robbed? No, it was a little late to be talking about confessions. They knew all they needed to know. Bell had better make up his mind to have it over with.

There is no record that Tom Bell flinched when he was told the verdict. He did ask time to write, which they gave him, telling him to be quick about it. He wrote two letters, one to Mrs. Hood, the other to his mother. A week later the San Francisco *Alta* printed the communication to Mrs. Hood, describing it as "written in a bold, elegant style, such as would be called a 'business hand,' carefully punctuated &c." It ran as follows:

Firebaugh's Ferry, Oct 4, '56

Mrs. Hood, my dear and only friend now in this country:

As I am not allowed the liberty of seeing you, I have been given the privilege of writing you a few lines, as I have but a few moments to live. I am at a great loss for something to say. I have been most foully betrayed. Bill and John have told things that never took place. I am accused of every robbery that has been committed for the past twelve months, which is entirely false. I have never committed but three highway robberies in my life; but still I am to blame and my fate is sealed. I am to die like a dog, and there is but one thing that grieves me, and that is the condition of you and your family. Probably I have been the instrumentality of your misfortunes. In my last moments I will think of the many favors you have done me, and if I had fifty kingdoms to present, you should have them all. But alas! I am poor and my fate is sealed. I would like to give you some advice but I fear you may think me presumptuous. What I would say is this: That you had better send the girls to San Francisco to the Sisters of Charity. There they will be educated and taken care of. Tell all the girls farewell! Tell them to be good girls and to be very careful to whom they pledge themselves for life. All the money I have is ten dollars, which I have given to Mr. Chism for Sarah. If you ever see Edward S., tell him my fate. I must come to a close, for the hounds are thirsting for my blood. Good-bye forever.

THOS. J. BELL.

His letter to his mother was shorter:

Dear Mother:—

As I am about to make my exit to another country, I take this opportunity to write you a few lines. Probably you may never hear from me again. If not, I hope we may meet where parting is no more.

In my prodigal career in this country, I have always recollected your fond admonitions, and if I had lived up to them probably I would not have been in my present condition; but dear Mother, though my fate has been a cruel one, yet I have no one to blame but myself. Give my respects to all my old and youthful friends. Tell them to beware of bad associations, and never to enter into any gambling saloons, for that has been my ruin.

If my old Grandmother is living, remember me to her. With these remarks, I bid you farewell forever.

Your only boy,

TOM.

By the time Tom had finished these two epistles it was almost four o'clock in the afternoon. One of the party came to ask him if he was ready and Tom said he was, adding that now his life was worth nothing to him. He was told he might have a drink of whiskey if he wished and he said he thought he would like that. They asked him once more if he had anything to say about the others concerned with him in his career of crime, and he replied that he had no revelations to make; he would be gratified, however, to drink to the health of the party present and hoped that no personal prejudice had induced them to execute him. After this pleasant gesture he asked one more favor. Would they permit him to read aloud to them the letter he had written to his mother? No one objected, and Tom read from the paper in his hand, the members of the posse standing respectfully silent as he did so. After he was finished, he added a few rambling remarks about his past life, saying that his first experience in crime had followed upon his ruin at gambling, and that it had been the theft of eleven mules from a Mexican *vaquero* near Mariposa. It was his success in this crime, he said, that led him to continue in his evil ways—that and the fact that Mexicans had always seemed to him natural enemies. If circumstances had not made it necessary he would never have robbed any American of so much as one cent.

It is hard to believe that Tom Bell could have thought such a plea would soften the hearts of the men who caught him. Perhaps he did not really think so; the chances are he was just talking. For all the bold face he put upon it, the knowledge that a rope was awaiting him not fifty feet away must have struck coldly at his heart; even a minute or two more of life was something; they wouldn't walk him out to that tall sycamore as long as he told them anything they wanted to hear. But apparently they had heard enough. Two men took him, one at each elbow, and turned him toward the door. Between the cabin and the tree, he said desperately that he was only twenty-six years old. The information did not seem to interest anybody. As they settled the noose around his neck, he appeared to get hold of himself and began to pray in a low, controlled tone of voice. He was still praying when they walked away with the other end of the rope.

Ten minutes later, Sheriff Mulford and his Stockton men rode into Firebaugh's Ferry, conveniently late for the ceremonies.

5

As Tom Bell in life had been a source of conflict and confusion, so he was in death.

By Monday, October 6, some of the foothill papers had the story, among them the San Andreas *Independent*, which printed a reasonably factual account together with a brief sketch of Bell in which the reporter noted that Tom had made a point of his youth when he was caught. Evidently it did not occur to the editor to check back on Tom's plea that he was so young; if he had, he might have wondered just how the bandit had become a doctor so early in life. If he was no more than twenty-six when he was caught, he had begun his medical career at the tender age of eighteen. Even in those days of easy diplomas, that would have been stretching it.

Three days later the Stockton *Argus* felt that the story of Bell's capture and execution was sufficiently authenticated so that it might be stated as a fact. This paper added that most of the Bell gang had been captured, though there were still a few at large. Down in San Francisco, the *Alta* copied that report from the Sacramento *Union*, which had quoted it, but added that it was probably untrue, a rumor only, which had been spread by the gang in order to give Bell freedom to get away.

One paper gratuitously injected a scalping into the proceedings; Bell, it said, had been "hanged and scalped on the upper San Joaquin." The San Francisco *Alta* repeated that it was all nonsense, that Bell was still alive, and that a man who knew him quite well had actually seen him since the date on which he was reported hanged. Further, the *Alta* noted, the grand jury of Placer County had recommended that a reward of one thousand dollars be offered for the arrest and detention of Tom Bell. The editor implied that in the face of such evidence no one could believe the story that the bandit had been caught and done away with.

Nevertheless it was true, and before long the public— even the *Alta*—was convinced. Indeed, its editor did the handsome thing by his readers, confirming the story and adding a fine, wordy moral homily in which he made note of the sad fact that the discoveries of gold in California and the "eager chase after the butterfly of wealth" had led to such evils as avarice, recklessness, and in this case to out-and-out crime. "Temptations," he wrote, "are about the gold-seekers on every hand. They drink and they gamble. They associate with men who, in their Eastern homes, would be shunned by them as the worst of their kind. Still worse, they forget the admonitions of mothers and sisters given them at parting. Will not this be a warning to our young men?" In case the caution might not be sufficiently strong, the editor added two sentences in which he put the matter on the strictest practical basis. "The fate of the desperado in California is becoming a certain one," he wrote. "Let Tom Bell's end be a warning to all who today are treading in the path which led him to the gallows." If one plea, on mere ethical grounds, wasn't enough, certainly two, the second issued in all logic, should take root in the hearts of California's youth.

Tom Bell was dead, his gang was scattered, most of them were in jail and the rest would be run down within a few weeks. Yet the case was not quite closed. There were two postscripts.

One came in the form of a letter from Mrs. Elizabeth Hood to the *Bulletin* in San Francisco. That paper had printed the confession of Bill Gristy, *alias* White, as he gave it, and there was a statement in it that irked Mrs. Hood greatly. The *Bulletin's* editor evidently felt that in this case an injustice had been done, for he gave Mrs. Hood the freedom of his columns. Her statement was dated Stockton, October 24:

> Bill White states that my children are, respectively, aged nine, eleven and fourteen years, and that Sarah, the eldest, was kept by Tom Bell as his mistress. The whole story is

totally untrue. My daughters are aged eight, nine and eleven years respectively, and Sarah, instead of being the eldest, is the second child and nine years old. Anyone who has seen the children cannot but be convinced of the falsity of White's statement. The disagreeable duty of thus appearing in the public prints is forced upon me from the fact that my daughters were dismissed from school on the strength of the statements contained in the confession above alluded to, as unfit associates for children of a like age. As a mother I could not pass by in silence a slander so infamous on an artless child.

Perhaps Mrs. Hood was telling the truth. If so, she must have been forcibly reminded of the proverb about people being known by the company they keep. Her daughters may, as she said, have been mere children and no more than that to Bell. But Mrs. Hood herself was by no means free from blame in the matter. After all, she had been closely associated with Bell for more than a year. She knew very well what business he was in, and had helped him conduct that business on many occasions. It was too bad that some of the pitch should have stuck to her children through no fault of theirs (if the facts were as she put them), but the mother who "could not pass by in silence a slander so infamous on an artless child" would have done better to think about such things long before.

The second after-event was perhaps the most tragic in the whole Bell saga. On November 3, almost exactly a month after the quiet execution on the banks of the Merced, five men in the Northern Mines, to which the news had not yet penetrated, heard a rumor that Tom Bell was concealed in a cabin near Gold Flat. It was after nightfall when they got the story, but the deputy who led them out into the dark was a man who took his duty seriously. If they waited until morning, the outlaw might be gone. Now was the time to get him.

The little party set out, splitting into two groups as they came to the small ravine at whose head was the cabin for which they were looking. The deputy and the men who remained with him made their way through the brush for some minutes, when suddenly they came upon two horses tied to a tree. This, obviously, was the place to lie in wait; when Bell and his companion came to recover their mounts they would have them. They waited for half an hour, and then the deputy heard a rustle in the bushes ahead. "Who is there?" he called, adding, "Move and I shoot!" The answer was a blast of rifle fire from the thicket, to which the deputy and his friends replied. The counter-fire killed the deputy and wounded one of his aides. It was only then that the men in the brush came forward. They were the two other members of the party who had tethered their horses and gone forward on foot, to find the rumor false and the cabin empty.

As to later views of Tom Bell and his brief, violent career, it is curious to note that Bancroft, who mentions him in his history of California written thirty years afterward, seems to have missed the one important point about him and to have gathered a wholly erroneous notion of his nature. Maybe it was one of the great historian's staff writers who made the mistake, but the veritable Hubert Howe Bancroft who set his name to it must bear the responsibility. For the fact that Tom Bell was the actual pioneer in organized stage-robbery in California—even though unsuccessfully—seems to have escaped the historian entirely. What he saw instead was the shining halo of knight-of-the-road-errantry which descends sooner or

later on all bandits. The reader, who has here seen Tom
Bell as the record shows him, may come to his own conclusions about Bancroft's statement that Bell was "by
far the most intelligent, accomplished and kind-hearted
American gentleman who ever took the road in California."

The halo—if the metaphor may stand—must have
shone uncommonly brightly in Bancroft's eyes.

# RATTLESNAKE DICK

THERE IS NOTHING MUCH AT Rattlesnake Bar nowadays. It is merely a shallow bend in the North Fork of the American River, more gravelly than most of the bottom thereabouts perhaps and dotted with weatherworn humps of old stone. Back from the banks there is a little scattering of spindly second-growth pine and stunted live oak, a mangy fur on the back of the red earth that marks the gold region. The river, too, loses its earlier vigor and dash, readying itself for its departure from the foothills into the wide valley of the Sacramento only a few miles farther west. It is a lonesome spot now, too bare for worthwhile cultivation, too far from towns for anyone to want to live there.

In the early 1850s Rattlesnake Bar was another matter. Hundreds of cabins clustered in the ravine of the American, spread themselves on both banks, clotted in small groups near the river. For Rattlesnake Bar was heavy with gold, inexhaustible, men thought, and the California gold-seekers swarmed there to wash their fortunes from its gravel. One of the richest placers in an area notable for richness, it was known as the best spot in the Northern Mines for a man to make his first try.

The trouble was that this kind of mining had no real permanence. The gold caught in the river beds where the glaciers had dropped it was easily available, though at the cost of back-breaking labor with shovel and Long Tom. But there was just so much of it and no more. And with half the world coming to work the streams, it could not last forever. By 1853, even Rattlesnake Bar was thinning out. Now and then a big pocket would raise the hopes of the miners when they happened on a spot that had not been turned over, but the riffles in their sluice-boxes caught fewer and fewer of the heavy grains, and there was less and less chance for a new man to get hold of a claim. As the year grew older Rattlesnake Bar lost its thousands. Some few stayed; it was possible to make a reasonable profit still, if a man was willing to keep at it. But miners were restless, and there was always some rumor of a new strike in the air. Most of them moved on; the foothills were wide and long; somewhere else they would find the Golconda they knew was just around the corner.

Nobody had told the two Barter brothers that the California rivers were like this. Sons of a British Army officer stationed in Quebec, they had the black hair and dark eyes, the mercurial spirits, the adventurous, reckless temperament of their French-Canadian mother, and when their father died they went looking for their fortunes in the United States. The spirit of the Oregon Trail was in the air then, and that bright land seemed to them just what they were looking for. California and its gold were not far from Oregon, either, and perhaps when they had seen the Northwest they might try the gold country and discover what it had to offer. With their sister, her husband, and an elderly cousin, they joined a caravan and rolled westward to find the end of the rainbow most of America seemed to be seeking.

It was a foregone conclusion that Oregon would not hold two such lively young men. Their sister and brother-in-law well established in the tiny settlement of Sweet Home, they began to think of the riches to the southward —easy riches, to be had for the trouble of picking them up. Richard, the younger, was especially anxious to have a try at the mines. Just under twenty, handsome, daring, undisciplined, he was bound to go and he won his more conservative brother over to his scheme. They assured their anxious sister that it would be only a short trip. A few months and they would be back with enough gold to make the whole family rich. How could they fail when thousands were picking up more gold in a day than they could spend in months? The sister who did her devout best to take care of these dashing brothers finally agreed. But they mustn't disappear, as so many gold-hunters were doing. They must keep in touch with her, let her know how they fared. After all, they were her only close kin. The brothers promised; of course they wouldn't forget her. But she would see. They would be back in no time, wealthy men.

What in another era might have sounded like nonsense was a commonplace in the 1850s. Even the elderly cousin took fire from the boys' enthusiasm. He would go with them and get his share of the easy money too. In a fever of happy anticipation the three set out for California.

They were on their way to an adventure even bigger than
the westward trek they had just finished. So they came
to Rattlesnake Bar on the American River. The newest
and richest placer yet, its name was on every man's
tongue. Obviously it was the proper place to begin getting rich.

It took a little less than twenty-four months to convince two of them that their dream was not going to
come true. Rattlesnake Bar itself was just about placered
out, and anyway the brothers had no opportunity to take
up a good claim of their own. They worked on shares
here and there and learned something about the hard
labor that went into this game of "easy pickings." They
found out what it meant to stand hip-deep in the icy river
all day for perhaps as much as fifteen or twenty dollars
if they were lucky, and then to have to spend all they
made for food at the fantastically high prices that prevailed in the mines. They discovered that it was almost
as bad to broil in the sun, to carry water when the river
ran low in the dry season, to slave at building flumes that
the storms of autumn would probably reduce to match-
wood. Like thousands of others, they made their private
prospecting trips into the hills, following up smaller
streams, washing the dirt in dry diggings in the hope of
finding the telltale "color" that meant gold in paying
quantities. But they had no luck. And finally, the older
brother and the cousin concluded that Oregon looked better to them. A man might not make a fortune overnight
at farming, but anyone who was willing to pay attention to business could get a good living out of that fine
rich country of the Northwest. Their sister wrote that

she and her husband were doing well, and that the sensible thing was for the brothers to come back and join them. There was plenty of room on the new homestead, and any amount of land to be had if they wanted their own. Why continue to pursue the golden will-o'-the-wisp when it was very clear that they were no nearer to wealth than on the day they left Sweet Home? The two made up their minds to go back. As the phrase went, they had "seen the elephant." But there was no budging the younger. Dick Barter was going to stay. He had come to California to make his fortune and he was going to remain until he did. They left him at Rattlesnake Bar, still obstinately convinced that somehow he would succeed where his brother and cousin had failed. He would show them. They shook their heads, but understood that nothing they could say would make him change his mind. Dick was always like that—headstrong, proud, certain he knew better than the next man. Those were good qualities, too, in their way, and maybe after all Dick would have the luck they had missed. They said good-bye and turned northward. Dick was twenty-one now and a man; he could find his own road.

For another year Dick Barter stuck to mining, working for men who had claims, doing a little prospecting on his own. Miners began to move away, to try other rivers, to tackle some of the new quartz veins that people were talking about over in Nevada City. Rattlesnake Bar was losing its prestige rapidly. A handful of men clung to their river; there was still gold enough if a man didn't insist on growing rich all at once, and besides habit is strong. None of them, however, expected to get more

than good wages out of it; they understood the ways of
these streams and knew that by patient hard work they
might make a living for some years yet, but that was all.
Young Dick Barter was the only one who kept the enthusiasm with which he had come. Rattlesnake Bar would
yet prove itself the best town in the placers; he knew it.
Over in Auburn on Saturday nights he expatiated on his
theme until he became a standing joke among the older
miners. "Rattlesnake Dick," they called him. There was
no malice in their jest, merely the rough frontier humor
that passed for wit in that time and place. Nor did Dick
mind. The name was a tag, a label, an identification
mark, that was all. In the mines men who were honestly
disliked had less pleasant nicknames than that.

Writing of Dick twenty years later, a Nevada County
historian described him as "naturally able, clever but
selfish, vain, and devoid of the ordinary sense of right
and wrong—one of those men whose course in life is gov-
erned by circumstances."

Perhaps that old historian was right about it. Yet looking back after three-quarters of a century, his judgment
seems a trifle on the harsh side. True, Dick Barter did
go wrong, hopelessly and irretrievably to the bad. But
he was tried in ways that his judge can hardly have experienced. Probably a stronger character might have bent
circumstances to his will; a better man could have thrown
off the bad luck, made his life come right in spite of everything. Maybe he could. It is hard to say. A man is what
he is; it is not intelligent to demand that he be something
else. Incredibly difficult circumstances did govern Dick's
course. He learned, not once or twice but three times, that
men can be unbelievably callous, revengeful, cruel, and

for little or no reason. The knowledge made him an enemy of society. Yet—well, the reader may judge.

It began in the early spring of 1853.

Somehow Dick had earned the ill will of one of the miners on the North Fork. The man's name does not appear in any of the records nor is there any explanation of his grievance. There is only the bare fact. The proprietor of the small camp store at the Bar had reason to believe that someone was stealing his stock, and a man who hated Dick reported to the authorities that he was the thief. He was arrested and tried on the charge, but a local attorney, "Judge" B. F. Meyers, defended him so successfully that the jury found him not guilty. The sentiment in Rattlesnake Bar was that young Dick had been made the victim of spite, and his trial in no way damaged him among his friends.

But this was only the beginning. Later that year Dick was in trouble again. A Mormon named Crow missed his mule and declared flatly that Dick Barter had stolen it. This was a far more serious charge; in those days it was a high crime to rob a man of his means of transportation —horse or mule, it was all the same. This time Dick was not so well defended. Sentiment ran strong against him, and he was convicted and sentenced to State's Prison for two years. He did not get as far as Angel Island, then the California prison. For, once more, evidence was produced to show that Dick had been falsely accused. It was strong enough so that he was released before his guards had taken him out of town. Then conclusive proof turned up. The mule was found, and the man who had stolen it was arrested and confessed his crime.

It is hard to believe that one young fellow, no matter if he was vain, too clever to please some of his acquaintances, even (as the historian calls him) out-and-out selfish, could have been so badly used. But it is not hard to see what could and did happen afterward. Whatever Dick did, he was remembered as the man who had twice been in trouble over a matter of theft. To be sure, the courts had set him free but, well, the relationship between smoke and fire is well known. So the whisper ran. There was nothing for Dick to do but leave that part of the country and begin again somewhere else.

Even the historian who judges him so harshly gives Dick full credit for making the attempt to start a new life, to conduct himself so uprightly that thereafter no one could so much as accuse him of any crime. Shasta County was a good hundred and fifty miles away. Perhaps there he would have a chance to commence a new career which would bring him the luck he had failed to find so far. To make doubly sure, he would even change his name. As "Dick Woods," he could be born again, begin where he began when he had come to California three years earlier, all the way down from Sweet Home in Oregon, hope high in his breast.

There was nothing the matter with his plan. Many another man had done the same thing, and for reasons less honorable. People did not inquire too closely into another man's past in those days; too many had their own secrets which were just as well buried. For more than two years, Dick Barter succeeded in living quietly and industriously as "Dick Woods" up in Shasta. His luck, apparently, was no better than it had been, as far as mining went. But he got along, found himself in no trouble, lived an uneventful life like a thousand other miners about him until the spring of 1856.

In that year a new lawlessness seems to have sprung up throughout the foothills; perhaps it was a reflection of the state of affairs in San Francisco, which was steadily growing worse. Convicts from Australia, known in the mines as "Sydney ducks," had begun to wander into California, and more and more riffraff from all quarters of the earth made the State their goal. Once honesty had been the rule throughout the canyons and gulches. A man could leave his tools, even his gold, unguarded on his claim or in his cabin and no one thought of disturbing them. Now everything was different. The early community of friendliness was being replaced by suspicion. It was every man for himself, and no one knew when a stranger might turn out to be no decent miner but a thief or worse. As the year grew older, too, crime began to organize itself. Men like Monte Jack allied themselves with such leaders as Tom Bell, and swept through the foothill counties, robbing wholesale. Often an unlucky miner gave up scratching the earth in disgust, feeling that he could do better in illegal ways than by hard work where there was so little reward.

Dick, however, seems to have meant it when he determined on leading an upright life. He was growing no richer, but he was getting along. And though other men took to the road, he stuck to honest labor and kept sedulously away from the law. Perhaps he would have lived and died an honest citizen if it had not been for his unfortunate capacity for making enemies in his youth. Maybe it was the "vanity and selfishness" which the historian remarked in him, or it may have been merely his debonair good looks and high enthusiasm, so irritating to men soured by ill fortune. Whatever the cause, he had left enemies behind him in Rattlesnake Bar. Now one such enemy took the opportunity to do him a bad turn. Someone who had known Dick in the Ratlesnake days came through Shasta County and saw him, and again the story got about. No one needed to tell him what had happened; it was evident in the conduct of everyone who pointed at him, whispered about him, avoided being seen with him. A third time his luck had done him down.

Many years afterward, a man who knew Dick testified that he had heard him say, "I can stand it no longer! I have been driven to it. Hereafter my hand is against everyone, and I suppose everyone's is against me!" This may or may not be accurate reporting, but undoubtedly it describes Dick's state of mind when he realized that the old slanders had caught up with him. Here he was, victim of an incredible series of thrusts of fate; young, strong, and ambitious, but cut off by a chain of fantastic accidents from even the chance to make a decent living. Meantime men who were frankly outlaws were ranging the highways, taking what they wanted, committing ever more spectacular robberies, yet inspiring fear and respect. People only sneered at Dick Woods who had stolen a mule and somehow got out of it. Like many another before him and since, Dick decided that if he was to have the name he might as well have the game too. At least he might prosper at the bandit's trade. His mind was made up. One night he poked his pistol into the face of a lonely traveler, getting enough money to help him southward to the country he had once known so well. Still young enough to require a seasoning of melodrama with his misdeeds, he told the victim that if anyone asked who had robbed him he might say it was a man who called himself Rattlesnake Dick.

Even that, however, didn't seem quite strong enough. There ought to be a handle to swing it by. Then he had an inspiration. "The Pirate of the Placers!" he added as he faded into the brush.

2

Ishmael or pirate, Dick lost no time in making himself known to the miners whose treatment had driven him outside the law.

Back in his old haunts on the American River, he roamed from Rattlesnake Bar down to Folsom, robbing on the highroad, cleaning out sluice-boxes, running off horses and cattle. At first he worked alone; after all, he had to learn the trade. But it was a day of gangs in the mines, and it was not long before Dick saw that he could do better if he fell in with the trend of the times. Near Folsom, on the Auburn road, was the Mountaineer House, run by a Sydney man named Phillips; the rumor was that Tom Bell used the inn as one of his rendezvous. Whether or not Dick knew Bell is not recorded. He did know Phillips. And it was through the kind offices of that unsavory gentleman that he got together his first gang in the early summer of 1856. He had a plan in his mind, and he needed help in carrying it out. If the crew of rascals that he now gathered round him proved to be even reasonably stout fellows, he believed he could stage what would be the biggest robbery California had ever seen.

There were five of them altogether. One, Dick's most trusted lieutenant, was a choice scalawag named George

Skinner. Sometimes he called himself "Walker," and occasionally he chose "Williams" as his alias. He had been in and out of California jails ever since he had come West, had twice been sent to State's Prison on larceny charges and had escaped once. His brother, Cyrus Skinner, was hardly less notable a criminal; he had been in State's Prison but had escaped, and had a long record of jail sentences before that last incarceration. To this precious pair Dick added a husky horse-thief, one "Big Dolph" Newton, an Italian named Romero (sometimes called "Nicorona"), and a nondescript small-time robber, Bill Carter. Together these six inaugurated a regime of wholesale banditry and theft throughout Placer and Nevada counties, even going so far as to rob stores and cabins. The populace was thoroughly irritated by their performances, and random posses occasionally went out to trace them after a robbery. But nothing came of their efforts to catch up with the gang. Men like Phillips in the Mountaineer House always knew when a pursuit was in the wind; once warned, Dick and his crowd were able to go into hiding until the angry citizens had cooled down. What no one knew was that Dick's big plan was slowly maturing. The months of varied depredations were giving him a chance to try out his men, accustom them to his ways, make sure they could be relied upon when the time came. By midsummer of 1856, Dick was pretty sure his gang could take orders, and he was ready for his master stroke.

The plan had its inception in a bit of information Dick had picked up in his honest days in Shasta County. There he had heard of the manner in which gold was shipped out from the mountains in the north. From the mines up near Yreka there was no road good enough for stages, and the habit was to send out the bullion packed on mules. The mule trains were usually guarded by a convoy, but a few well-armed men acting in concert should be able to surprise the guards, tie them up, and make off with the treasure. There was only one hitch in such a proceeding. The express mules all bore the express company's brand and would be recognized anywhere. That meant a transfer of the bullion to a new lot of pack animals. Dick had thought about it, and had his scheme ready. George Skinner, whom he could trust, would head the gang; with him would be Carter, Big Dolph, and Romero. In the meantime, Dick and Cyrus Skinner would raid a corral they knew about, down near Auburn, steal the necessary mules and drive them up through the foothills to an appointed meeting place. There the two groups would join forces, transfer the gold, and skip. Dick went over the scheme carefully for flaws, but there seemed to be none. It would work, he was sure.

First, all six scouted the terrain and pitched upon the spot at which they would intercept the loaded mule train. They chose the side of Trinity Mountain, a spur of the basaltic formations that line the northern Sierra's western slope, and as lonely and desolate a stretch as any in the hills. It would have been hard to find a better place for the attack. The ground was broken and rough; all the mountainside was cut and scarred with small ravines and gulches where the robbers with a secretly marked trail to follow could throw off any pursuit if they should have to run for it. But they did not expect it to come to that. Lying in wait at a sharp bend in the rocky trail, they could pick off the convoy very easily as the string of mules wound round the curve. George Skinner was certain he could handle the job perfectly. All that Dick and Cyrus Skinner needed to do was to be at the appointed spot with the unbranded animals.

As a matter of fact, George Skinner had not over-estimated his talents. He came near making one mistake when, as an afterthought, he augmented his party of four with a Mexican he knew. Perhaps, as will appear, it was the Mexican who made the mistake. But Skinner and his men carried out their part of the plan with precision. As a contemporary reporter put it, "the demeanor of the robbers was so fierce and the attack so sudden that the men with the train could not resist." Working fast, Skinner and his companions tied the guards to trees, unloaded the treasure from the mules, and made off across the mountain to the rendezvous. The gold was too heavy to carry very far; there was something like eighty thousand dollars' worth of it altogether. But they had chosen their spot well. Though it was only a short distance from the trail it was well concealed, and in any event the disarmed guard would not dare to follow, even if its members managed to work themselves loose. Skinner congratulated himself on a job well done, and he and his men settled themselves to wait for the arrival of Dick, brother Cyrus, and the new mules.

They waited all night and the next day. George Skinner then sent out a party of two, instructing them to scout down the mountainside, parallel to the trail and keeping it in sight, in order to learn whether by some chance Dick and Cyrus had missed the markings which would lead them to the spot agreed on. The scouting party returned on the second day, having seen no sign of Dick, Cyrus, or the mules. On the evening of the third day, the Mexican's nerve broke. He was not accustomed to operations on as grand a scale as this, and with every hour he had grown more apprehensive. Now he demanded that he be given his share of the plunder and the chance to leave. The convoy had worked itself loose on the first day, taken its branded mules, and ridden away; Big Dolph Newton, posted as a sentry on a high peak, had seen them go. They would be back any day now with officers from down below, and even five desperate outlaws would have no chance against them. For himself, the Mexican said, he did not want to be there when that happened. He would take his cut and go.

George Skinner saw that the unaccountable failure of Dick and his brother to appear had jeopardized the success of the entire scheme. Nevertheless he was enough of a tactician to see also that it would never do to turn this excitable fellow loose, with or without a share of the gold. He might be caught; he might weaken and give the whole show away. Peace officers were sometimes not too particular about the means they used to induce a man to betray his fellows, and the chance was too great. He told the Mexican he would have to stay and see it through with the rest of them. He had been brought into the robbery and given an opportunity at some real treasure. Now he would have to take the bad luck with the good. Perhaps the Mexican did not believe Skinner meant what he said; he may have thought, too, that he would not dare to risk the sound of firing when officers might be near. For he drew his knife and informed the other four that he was going, share or no share, and no one would stop him. That was his last move. Skinner shot him dead on the spot.

The act brought matters to a head. It was clear that something must have happened to Dick and Cyrus. Between them, the four now on the ground could carry half the gold they had stolen. The thing to do was to bury the other half and mark the spot. Some time later they could come back and recover it; just now this part of the country was likely to be too warm to hold them. The other three agreed that Skinner was right.

Somewhere on the side of Trinity Mountain that forty thousand dollars may still lie hidden. For when the gang got their half of the gold back to Folsom, they found that the law had been too smart for them. Instead of trying to trail the robbers through the rocky Trinity countryside, the officers had taken the word of the convoy guards who were sure that the men concerned were associates of Rattlesnake Dick. Acting on this belief, a posse had gathered near Jack Phillips' place on the Auburn road. After depositing the portable half of the stolen gold in the Folsom hideout, Skinner had led his men toward Auburn to see if he could learn what had become of Dick and Cyrus, and shortly after dark they met the posse under Detective Jack Barkeley of Wells, Fargo. The fight was over very quickly. George Skinner was instantly killed, and Newton and Carter threw down their guns in surrender. Romero, badly wounded, made off through the trees; but Barkeley went after him and fished him out of the American River into which he had plunged, with the notion of swimming across. All three of the robbers were taken down to Folsom and tried in short order. Romero, his wound healed, got ten years in the penitentiary. Big

Dolph Newton received the same sentence. Carter would have been there beside them but for the fact that both Dick and Skinner had judged him wrongly. He was the weak one. When the officers told him what he was up against he led them to the Folsom hideout, where they recovered the forty thousand dollars that had been carried so painfully all the way from Trinity Mountain. As for the buried half of the treasure, Carter could not help them there. George Skinner had dug the hole, marked the spot in his mind, and told the others it was none of their business. Now he was dead and the secret had died with him. The law kept an eye on Carter for some time, but apparently his story was true. Given a full pardon, he settled in Placer County, and, as far as the record goes, turned honest. At least he was never known to go within a hundred miles of the mountainside where the gold was hidden, and he died a poor man.

As for Dick and Cyrus, the law knew nothing about them. Perhaps Carter had been afraid to tell; he may have known Dick well enough so that he could be sure he would get even for any treachery toward him. And the officers had known nothing of Dick's part in the affair; all they had heard was that the robbers had been Dick's associates. Perhaps they never asked Carter. At any rate, it was left for the editor of an Auburn paper to solve the mystery of what had happened to Dick and Cyrus, though he did not know his little item bore any relation to the gold-train robbery that had startled all northern California. He printed it, in fact, on the Saturday before the robbers had got back to Folsom with their half of the treasure. George Skinner may or may not have read the story before Barkeley's bullet finished him. It was only a stickful of

type, to the effect that earlier in the week Rattlesnake Dick
and a companion, one Cyrus Skinner, had been lodged in
the Auburn jail for stealing mules.

### 3

Once committed to his career of crime, Dick was nothing if not resourceful.

Obviously he could not carry on his profession of highwayman while he languished in Auburn jail. The thing to
do was to get out. He found Cyrus Skinner willing to listen. Cyrus, as a matter of fact, had been committing his
recent crimes on borrowed time; he had served only a few
weeks of a fourteen-year term in State's Prison when he
escaped and joined Dick. Now he was faced with the
prospect of going back to Angel Island, and for a much
longer stretch. He was more than anxious to hear any
scheme Dick might put forward.

As it worked out, the escape was a simple one: a matter
of a key mistakenly left in a lock, and a quick dash into
the darkness. The two had agreed to separate and meet in
San Francisco. Dick fulfilled his part of the bargain, but
Cyrus was not so fortunate. They caught him next morning hiding in the brush outside Auburn, and he went back
to the Island after all. This time it took him four years to
work out a plan of escape. When he succeeded, he wisely
came to the conclusion that California was not a good
place for him and made tracks for Montana. He might
better have stayed, for the good people of that part of
the country had even less patience than the Californians.
The first time Cyrus tried his little tricks they strung him
up to a tree.

Even Dick might have picked a better spot than San Francisco at that particular time. Just a month earlier, James Casey had shot and killed the crusading editor of the *Bulletin*, James King of William. And that cold-blooded murder had proved the last straw. Once, five years before, a Committee of Vigilance had been formed to clean out the town. Now a group of outraged citizens brought the old Vigilante principle to life again and proceeded to give San Francisco another rousing shake-up. For the most part, they were after bigger game, but the reform wave washed into all sorts of unexpected corners, and Dick found himself seriously hampered in his efforts to get about in the city's underworld. Half a dozen times he was hauled down to the city prison on suspicion. He was indignant about it, standing on his rights and insisting that he had committed no crime. No one seemed to care; they looked him over and turned him loose when they got ready. It was inconvenient to be so closely watched, but finally he managed to scrape together a little band of four men who were willing to listen to his grandiose plans and in the meantime help him in such petty crimes as would serve to keep them going. But when Dick was arrested yet again, this time for the "show-up" in the public Plaza where police officers were given the opportunity to look well at the faces of known shady characters, he felt that matters had gone far enough. A city in the throes of reform offered poor pickings for a man in Dick's business, and he persuaded his followers that they would do far better up in the foothills where he knew his ground. The five—George Taylor, Aleck Wright, Billy Dickson, Jim Driscoll, and Dick himself—left the city and headed north and east. There were sheriffs in the mining counties, but Dick had experience dodging sheriffs. He assured his new gang that he would show them what was what, once they got to the mines.

For a year or two they did well enough.

Dick was still small potatoes compared to other rough characters who were making the gold country their center of operations, and public attention was focused on the more notable outlaws. By the autumn of 1856 the infamous Tom Bell had been caught and hanged, but some of his men were still loose and had formed bands of their own. In 1857 and 1858, the mines were easy pickings for dozens of the criminally minded who had been swept out of San Francisco by the Vigilance Committee's new broom. The foothill roads swarmed with them; and with so many to worry about, the peace officers had no more than a routine interest in Dick and his friends. Sometimes the gang worked together on big jobs; often its members conducted independent forays as the spirit took them. One such was the robbery of the Folsom stage by Jim Driscoll and an outsider known as "Cherokee Bob." On this occasion the two adopted the unusual method of concealing themselves in a ditch part way up the bank beside the Folsom road. When the stage passed, both leaped to the boot, crawling thence to the roof of the vehicle and catching driver and messenger from behind. It was a good trick, but it cost Dick one of his men. For after the robbery Driscoll made the mistake of repeating his technique once too often. His favorite habit in throwing off pursuit was to let the word get round that he had left the State. This time an intelligent officer put two and two together. There had been a robbery; Jim Driscoll was said to have left California. Wherefore, even though there was no circumstantial clue, Sheriff Bullock took a long chance and clapped a hand on the shoulder of Driscoll as he innocently stepped ashore from a river boat at the little town of Vernon. If the bandit had thought it over more carefully, he might have gone free; Bullock had no actual evidence. But the surprise upset him, and before he realized what he was saying he blurted out, "Damm it, Bullock, how did you pin that job on me?" Bullock was content to answer that so noted an outlaw could hardly hope to go unidentified. Flattered in spite of himself, Driscoll admitted his guilt. After he had received his prison sentence he suggested to the authorities that if they would guarantee him a free pardon, he would show them where he and his companion had concealed the treasure, a matter of some six thousand dollars in gold. His offer was turned down. The natural assumption is that "Cherokee Bob" was three thousand dollars richer.

Dick, however, was credited with planning most of the robberies in which his men were involved, and it is likely that he took an active part in many of them. Indeed, it seemed that his luck had changed. Try as they might, the officers of the law could not get him into State's Prison. Now and then they would jail him, but he always got away. An early historian writes of him that he "broke out of every jail in Placer and Nevada counties" in his time. It began to look as if he would go on with his illegal career as long as he pleased. In fact, he might have done just that if it had not been for a gentleman named John C. Boggs.

Mr. Boggs was Deputy Sheriff in Placer County, and he took his job seriously. Moreover, he took a very special interest in Rattlesnake Dick. Other officers might occupy themselves with banditry in the large if it pleased them; Boggs was a man of one idea, and he regarded Dick as his own peculiar problem. They had clashed innumerable times, and Dick often declared his particular hatred for Boggs, saying that the deputy had once sworn falsely against him and had been his enemy ever since. This may have been a reference to the early days in Rattlesnake Bar, though one cannot be sure about it now. Boggs might have been one of those who accused Dick of stealing Mormon Crow's mule, that wretched animal which was the original cause of all Dick's troubles. Whatever the real reason, Boggs was determined to make Dick his prisoner, and Dick was just as determined that no Boggs would ever put him behind bars.

In the long run, honors were even. Boggs did catch his man once, when the sheriff took him in pursuit of Dick who had been reported near Nevada City. There was some gunfire, but no one was hurt, and Dick had turned to run for it when he caught his foot in some vines, sprawling full length on the ground. The two were on him before he could rise, and bundled him off to the Nevada City jail. He did not stay there long; as usual, before they were ready to try him he had escaped. For a while they thought they were through with him at last, for Dick cunningly put about the rumor that he had fallen down an unused mine-shaft in the dark and been killed. Officers found no corpse there when they went to look, but it was said that Dick's friends had thrown quantities of rubbish down the abandoned hole in order to conceal his remains. The story gained currency for a short time, until

Dick held up a store near Auburn and was recognized by his victim.

Boggs was one up; but Dick evened the score a little later when the deputy tried to take him off the Nevada City stage.

Word had come to Boggs that Dick and George Taylor of his band were boldly riding the stage down to Folsom, and he decided that he would go out and get both outlaws at once. He armed himself with a derringer, two pairs of handcuffs, and a warrant, and waited for the stage on Harmon Hill. The trouble with Boggs was that though he deserved high marks for pertinacity, his wits were not as sharp as they might have been. The stage-driver stopped as he was told, but when Boggs called upon Dick and his friend to alight, they proceeded to confuse him with words, first denying their identity, then inquiring what right he had to arrest them. A contemporary historian writes that they "began to parley with him, Taylor finally demanding to see his warrant." Boggs fumbled for the document, and both highwaymen opened fire on him with their revolvers. The deputy may have been slow-witted but he did not lack courage; in the face of their fire he leveled his derringer and let fly. Unhappily his aim was bad, and when Dick and Taylor saw he had no other weapon they calmly descended from the stage and struck off over the hill, tossing back insults at Boggs as they went. The reporter who wrote the story notes in his genteel prose that Boggs' friends "smiled heartily" when they heard of his failure. His enemies, if he had any, must have gone even farther than that.

But Dick's streak of luck did not last. One by one, the bandits of the foothills were being run down, hanged, shot,

sent to prison. By the summer of 1859 the mining country
had swung back to law and order. Highwaymen were to
appear there in later years; as long as there was gold
shipped along those mountain roads there would always
be some who were willing to take the chance. But the hey-
day of the gangs was past. And Boggs was bent on removing the name of Rattlesnake Dick from the ever-shortening
list of criminals at large in his county. Methodically he
went over the ground, arresting smaller fry who might
help Dick to hide, checking up from town to town, press-
ing Dick himself more and more closely. It was no wonder
that Dick finally broke into the open and took the chance
that brought his career to a bloody end. Curiously, Boggs
was not in at the death.

Monday night, the eleventh of July, 1859, was clear
and there was a bright moon. After half-past eight on
that evening, an unidentified man knocked at the door of
George W. Martin, Deputy Tax Collector of Placer
County. When Mr. Martin answered the knock, the man
told him that Rattlesnake Dick and a companion had just
ridden through Auburn headed for Illinoistown. He did
not explain why he had chosen to take his story to the tax
collector instead of the sheriff's office, and Mr. Martin did
not stop to ask. He saddled his horse, rode over to the
jail, and told Deputies Johnston and Crutcher what he
had heard. The three agreed that it was best to lose no
time. Together they took the road over which Dick was
said to have gone.

Either their informant had been remarkably quick in
bringing them the news, or Dick and his fellow outlaw
had dawdled on their way. For the officers were less than

a mile out of town when they saw two horsemen ahead of them. Johnston, who was in the lead, called on the riders to halt. As they did so, he recognized Dick and added, "I am looking for you." The taller of the two turned in his saddle, saying, "Who are you, and what do you want?" and Crutcher had barely time to see that it was Rattlesnake Dick when the man fired, the bullet cutting Johnston's rein and shattering his left hand. Dick's companion fired at almost the same instant, and Mr. Martin dropped from his horse. For a moment it looked as though both bandits might get away without so much as a shot being directed at them, since Johnston, with one useless hand and no rein, was unable to control his horse and Crutcher had dismounted to look after Mr. Martin. But as the outlaws turned to ride for it, Johnston succeeded in quieting his mount, and Crutcher straightened up from Martin's body. The two blazed away together, and both were sure that Dick swayed and came near falling. They were astonished to see him rise in his saddle again and spur his horse down the road, his companion after him.

Martin was dead and Johnston badly wounded. It would have been folly for one man to ride in pursuit. While the injured man watched beside his friend, Crutcher went back to Auburn and found help. All night posses scoured the countryside. One group encountered a man with a curious story to tell. He had been sitting on his cabin porch by the roadside, he said, and had been startled by the sound of galloping horses. He had looked up just in time to see two men riding past at a furious pace, one of them reeling in his saddle, the other supporting him. That was the only clue anyone found that night.

But next morning when the Iowa Hill stage was approaching the Junction House, a mile or two out of Auburn, driver and passengers were startled to see a corpse lying beside the road. There was no horse anywhere in sight, only the dead man, and he was very dead indeed. A brief examination showed that he had been shot twice in the body, both bullets having passed through from breast to back. Either wound would have proved fatal, but there was also a third bullet through the brain. The clothing of the dead man was remarkable for its quality; the newspapers recorded the fineness of the black cloth trousers, the light-colored vest and coat, and remarked upon the soft kid gloves. None of the passengers could identify the man, but the driver was able to tell them that it was Rattlesnake Dick.

They took the riddled body into Auburn, leaving it on the sidewalk in front of the Masonic Hall while the driver walked round the corner to the sheriff's office with the news. It was while the curious crowd waited for the authorities to appear that the body of reckless, vain, ill-balanced Dick Barter suffered one last indignity. A prominent citizen of the town, one Sam Whitmarsh, deliberately raised hs heavy boot and kicked the dead man in the face. It is pleasant to record here that, according to a contemporary newspaper, the act was generally conceded to have been the cause of his defeat at the polls a year later when he ran for the office of Supervisor.

The editors of the region made much of the fact that Rattlesnake Dick had met his end, though they could not get together upon the precise manner of his death. He must have realized that he was too badly wounded to live; they could all agree on that. But had he then shot himself, or had he ordered his companion to perform that office? The debate was never satisfactorily settled. Neither was the question of the message supposed to have been found with the corpse. One reporter stated flatly that by Dick's side, when he was found, there had been a scrap of paper on which were scrawled with pencil the words, "I die as all true Britons do!" Others scouted the message as sheer nonsense. Later a story was circulated that there had been two messages; that on the other side of the paper had been written, "If J. Boggs is dead, I am satisfied," this being taken to mean that Dick had mistaken Mr. Martin for his chief enemy. There is now no evidence that either message existed; at any rate, none beyond the printed report which was vigorously denied at the time by those having quite as good an opportunity to know the facts.

There is no question, however, about the letter that was found in the pocket of Dick's coat. It was from his family in Sweet Home, and it was dated March 14, 1859. In it Dick's sister Harriet urged him to mend his ways, pleaded lovingly with him to pray that he be "restored to the paths of rectitude," and pathetically reminded him that he had once been a decent, upright boy. It is a very touching communication altogether, suggesting as it does that a young man who could hold a sister's affection so firmly in spite of his misdeeds could not have been altogether bad.

Another point remains. Who was Dick's companion on that moonlight night when he so foolishly shot it out with the officers? There were those who maintained it was George Taylor, while others stuck to the belief that it was Aleck Wright. No more was ever heard of Taylor, but nearly ten years afterward Wright was arrested and tried for the murder of Mr. Martin. Nothing came of it. The proofs offered were of the slightest, consisting of no more than the opinions of several gentlemen who happened to believe that Wright was guilty. The jury could only acquit the prisoner. A decade later, a Placer County historian was to write, "It is generally believed that Wright was the man," but he brings forward no evidence in support.

At any rate, Dick Barter was buried by the county, and that was that. Or almost. A month afterward, on August 15, 1859, the Sacramento *Union* carried an obscure item, a mere six lines of type which put a sardonic exclamation mark at the end of Dick's career. This is the item:

> RATTLESNAKE DICK:—The horse of this highwayman was lately found near Grass Valley, alive but with a shot in the neck. It was claimed by a man named Charley Smith, who was arrested as an old prison bird.

Irony, yes, if you like. It also, purely accidentally, points to what is perhaps the most tantalizing mystery in the whole story of Rattlesnake Dick. On that fatal night of July 11, Johnston and Crutcher each fired once. Mr. Martin had no time to shoot. When Dick's body was found, there were two wounds in the breast and one through the head—the last supposedly his own or his companion's mercy shot. But whose bullet wounded the horse?

GALLERY

"Joaquin, The Mountain Robber", drawn in 1853 for a Sacramento newspaper. Though it does not pretend to be a likeness of Murieta, the picture
is accepted by devout believers as an authentic portrait.

A later conception of Murieta, painted in the 1860s by Charles Christian Nahl. It now hangs in San Francisco's Union League Club.

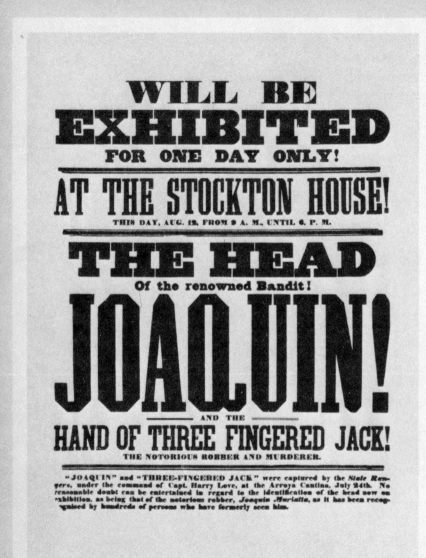

The only known copy of the first poster advertising the pickled head of "Joaquin".
Note that the text refers to "Muriatta", a spelling for which no other authority exists.

A newspaper sketch of the "Head of Murieta" said to be drawn directly from the head-in-alcohol.

R. HYENNE

# EL BANDIDO CHILENO

## Joaquin Murieta en CALIFORNIA

V. Acha - Córcega 238 - Barcelona - editor

Cover of a pirated Spanish edition of the Murieta story. Since it was lifted from a Santiago issue, Murieta is called a Chileno.

John Rollin Ridge, San Francisco journalist of the 1850s, whose fictional "Life" of Joaquin Murieta created the Murieta legend as it is today.

☞ Agents of W., F. & Co. will **not** post this circular, but place them in the hands of your local and county officers, and reliable citizens in your region. Officers and citizens receiving them are respectfully requested to preserve them for future reference.

Agents **WILL PRESERVE** a copy on file in their office.

# $800.00 Reward!
# ARREST STAGE ROBBER!

1.

On the 3d of August, 1877, the stage from Fort Ross to Russian River was stopped by one man, who took from the Express box about $300, coin, and a check for $305.52, on Grangers' Bank of San Francisco, in favor of Fisk Bros. The Mail was also robbed. On one of the Way Bills left with the box the Robber wrote as follows:—

    "I've labored long and hard for bread—
        For honor and for riches—
    But on my corns too long you've trod,
        You fine haired sons of bitches.
                BLACK BART, the P o 8.

Driver, give my respects to our friend, the other driver; but I really had a notion to hang my old disguise hat on his weather eye." (*fac simile.*)

It is believed that he went to the Town of Guerneville about daylight next morning.

2.

About one year after above robbery, July 25th, 1878, the Stage from Quincy to Oroville was stopped by one man, and W., F. & Co's box robbed of $379. coin, one Diamond Ring, (said to be worth $200) one Silver Watch, valued at $25. The Mail was also robbed. In the box, when found next day, was the following, (*fac simile*):—

[Courtesy Wells Fargo Bank History Room]

Above: Reward poster issued by Wells, Fargo & Co. on Black Bart in the late 1870s.

Right: Black Bart, greatest stage-robber of them all, photographed after his capture in 1883, the very picture of a retired and respectable mining man.

This Beadle Dime Library item was rushed into print within three months of Black Bart's capture. It is, of course, pure fiction.

Above: James B. Hume, once
Sheriff of the roaring camp of
Hangtown, later Chief of Detec-
tives for Wells, Fargo & Co.

Right: Harry N. Morse,
scourge of the California outlaws in the 1850s, afterward
hired by Hume as a special
detective to track down Black
Bart.

Stage-coaches like these carried passengers and treasure-box.

The house of "Greek George" where Tiburcio Vasquez was captured.

Dick Fellows, California's most spectacularly unsuccessful highwayman, whose troubles all stemmed from his conviction that he could ride a horse.

Above:  Tiburcio Vasquez, cold-blooded killer and robber, one of the last of the outlaws to be run to earth and hanged.

Right:   John Allen, known as "Sheet-Iron Jack", the barber-horsethief, finally sent to Folsom Prison for his crimes.

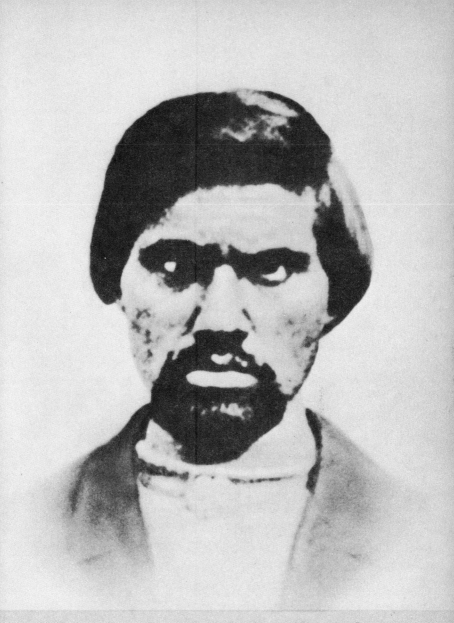

Juan Soto, Indian outlaw, killed in a hand-to-hand duel with Sheriff Harry N. Morse.

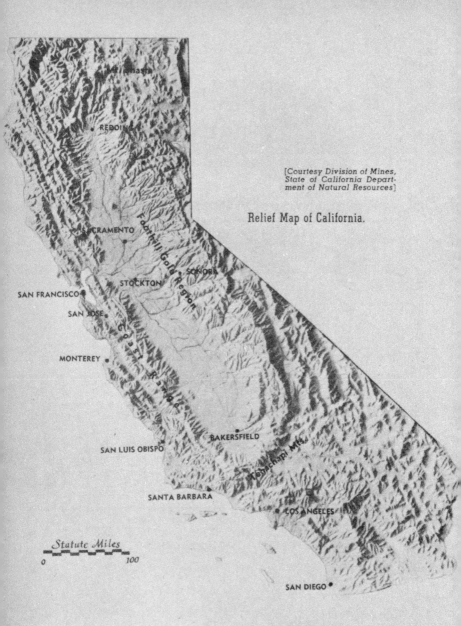

[Courtesy Division of Mines,
State of California Department of Natural Resources]

Relief Map of California.

Statute Miles
0          100

[Prepared by N. F. Drake, Department of Geology, Stanford University]

HE STAGECOACH DRIVER OF California's early days drove like Jehu (the record proves it), scorned the yawning abysses so close to his rolling wheels, swore like a trooper, and brought the stage in on time. Now and then he drank too much. Swaggering was his specialty. Sometimes he died in line of duty, always he risked death a dozen times a week. In short, he was a very devil of a fellow.

But even a devil of a fellow may quail when a double-barreled shotgun is presented at his breast. When that weapon is in the steady hands of a robber masked in a flour sack pierced with eyeholes, the greatest rakehell ribbon-twister of them all may be forgiven if he does what he is told.

Between 1875 and 1883, twenty-eight California stage-drivers altogether saw that masked man and knew him for the most famous bandit California ever boasted. All twenty-eight halted their sweating horses as they were bid and listened for the four words in which Black Bart invariably announced his reason for stopping the stage. "Throw down the box!" he used to say, in a voice his victims unanimously declared to be both resonant and deep. Most of the drivers threw down the box. The twenty-eighth could not comply. This time the Wells, Fargo Express Company had decided that perhaps their treasure would have a better chance if it were bolted fast to the stage floor. It hadn't. Bart got it just the same. But the job took him just two minutes too many.

The Black Bart legend was a long time growing.

On August 3, 1877, the stage coming in over the low hills between Point Arenas and Duncan's Mills on the Russian River was held up by a lone bandit. There were no passengers; there was no shotgun messenger riding beside the driver to lend him support. There was the driver and there were his horses. He could start them quickly, but bullets were quicker. When he was told to throw down the box he threw it down. The bandit got the Wells, Fargo treasure, amounting to no great sum. The official report listed three hundred dollars in coin, and a check for $305.52 drawn on the Grangers' Bank of San Francisco in favor of the firm of Fisk Brothers. There was no shooting, no rough language; indeed, this lone highwayman was unusually polite, though firm. The driver was informed that he might proceed, and gladly took the hint. When he told his story, all he knew was what he had seen; a man in a long linen duster with a flour sack over his head and a double-barreled shotgun in his hands, who had told him to throw down the box. He had thrown it down. As for identification, who could tell anything about a man under a flour sack? He did remember that the bandit's voice was deep and hollow. That was all. Perhaps a posse might find some clue on the ground.

They found a clue, though in advance none of them could have hazarded the wildest guess as to its nature. It was—no less—a poem. What was more, it recited something of the history of the lone bandit and explained his motive. A clue of clues it was, the kind of clue the amateur detective dreams about. This was the verse, painstakingly written out on the back of a waybill:

> *"I've labored long and hard for bread,*
> *For honor and for riches,*
> *But on my corns too long you've tred*
> *You fine-haired sons of bitches."*

The last word of the third line is universally printed "trod"; the urge to correct proof is a common human itch. But Black Bart wrote "tred," as an old facsimile reproduction plainly shows. A practicing poet, he knew what rhymed and what didn't.

The first obstacle in the way of the officers was that, in a spirit of waggishness, the author had carefully written each line in a different hand. However, as though to make up for this willful bit of contrariness, he had accommodatingly signed his name. "Black Bart," the signature read, "The PO8." This was Obstacle Number Two, until some enterprising gentleman suggested that, whoever "Black Bart" might be, the remainder of the signature clearly referred to his own estimate of his literary attainments. Obviously this doggerel-writing, flour-sack bandit considered his effusion to be PO8ry. The dullest saw the point. As for "Black Bart," doubtless the robber's name was Bartholomew, or some such matter. He had added a prose postscript to his gentle little quatrain: "Driver, give my respects to our friend, the other driver; but I really had

a notion to hang my old disguise hat on his weather eye."
This was signed "Respectfully, B. B." Detectives on the
case deduced that the postscript was in the highwayman's
natural handwriting and said further that it showed the
writer to have had large experience in some clerical position. They would soon run him down and prove their case.

But finding the mysterious robber-poet was not so
simple as all that. There was really nothing much to go
by. There was a man who had a shotgun and a deep voice.
That description would have fitted ten thousand men in
California. Perhaps the officers on the case mentioned
dragnets. Doubtless they announced from time to time
that the press might expect an interesting bulletin in the
matter very soon. But the facts were that the trail was
stone cold. The check on the Grangers' Bank was never
presented. As for the three hundred dollars in currency,
that was no easier to trace than a shotgun and a deep voice
saying, "Throw down the box!"

No more was heard of Black Bart for almost a year.
There were various robberies committed about the State
in that time, even several stage holdups. But none bore
the authentic Black Bart stamp. There was no flour sack,
no linen duster, no poetry. Then, high in the Sierra, in the
green canyon of the brawling Feather River, Black Bart
turned up again.

On July 25, 1878, the stage from Quincy to Oroville
was held up. A lone bandit, masked in a flour sack, stepped
out of the bushes at a difficult and slow turn, and suggested
hollowly that the box be thrown down. It was thrown
down, and the driver was told to be on his way. This
time the bandit did better. The Wells, Fargo chest held
$379 in coin, a diamond ring said to be worth two hundred

dollars, and a silver watch valued at twenty-five dollars. On this occasion also the mail was robbed, though there is no information on what the pouch contained. But the record is exact on what the officers found when they reached the scene and discovered the broken treasure-box. Once again it was a poem. Encouraged, perhaps, by his success the year before, Bart had really outdone himself. He may have been reading in the meantime, very likely in the files of Hutchings' *California Magazine* which had specialized, twenty years earlier, in similar melancholy sentiments expressed in just such dying falls as met the eyes of the posse:

> *"Here I lay me down to sleep*
> *To wait the coming morrow,*
> *Perhaps success, perhaps defeat,*
> *And everlasting sorrow.*
> *Let come what will I'll try it on,*
> *My condition can't be worse;*
> *And if there's money in that box*
> *'Tis munny in my purse!"*

Again the lines of doggerel were written in varying hands. To confuse his pursuers still further, Bart had deliberately misspelled "money" in the eighth line, though he managed it well enough in the seventh. For of course it was the rhyming bandit. Like its predecessor, this longer effort was signed "Black Bart, The PO8." One newspaper reporter, plainly with no feeling for the niceties of either crime or art, went so far as to refer to the poem as "adding insult to injury." The reader of today may make up his own mind about that. It seems unlikely that Bart so much as thought of insulting anybody. He had got that out of his system the first time, with his lovely last-line epithet.

Here he was obviously in a plaintive mood. He might succeed; he might fail. It was, so to say, on the knees of the gods. He could not even be sure whether, after all his trouble, the box had any money in it. Or "munny."

The sheriff of Plumas County was nothing if not a practical man. It was clear to him that these two men who operated alone, decorated themselves with eyehole flour sacks, possessed deep and resonant voices, and wrote such poetry, were not in fact two bandits but one. As a newspaper of the day put it, in a perfect passion of understatement: "The two robberies, though a year apart, are so alike in their characteristics that they have founded a belief both were committed by the same person." The Governor of California, therefore, one William Irwin, announced a reward of three hundred dollars for "capture and conviction." The Wells, Fargo Company added another three hundred dollars and the postal authorities contributed two hundred dollars more. Black Bart was now worth eight hundred dollars to anybody who could (a) put him under lock and key, and (b) produce the evidence to convict him.

Nobody could. Everybody knew about him by this time; his name was one to conjure with. And he grew more and more daring. In less than a week the down stage from Laporte to Oroville was robbed by one man who took from the express-box a package of gold specimens valued at fifty dollars and a silver watch. It was Black Bart again; the driver was ready to swear it. Twice in October there were stage-robberies in the north; in both cases the holdup was conducted by a single bandit disguised in the now familiar flour sack. In the second case the sheriff was a

trifle brighter than most of his colleagues. He took expert
trackers with him, and succeeded in trailing Bart some
sixty miles from the scene of the robbery. This time there
was no poetry. In spite of the latter-day legend which hints
at reams of verse, there was never any more poetry. Like
a wise man, Bart seemed to know when he had written
enough. But there were signs that mountain men could
follow. And though they lost the trail eventually, they
found enough to give Wells, Fargo's Detective, J. B.
Hume, something to go on.

Hume was a man diligent in his business. A photograph
taken at this period shows him to have been tall and wiry
with high cheekbones, a fine expanse of forehead, and the
eyes of a man accustomed to notice even little things.
Oddly enough, his moustache—an overhanging waterfall
in the fashion of the day—lends him a curious resemblance
to his quarry. Perhaps it would be better to say that the
pictures of Bart look like a less intelligent, less forceful
Hume. Bart's imperial, of course, was his own private
whim; Hume left his chin bare. Bart, too, was several
inches shorter than Hume. Yet the likeness is there, slight
but clear enough; sufficient to suggest to the philosophical
reader that, but for the grace of a small chin whisker, a
few inches in height, and a dash less of character, the
robber might have been the special officer. The notion, to
be sure, is not precisely new; something like it must have
occurred to everyone who has seen a policeman.

At any rate, it was plain to Hume that if Bart himself
had disappeared, leaving behind only a poem or two, the
echo of a deep and hollow voice, and perhaps the faintest
whiff of brimstone, there might at least be a chance to discover what he looked like, that is if anyone had seen him.

Someone had. Up near Eel River a Mrs. McCreary, like Old MacDonald, had a farm. To that farm (Mr. Hume learned) had come a man on foot; a "gentleman tourist," the good lady had taken him to be. The Mc-Creary place was off the beaten track and a visitor was a rare treat, wherefore the stranger was prevailed upon to stop and eat noonday dinner. Mrs. McCreary's sixteen-year-old daughter had waited on him. If Mr. Hume would like to speak with her he might do so and welcome.

The girl—her name does not appear in the records— was glad to tell Mr. Hume what she knew. She remembered a good deal about the "tourist," so much in fact that one might think she regarded him with at least a tenderly maternal if not an actually romantic eye. She was able to tell Mr. Hume, for instance, that the stranger's coatsleeve had been slightly ripped and mended with white thread. His shoes had been split with a knife over the ball of the foot, she supposed to ease walking, and his watch chain was broken and mended with a leather thong. She was precise, too, about his physical appearance. He had graying brown hair, thinning above the forehead with wedges of baldness at the temples. At least two of his front teeth were missing. And she was sure about his eyes. They were deep set, under heavy eyebrows, and they were a piercing, brilliant blue. He used no tobacco nor liquor while at the farm, but asked for a second cup of coffee with his dinner. She had noticed his hands especially; they were slender and genteel, showing no evidence of hard work. At the mention of this patent of gentility, Mrs. McCreary added that the gentleman had spoken well and fluently, and had carried on what she described as an "intellectual conversation," well flavored with polite

jokes. A comical sort, she would call him. All of them—
was there a Mr. McCreary one wonders?—ridiculed the
notion of the stranger's being any kind of robber, much
less the notorious Black Bart. They said he was more like
a preacher. Mr. Hume thanked them and went back to
San Francisco. Preacher or robber, there was now a description to go by. Perhaps the man was Bart, perhaps not.
At least they could look for him.

They looked hard and long. They went on looking for
five years. At intervals, often more than six months apart,
then suddenly three or four times in as many weeks, Black
Bart would reappear, rob a stage treasure-chest and the
mail, and vanish. The whole area of the Northern Mines
was his stamping ground. Always the flour-sack technique
distinguished him; invariably his voice struck fear into
the hearts of driver and passengers. The latter might have
omitted the palpitations; Bart never annoyed any of them.
There is an uncertified legend (Bart himself told the story
later to a detective) that once a frightened woman threw
him her purse. Bart, if the tale is true, courteously threw
it back, saying that he did not want her money, that he
was interested only in the Wells, Fargo box and the United
States mail. Be that as it may, there was never a report
that he had touched anything else. But no one doubted
that he was completely in earnest when he said, "Throw
down the box!" Drivers continued to obey his orders with
alacrity.

Now and then his face was seen, though never by victims
or at the scene of a robbery. On September 1, 1880, the
stage from Weaverville to Redding was stopped by one
man, and the express and mail robbed. The next day a
rancher on Eagle Creek in Shasta County reported that

a man on foot had come to his cabin and asked for breakfast. Offered a wrapped lunch to carry him on his way,
he accepted with thanks. Yes, he had had graying brown
hair, and the wedges at the temples were noticeable. It
was true, too, that his eyes were blue and piercing. His
manners, however, were excellent, and his host was of
the same mind as the McCrearys who had felt that politeness could not go hand in hand with banditry. Surely this
could not have been Black Bart. Which way had he gone?
The rancher was vague on that point. In the general direction of Tehama County, he believed. Since Tehama
County borders Shasta County on the south, and in a
straight line from east to west, this was equivalent to
stating that the breakfast guest had headed directly for
Patagonia. The information was of very little use to
Shasta's sheriff or to Mr. Hume of Wells, Fargo.

The next two years saw Black Bart here, there, and
everywhere. Either he was in need of money or he just
enjoyed robbing stages. Toward the end of 1881 he held
up three drivers within two months and got clean away
each time. Once, in 1882, on the Laporte-Oroville road,
a Wells, Fargo messenger named George Hackett got to
his gun before Bart was quite out of sight and managed to
fire two shots. One report on the incident says that in his
flight Bart lost his hat which was later found with three
holes in it made by buckshot from Hackett's shotgun.
Another story declares Hackett to have had a rifle, and
that one of his bullets creased Bart's skull, leaving a scar
which he carried for the rest of his days. A "scar on top
of forehead, right side" does appear in the detailed description of Bart after he was caught. Buckshot or bullet,

Bart got away. Hackett conscientiously reported that when last observed the robber had been headed south. Next day there was a rumor that he had been seen forty miles away, near Camptonville, over in Yuba County. It may have been true. It was Bart's unique talent to cover, on foot, extraordinary distances in impossibly short times.

By the autumn of 1883 Black Bart had begun to assume in the minds of the people of California something like the stature of a giant.

The Wells, Fargo people knew better. So did their agents and the peace officers up and down the State. The Express Company had printed a four-page circular which listed sixteen robberies believed to have been committed by Bart, and which also carried a good deal of general information about him. It noted the flour sack, of course, and made a special point of his habit of jumping out in front of the team in a stooping position, shielding himself in front of the lead horses. It spoke of the double-barreled shotgun and pointed out that he used to unbreech it and roll it in his blankets; it noted his custom of bringing an old axe to the scene of his holdups, using it to break open the box, and leaving it on the ground when he was finished. Further, the Express Company said: "In opening the mail sacks he cuts them with a sharp knife; thus—T—on top of the sack near the lock. He has never manifested any viciousness and there is reason to believe he is averse to taking human life. He is polite to all passengers, and especially to ladies. He comes and goes from the scene of the robbery on foot; seems to be a thorough mountaineer and a good walker."

Following this were the details Mrs. McCreary's daughter had given Mr. Hume, and those the rancher in Shasta

County had been able to remember. Bart was described as an American, over fifty, about five feet, eight inches in height and of slender build, with high forehead, deep-set light eyes, heavy eyebrows, gray hair, a heavy moustache and chin whiskers well mixed with gray. There was the information that two of his front teeth were missing, that he had long slender hands, that he sometimes complained of throat disease, and that he talked as though well informed on current topics. Still further the circular explained that Bart "is believed not to be addicted to the use of liquor or tobacco, but is a great lover of coffee," and for good measure Mr. Hume threw in the statement that "when reading without glasses he holds his paper off at full arm's length." As a final touch, the circular added that "At no place where he has stopped for food has he been looked upon as suspicious in deportment or appearance, and it is most probable that he is considered entirely respectable wherever he may reside."

Such was the official picture of Black Bart, astonishingly close to the facts as they later developed. Hume, as has been said, had the genius for detail that lies behind all first-class police work. But for reasons best known to itself, Wells, Fargo specifically ordered its agents not to post this descriptive circular. They were to read it carefully and file it for future reference. They were not to make it public.

The people of California, then, knew of Black Bart only what rumor and story spread about, and what imaginative reporters printed in the newspapers. Over and again he had calmly walked out of the brush, uttered his resonant command, pouched his loot and disappeared. Time after time—the story grew to hundreds—he had

proven himself gallant to the ladies, courteous to the
gentlemen so long as they were passengers, but determined to have the Wells, Fargo box and the mail. Not
once had he fired a shot; in every case his steadily leveled
gun and blankly resolute flour-sack visage had been sufficient to make it understood that he meant what he said.
Sometimes drivers had not even waited for the word of
command. Was it not common knowledge that Black
Bart never failed? There had been bandits before in California, plenty of them. Those had been mere ordinary
men, and the law had caught up with them quickly
enough. Sometimes angry groups of victims had not
waited for the law, had taken justice summarily into their
own hands. But a man who could be jailed, a man who
could be strung up to a tree or brought down in a running
gun fight, such a man was one thing. A man who could
not be caught was another. And it was becoming increasingly and uncomfortably clear that Black Bart could not
be caught. The law never so much as came close to him.
He was here one day and fifty miles away the next, and
nobody knew how he did it. He was a superman, that was
the long and short of it; a matchless, transcendental highwayman, a very paragon of robbers. "Throw down the
box!" he said, deep and slow, and they threw it down.
Even his two lonely bits of rattle-trap verse, revived and
reprinted every time he held up a stage, were no longer
funny but grotesque, monstrous, threatening. He was
Black Bart, and he had become a legend.

Then suddenly the blurred, enormous shadow of the
legend swam into focus and turned out to be a simple
two-legged fact. Mr. Hume had been right. The giant
was only a man—a smallish, dodging, frightened man

at that. It was not the power and majesty of the law that burst the bubble. Given its essential clue, the law did run Bart down. But the primary factor was a plain citizen with no thought of bandits in his head. A young Italian boy had lugged his rifle out into the hills to see what he could find to shoot. That was all. The sheerest accident, the one-in-a-million chance, brought boy, stage, and bandit together in the same place at the same time.

2

In the California foothills November is chilly, bleak, showery. There is no snow, though nights are long and cold. In another month or two the hills are fresh and green, but light fall rains are not enough to start the new grass, and the bleached brown summer carpet still covers them. There are few pines, and those small and insignificant for the most part; the magnificent growth of the Sierra does not begin at foothill altitude. Scrub oak is the best these hills have to offer; in late fall their twisted branches are clotted with mistletoe, sometimes blanketed in autumn-yellow wild grape. An occasional late-turning poplar blazes orange fire, and scattered ailanthus trees spring out in pale lemon against the dark background of the oak. Where the dry creek beds mark canyon bottoms there are feathery willows, and everywhere is a tangle of low-growing wild peach, dense man-high manzanita, and red-berried toyon. Down in Calaveras County the hilltops are often bare and usually littered with chunks of dark porous rock. A volcano spouted here countless ages ago, and the broken lava mixed with fragments of slate makes hard going for man or horse.

Yet one who knew the country might find it ideal for certain purposes, particularly if he wanted to get away and leave no trace. Given a fair acquaintance with the terrain, a quick and clever man could throw off pursuit with ease. There are a thousand folds in the hills, little arroyos and gullies that twist and turn, even trails of a kind, plain enough to the eye that has once marked them down.

In early days one of the main stage roads ran through just this kind of country, from Sonora, county seat of Tuolumne, to Milton in Calaveras County. At Milton, passengers changed for Stockton, whence they could make direct connection by train or river-boat for San Francisco. The road is little used now. A fine new highway comes round another way; development of irrigation and the consequent shift in population have redrawn the map, and only a few farmers and mining men with business in Copperopolis take the old road in these times. But in the 1880s it was Sonora's chief link with the Valley, the regular route for travelers.

The morning of Saturday, November 3, 1883, was cold and clear with a sharp wind.

President Chester A. Arthur, always a careful and fore-handed gentleman, had been well ahead with his proclamation that on Thursday, November 29, the nation would observe its Thanksgiving for a year "replete with evidence of divine goodness, such as the prevalence of health, stability and order." The rest of the day's newspaper hardly bore him out. There was no stability, but rioting in Reading, Pennsylvania, where Hungarian millworkers had struck. In San Francisco Bay the steamer *San Blas* was quarantined because there was yellow fever aboard, and there was an epidemic of diphtheria in Massachusetts. In Sacramento, the editor of the *Union* had a minor complaint; the wind of the last few days was blowing strange odors from Chinatown over into the better residential districts. Like all his tribe, he was convinced that something should be done. It did seem, however, that order prevailed in the mining country of California. At least there had been no stage holdups for a long time.

Mr. Reason E. McConnell, driver for the Nevada Stage Company, may have read these items over his six-thirty cup of coffee at Reynolds Ferry. He had been up early. Making connections at Milton meant starting before dawn; he had tooled his stage out of Sonora at four o'clock that morning. Moreover, he had to make a stop at Tuttletown. The reason for that stop was now snugly packed in the Wells, Fargo chest, fastened to the floor of his stage; 228 ounces of amalgam from the mill at the Patterson Mine. With it in the box were five hundred and fifty dollars in gold coin and a small amount of gold dust, some $3\frac{1}{4}$ ounces worth sixty-five dollars. There were no regular passengers; but as the stage climbed the grade from the river, McConnell had company. At Reynolds Ferry, where the Copperopolis road crossed the Stanislaus, the ferry and small hotel were owned by one of the best-loved women in all the Mother Lode country— "Grandma" Rolleri, whose Calaveras Hotel in Angels Camp later became famous from one end of the mines to the other. Her son, nineteen-year-old Jimmy, had the ferry job, and this morning, after taking McConnell and his stage across, he suggested that he ride over to Copperopolis with him. He could take his Henry rifle and maybe he would find something to shoot—a rabbit or a squirrel, even a deer if he was lucky. McConnell was glad enough to have someone to talk to, and told the boy to come along.

The time must have passed pleasantly. Jimmy and McConnell were old friends, the air was cool and exhilarating as the sun rose higher. There is no record that Jimmy saw any targets; indeed the chances are against it, because as the stage wound through the hills he made up his mind to get off. McConnell's road led over Funk Hill ahead. The horses had to take it slowly, and it occurred to the restless Jimmy that he might easily cut round on foot, meeting the stage as it came down the grade on the other side. That way he might scare up a shot in the scrub. A loaded repeating rifle and nothing to shoot at make a combination to fray the patience of a grown man, let alone an eager boy. So Jimmy got off three or four miles from Copperopolis to try his luck. Nothing told him that he and his rifle were to bring an end to the career of the most successful and the most greatly feared stage-robber California ever saw.

There was nothing to disturb McConnell either. He may have smoked as the stage swayed along; there being no passengers—particularly no ladies—etiquette was not involved. At all events, his mind must have been at ease; there were no bad curves, the reins hung loosely from his fingers as the horses plodded and steamed up the grade. He was nearly at the top when a rustle in the brush made him turn his head. He looked straight into the muzzle of a gun. Behind it was a man, a flour sack over his head, steady blue eyes visible through two holes cut in front.

No driver in the mines could have been mistaken. McConnell knew he was held up by Black Bart.

Perhaps this was the only time in his career that Bart did not open the conversation with his customary command. For one thing, the driver had no box up beside him, wherefore he could not throw any box down. But Bart had something else on his mind. The best stage-robbing technique does not include asking questions; the highwayman who understands his business asks his victims nothing, he tells them. But there was something Bart had to know, and quickly. His voice lacked its usual resonance as he put the question. "Who was that man—the one who got off down below?" he asked.

In such situations there is a delicate psychical balance, naturally in favor of the man who holds the gun. But it must have shifted a little then. For where there is any parley there is time for the defensive side to think. McConnell answered (and he surely felt better as he said it) that it was no man but a boy, a young fellow who had ridden out with him to hunt some cattle that had strayed.

Still Bart was uncertain. Here was a new set of circumstances. There was no precedent to follow. You couldn't say, "Throw down the box!" when it wasn't there to throw down. As it turned out, Bart knew very well that in this case the chest was inside the stage and fastened securely to the floor. He knew, too, that the amalgam was inside it. He had visited Tuttletown— doubtless as a "gentleman tourist"—made friends with Dr. Drake, in charge of operations at the Patterson Mine, scraped an acquaintance with the millman and learned all about the shipment and when it would go out. But he had to do something. If the box wasn't up there, the driver was. "Get down!" Bart said. He had thought out his plan of action in the case of stages with the box fastened to the floor. It was that business of the unknown person, the boy with the rifle who had disappeared while the stage rounded the bend below, that had thrown him off for a moment. Now the scheme came back to him. "Get down!" he repeated, and motioned with the barrel of his gun.

Examining the affair now, in the light of what we know, it is easy to see that the balance was shifting; slightly yet, but toward McConnell. Bart had lost ground with his question. His timing was off, not much, but a little; and McConnell must have sensed it. For he replied that he couldn't get down. The brake was bad; it wouldn't hold. If he got off, the stage would roll back downhill.

If Bart had ordered McConnell to back his horses, turning as he backed, the driver would have had to admit that a stage couldn't very well roll downhill while it was broadside on, across the road. But Bart's temperament played him false. He loved to argue, to talk, to set fact against fact. The trouble was that he did not really think fast; he merely thought of many things. And this time he thought of something—the wrong thing. "It will not roll downhill," he said reasonably, "if you put a rock behind the wheel." McConnell must have known then that he was the smarter man. "You do it," he said. And Bart did.

If McConnell had been armed, had had a pistol anywhere within reach, the career of Black Bart would unquestionably have come to an abrupt end then and there.

You can shoot it out with a temporizing bandit and the advantage will be all on your side. McConnell had no gun, and Bart's hand looked steady. He dismounted and unhitched as he was told.

To the reader looking back at the little drama from the vantage point of half a century, it is interesting to know that though Bart kept the driver covered with one hand he helped him loosen his straps and buckles with the other. It is plain as a pikestaff that Bart was flustered, trying to hurry the business along. It was a new situation to him, and Bart did not do so well in new situations. Always he had followed his simple and effective routine: the mask and gun, the stride forward out of the brush on a hill or at a bad turn, the stooping position by the lead horses so as to be out of the line of possible fire, the command to throw down the box, the second command to get going, the box left behind to be rifled at leisure. He understood how to do it that way. Even when ladies excitedly threw him their purses, he could handle the interruption with éclat; after all he was in charge, his word backed up by his gun, the driver up on the seat, the passengers inside the coach. There was nothing to distract him; the proceedings ran smoothly in the same general channel. But here it was all different. There was that matter of the boy with his rifle. Maybe he was not dangerous, off there somewhere on the hillside, but maybe he was. He might be sneaking up through the brush at this moment, sights trained on Bart's back. There was the box itself, secured in place inside the stage instead of lying in the dust at his feet. There was this driver who didn't seem quite to realize his position, who made excuses, who had actually told him, Black Bart, what to do about a rock under the wheel. Worse, he, Bart, had done it. Certainly the quicker it was all over the better. He made his voice as firm as he could and told McConnell to take his horses on up the hill and over the crest out of sight.

At this point the student who tries to sift the truth from the widely varying stories of this particular robbery finds himself flatly up against a wild absurdity. Bart had to get the box open. It is a fact that he did so, as later events show. How did he open it?

McConnell could not have seen the process. Bart was working inside the stage; the box was never detached from the floor to which it had been so firmly fastened. Moreover, McConnell could not even see the stage itself; he had taken his horses over the hill and down a short way on the other side. Bart had watched him go. Newspaper reporters who wrote the story of the holdup took their facts straight from McConnell who told them only what he had seen and heard, and they wrote merely that "Bart then broke open the box." Yet there is a statement as to the method he used. It comes from what should be a reliable source—Harry N. Morse, the detective who afterward took Bart to the scene and had him reconstruct the crime. Morse says, in all soberness, implying that he had the information from Bart himself, that after the horses and driver were out of sight, "Bart then got out his tools, a sledgehammer, a big crowbar, a wedge for splitting wood, a couple of picks and an axe"! To this extraordinary equipment a later account adds "a miner's gad, drill and chisel"!

I suggest that the most willing reader can hardly credit this fantastic burglar's kit. It was Bart's custom to come to the scene of his robberies on foot, carrying a blanket-roll. In this case, as will appear, he had brought along a remarkably varied assortment of baggage, including a pair of field glasses, two pairs of detachable cuffs, a small round derby hat, and a package of provisions. Is it possible to believe in this picture of a small man (Bart's shoe size was Number Six), wearing a derby hat, carrying somewhere about his person a shotgun (it was found later in a hollow tree), a flour sack provided with eye-holes, another sack for the booty, two extra pairs of clean cuffs, a case containing field glasses, under one arm a bundle of miscellaneous provisions and under the other a pair of overalls he had "picked up somewhere in an old cabin," dodging cautiously through the underbrush up-hill and down on his way to the ambush, in his pocket a five-pound iron wedge and a knife to slit the mail-sacks, and over his shoulder this bristling, clanking fifty-pound hardware store consisting of a sledgehammer, a large crowbar, a miner's gad, drill and chisel, two picks, and an axe?

I am afraid not. Charming conception though it may be, it simply won't wash. Bart did break open the box. It was his habit to carry an old axe for opening boxes; the Wells, Fargo circulars all noted this. McConnell said later that from where he stood with his horses he heard the sound of heavy blows "for some time." What implement or implements made these sounds? Probably no one will ever be sure. The only certainty in the whole mad affair is that they were not a sledge, a crowbar, an iron wedge, a miner's gad, drill and chisel, two picks, and an axe. Not all those.

✦

What did McConnell think about, standing there with his horses over the hill? It would be interesting to know. Very likely he wished that he had brought along a pistol, just this once. Perhaps he tried to fix in his memory some details of the robber's appearance. McConnell was a level-headed man, and undoubtedly he realized that he would be asked for a careful description. It is quite likely that he tried to think of some plan or other by which he might capture the highwayman so busily cracking the Wells, Fargo box back there on the road. The Company ought to do pretty well by a driver who could lay Black Bart by the heels; and after all there was also the matter of the reward to be considered.

It is not at all difficult, however, to imagine what McConnell thought when he suddenly saw a movement in the brush below him. In that moment he must have realized how beautifully fate had played into his hands. Here was his weapon. Here was his scheme to capture the robber. Here, providentially, was his big chance. For the slight figure that had come into view, working its way along the western slope toward the road, was that of his companion of the early morning—young Jimmy Rolleri. And as McConnell knew, Jimmy had his Henry rifle with him.

When they asked McConnell about it later, he told the story of the next few minutes in less than thirty words. He said merely, "I attracted Jimmy's attention and signaled him to walk in a detour around the foot of the hill and come to me out of sight of Black Bart."

It must have seemed like hours before the boy made his way to where the driver was standing. There can be no question that he understood something was wrong.

Jimmy was a smart country boy, and anyway a driver doesn't stand on the road with his horses and no stage unless something very odd indeed is going on. McConnell knew that well enough. But supposing Jimmy should inadvertently make a noise that Bart could hear? McConnell could see his chances for promotion and pay vanishing into thin air. Or what if Bart should suspect something and come over the hill before the boy and his rifle were within reach? It could not have been a comfortable thought.

But Bart heard nothing. Jimmy at last came up to the driver, and the two made their way quietly toward the crest of the hill. As they tiptoed upward, both of them realized that the sounds from the direction of the stage had ceased, how long ago neither could tell. What had happened? Had Bart made his haul and gone? Still cautious, they eased up to a spot where they could look back down the road.

If the thing had been rehearsed, it could not have been timed more precisely. At the instant they peered over the crest, Bart backed out of the stage, his plunder in a sack, a bundle of papers in his hand. There he was, set up like a target, all unconscious that two men and a rifle were ready to stop him where he stood.

Two men and one rifle. On this uneven combination turns one of the interesting points of the story. "They fired at me," Bart said afterward. But which one held the rifle and pulled the trigger? Was it McConnell, or was it Jimmy Rolleri?

The newspapers of the time are unanimous. All put it in substantially the same words. McConnell, they say, "seized the rifle from the boy and opened fire on the robber." There were no witnesses, of course. Bart's indefinite statement, "They fired at me," has generally been taken to mean that he made no distinction, that in those panicky moments of flight he had other things to think of, as of course he did. And most of those who have looked into the curious story of Black Bart have accepted the newspaper accounts as they stand.

There is, however, another view. That is that Bart told the literal truth when he said, "They fired at me." The stories of Jimmy's own brothers and sisters, some still living, bear this out.

Various accounts of the holdup have McConnell firing anywhere from two to eight shots at the fleeing Bart. The best evidence is that there were three shots in all. And Jimmy's own story was that he fired the last one. According to his version, McConnell took the rifle from him, fired, and missed. As Bart ran for it, McConnell fired and missed again. Jimmy said that he then told McConnell, "Here, let me shoot. I'll get him and won't kill him either." It was at Jimmy's shot, so he always said, that Bart stumbled and dropped the bundle of papers, though he held on to the sack and disappeared into the scrub before Jimmy could fire again.

Evidence? Well, there is this: After Bart had been caught and convicted, Jimmy was offered a job with Wells, Fargo. He did not take it because his mother was against the idea; as she put it, she wasn't going to have her boy a target for anybody. But Wells, Fargo & Company didn't merely let it go at that. They presented him with a rifle handsomely inlaid with silver scroll-work and appropriately engraved with his name and the date. It would be pleasant to record that this rifle still exists, but it would not be true. For Jimmy decided to go hunting with it one day, and at the first shot it flew to bits. Jimmy was not hurt, but he was annoyed. Quite sensibly, he boxed up the fragments and sent them back to Wells, Fargo, whose officials expressed suitable regrets and in due time shipped him another, a fine Winchester with no fripperies about it this time, merely a chaste silver plate screwed to the stock, engraved "James Rolleri, Jr., For Meritorious Conduct, November 3, 1883." Jimmy died in 1903, but his sisters carefully preserved the souvenir until the autumn of 1938, when the Calaveras Hotel in Angels Camp was burned to the ground, the rifle with it.

The Company did not forget McConnell either. He was given a reward of one hundred dollars in cash. There is a story that he got a rifle, too, but there is no evidence in the records. As for the matter of who fired on Bart and how often, no one seems to have taken the pains to see that the newspapers corrected their statements about who did the shooting that day. Possibly Wells, Fargo thought it best to let sleeping dogs lie. Certainly there was no harm in allowing public credit to go to their driver.

In any event, three shots were fired. Bart ran like a rabbit for the brush, dropped the bundle of papers but held on to his more valuable loot. There was no time for a fourth shot. Bart was gone. Once more, it seemed, he had robbed a stage and made good his escape. McConnell and Jimmy followed as far as the package, which they picked up and found smeared with blood, a hint at least that Bart had been wounded. Then they did the only thing they could do. They hitched up and drove on into Copperopolis to report the robbery. Wires were dispatched to San Andreas for Sheriff B. K. Thorn of Cal-

averas County, and to San Francisco for Mr. Hume's
assistant, Wells, Fargo Detective John N. Thacker. Both
replied that they would get to the spot as fast as they
could travel. In the meantime a posse of Copperopolis
citizens rode out to the scene to tear up the underbrush,
trample such tracks as might exist and, in the immemo-
rial manner of the amateur, confuse the issue in every way
possible before the professionals got there.

3

Sheriff Ben Thorn was a thorough man.

When he arrived on the ground, which was early in
the afternoon of the same day, he went at the matter in
hand as a good policeman should. He organized the random posse and set its members to work in orderly fashion,
combing the side of Funk Hill to see what he could turn
up in the way of tangible clues.

He found a great many. First, close to the road, there
was "a small round derby hat." McConnell had reported
that as Bart ran his hat fell off. This leads to an amusing
speculation. Did Bart wear the derby underneath the
flour sack disguise in order to give him added height? Or
did he have it perched on his head over the sack, scare-
crow fashion? The chances are that the first assumption
is the correct one. Bart, as was later shown, possessed an
almost childlike sensitiveness to ridicule. He was a joke-
ster in his way, but like many another wit he was careful
about making himself the butt of a jest. It is unlikely
that he would have permitted himself to look as silly as
derby-over-flour-sack would have made him. The point
is not important, save as it helps build up or destroy the

picture of the dignified, gentlemanly little man Bart turned out to be.

But the derby was only the beginning. A little distance uphill from the road was a large rock which the Copperopolis posse must have seen for some four hours of rummaging in the brush, but behind which nobody had thought to look. Sheriff Thorn thought of it, however, and when he came to the spot he was rewarded by an amazing profusion of clues.

There were, for example, two paper bags containing crackers and granulated sugar. Both were stamped with the name of Mrs. J. G. Crawford who kept a grocery store in Angels Camp, a dozen miles or so from the scene of the robbery. There was a leather case for a pair of field glasses or opera glasses; Sheriff Thorn called them the latter in his report, but the Wells, Fargo men preferred the former term. Beside these there were a belt, a quartz magnifying glass, a razor, a handkerchief full of buckshot, three dirty linen cuffs, and two flour sacks, one bearing the mark of Sperry & Company's mill in Stockton, the other carrying the name of a Sonora brand. "Apparently," said Sheriff Thorn later, with fine conservatism, "a person had been lying at the base of the rock." For all his cautious language, though, Ben Thorn had a discerning eye. He noticed that in one corner of the handkerchief, in small letters, was what appeared to be the identifying mark of some laundry—F.X.O.7.

All this was excellent as far as it went. But Thorn was not one to leave a job half done. He and his posse, now augmented by two officials, Sheriffs Cunningham of San Joaquin and McQuade of Tuolumne, "tracked around," as Thorn put it, for the rest of the afternoon. They just might find some further trace of their man, even perhaps run across someone who had seen him.

Their thoroughness paid them well. They found a hunter named Martin, who had a cabin about three-quarters of a mile from the scene of the holdup. Martin had some very useful information. That morning, he said, he had met an "elderly man with gray whiskers" who, when asked whither he was bound, replied that he was headed for Jackson where he lived. Further, he had volunteered the statement that he had been visiting Chinese Camp and Jamestown, on the other side of the river in Tuolumne County, to see someone, unspecified, on business. Martin had thought there was something fishy about the fellow, for he had then asked which way one went to go to Jackson, and whether it was necessary to pass through Angels Camp to get there. Martin had told him no, that he could go round Angels Camp if he wished, and had given him proper directions.

Sheriff Thorn was interested. He asked Martin if he would know the man again if he saw him. Martin answered that he would. Sheriff Thorn was not only interested but pleased. This was the kind of evidence he liked.

Nor was it all. Fortune favors the thorough man, and Thorn had one more lucky encounter, this time with a certain "Doc" I. P. Sylvester. "Doc" was no physician. He had acquired his nickname from a private fancy which he never hesitated to make public—the notion that pills rolled from dried angleworms would cure anything. Aside from this crotchet, he was as sharp as the next man, and was glad to tell Sheriff Thorn what he could. He had been up in the vicinity of Bear Mountain, he said, on a little prospecting trip, and was coming back to his cabin in Nassau Valley when Thorn met him. Had he seen any strangers? Yes, as a matter of fact, he had: a medium-sized, sturdily built man with a gray moustache and imperial. Had this stranger seemed at all disturbed? No, "Doc" couldn't say he had. When asked where he was going he had replied that he was traveling north to Jackson and wanted to know how much farther it was to Angels Camp. "Doc" had told him that it was about twelve miles, and the stranger had thanked him and gone on. Was Thorn looking for a man like that? As the gray-moustached stranger had done, Sheriff Thorn thanked "Doc" Sylvester and went on his way, a man who kept his own counsel.

That night in Angels Camp he did some more looking round. For one thing, he talked to Mrs. Crawford who added her bit to the slowly growing accumulation of evidence. She remembered quite well a stranger who looked like the one that Martin and "Doc" had described. It was about a week ago she had seen him. He had come into her store on October twenty-fifth and bought a dollar's worth of Knic-Knac crackers and ten or fifteen cents' worth of granulated sugar. She had put these purchases into paper bags like the ones the sheriff had found at the rock. She always used these bags stamped with her name; they were her way of advertising her store. Ben Thorn thanked her too, and went on looking round Angels Camp. Before bedtime he had found several others who had seen a man corresponding to Martin's description, in and about town on the date mentioned by Mrs. Crawford. Now he was getting somewhere. Distinctly he had something worth taking down to San Francisco.

✦

In the city offices of Wells, Fargo & Company, Mr. J. B. Hume had had Black Bart pretty constantly on his mind. He was sufficiently interested, in fact, to hire a special detective, Harry N. Morse, some six months earlier, and instruct him to work exclusively on the robberies supposed to have been committed by Bart. When Detective Thacker came back from Copperopolis with his report Mr. Hume listened closely.

John Thacker had talked at length to driver McConnell and had got the details of the holdup and the attempt to capture the robber. There was no doubt in his mind that it was Black Bart again. McConnell's description of the bandit's appearance matched exactly what they already knew of Bart. The broken box, the slit mail sack, the garb of the robber—it all fell into place. It was the PO8; no doubt of it.

But Detective Thacker had also talked to young Jimmy Rolleri. And from Jimmy he had elicited a surprising bit of information. Black Bart had broken his rule never to stay overnight near the spot of any of his robberies. Late one evening about a week earlier, Jimmy had told him, a stranger had come to the Rolleri inn at Reynolds Ferry and taken a room. It was the same man at whom he and McConnell had fired; Jimmy was sure of it. He remembered the man particularly because of his unusual request that he be given a key to his door. Nobody had ever asked for a key before, and Jimmy's sisters were uneasy about it. In the morning the stranger ate breakfast with the family and Jimmy ferried him across the river. Asked to describe the man, Jimmy mentioned his gray moustache, the wedges of baldness at the temples, the deep voice, the brilliant blue eyes. The last Jimmy had seen of him was his back and his blanket-roll as he trudged up from the river. The last, that is, until he saw that same back over the sights of his rifle as he pulled the trigger on Funk Hill.

If Mr. Hume was interested when Thacker made his report, he was all attention when Sheriff Thorn of Calaveras came in with his haul of evidence. Here at last was something tangible, something a man could put his hands on. Mr. Hume took the derby hat and the case for field glasses, giving his special operative, Harry Morse, the handkerchief. It wouldn't be long now. Between them, they would surely unearth something. What Hume did with the hat and the leather case is not recorded. But Morse went straight to work. If the mark in the corner of the handkerchief was that of any San Francisco laundry, sooner or later he would run it down. This was an occasion for the slow, sure plodding in which the good detective excels, and Morse was a good detective. There were ninety-one laundries in the city. He would call on them all, no matter how long it took him.

It took just a week. On Monday afternoon, November 12, the mark F.X.O.7 came to light. Morse told a reporter later, "After diligent search I was rewarded by finding the identical mark on the books of a laundry agency, Mr. Ware, 316 Bush Street. The handkerchief had been left there three times—Saturday, July 21, and Saturday, August 11, were the first two. I found on inquiry that the washing belonged to one C. E. Bolton."

When the newspapers finally got the story, they didn't put it quite that way. One said that the mark was found to be that of the American Laundry, which sent Morse to Mr. Ware, its agent. Another said that Morse found

Ware through "a Chinese laundry on Valencia Street." Still another printed a note to the effect that it was the California Laundry, making no mention of whether it was Chinese or good California-American. Ware himself had a story different from any of them, and since he was widely accused of having turned over his friend Bolton to the police (no one actually said he had done it for a consideration, but the implication was there), it is only fair to his memory to quote from his statement to the press after Bolton had been arrested and proved to be Black Bart. Wrote Mr. Ware plaintively: "In order to show how innocently I was led into giving what information I did concerning Mr. Bolton, I here desire to state the true manner by which the laundry mark on the handkerchief led to his arrest. The handkerchief was never shown to me, but was taken to the laundry where the washing was done, and there identified by Mr. Ferguson, the proprietor, as the mark of C. E. Bolton sent from my office at 316 Bush Street. Morse then came to me and asked if I would be good enough to let him look at my book for the name of a gentleman who he understood had been getting his washing done here; said that he understood the gentleman was a mining man, and being a mining man himself he desired to see him on business. I asked him what name he wanted to find. He said Bolton. 'Why certainly,' said I, 'I know Mr. Bolton well. He is in the city now; just arrived from his mine two days ago, and if you will call later you will probably meet him here, for he is an old acquaintance of mine and makes this his headquarters when in the city.' "

Curiously, no one at the time thought to look up Mr.

Ferguson, discover if he actually existed, whether he operated a "Chinese laundry," what it was named, or what his version of the tale might be. Perhaps no newspaper considered it worth while. Mr. Ware had had his day in court and that was that. Fortunately it is possible now, more than half a century later, to solve the mystery of the laundry and to clear Mr. Thomas C. Ware of any charge that he betrayed his friend, even though he remains an almost incredibly naïve babbler. The San Francisco Directory for 1883 holds the answer to the puzzle. Morse's count was accurate; the classified business section lists exactly ninety-one laundries. It shows no "American Laundry," nor any "Chinese laundry" anywhere on Valencia Street. But it does show the California Laundry, and notes that it was operated by the firm of Ferguson & Biggy. Moreover, it was in the neighborhood, at 113 Stevenson Street, which was not more than half a mile from Mr. Ware's shop. Whether Mr. Phineas Ferguson or his son Walter, who acted as clerk, checked the telltale mark and sent Morse to the gossipy tobacco-merchant does not signify. The evidence tends to show that Ware's defense against the hint of treachery was sound enough.

The fact remains that Ware was a silly man. For, once having started gossiping, he went right on with it. Not at all surprised that this inquisitive stranger should be familiar with his friend Bolton's name, his business, and where he took his laundry, yet know nothing of what he looked like or where he lived, Ware undertook to supply that information too. He described Bolton in detail, Morse says, and added that he lived in a small hotel called the Webb House, at 37 Second Street; "In Room

40," he added. Morse thanked him and said he would be back later.

The first thing to do was to set a watch on the hotel. Captain Stone, of the city police, took care of that, glad to do Wells, Fargo's representative a favor. Satisfied that "Bolton" could neither get in nor out without being seen, Morse went back to talk some more to the communicative Mr. Ware.

He found him willing as ever, quite glad to step out of his shop for a few moments to have "a little private chat." Even Ware never attempted to explain what he thought this unidentified busybody could want with him in private. His letter to the press says merely, "When he asked me if I could spare a few moments from my business, I consented and we started down the street together." What further detail Morse might have added to his mining-man fiction of earlier afternoon is a matter for speculation only. Because none was necessary. Before Ware could get round to asking what Morse wanted of him, Bolton himself came walking up the street. "He spoke to me before I noticed him," wrote Ware earnestly, "and I then hailed him and told him the gentleman wished to see him; then turning to the stranger I said, 'I don't know your name, sir.' 'Hamilton is my name,' said he. I then introduced Mr. Bolton and they walked down the street together, and I returned to my business, not dreaming of the trap that had been set."

So Mr. Ware, never guessing he had proved once again that a stupid man is so much more dangerous than an enemy, felt himself happy in the knowledge that he had done two mining gentlemen a good turn. Perhaps this new Mr. Hamilton would henceforward buy his cigars at

Ware's, or maybe send out his washing through Ware, Tobacconist, to Messrs. Ferguson & Biggy. Dreaming not at all of traps, much less that his name would be forever entangled with that of California's most famous stage-coach robber, he stepped back into his shop and out of the picture.

In the story he gave the papers, Harry Morse left a very clear description of the dapper little man he had so fortunately met on San Francisco's Bush Street. He said, "He was elegantly dressed, carrying a little cane. He wore a natty little derby hat, a diamond pin, a large diamond ring on his little finger, and a heavy gold watch and chain. He was about five feet, eight inches, in height, straight as an arrow, broad-shouldered, with deep-sunken bright blue eyes, high cheekbones and a large handsome gray moustache and imperial; the rest shaven clean. One would have taken him for a gentleman who had made a fortune and was enjoying it. He looked anything but a robber." Not that Morse was in the least doubtful of his man. He adds, "I knew he was the man I wanted, from the descriptions." At any rate, he was sure enough to take him as quickly as possible to Mr. Hume. Could he, asked Morse courteously, spare a few moments to consult with him on a mining matter? Mr. Bolton said that he could. What the two talked about as they walked down Bush Street to Montgomery, then to California and Sansome streets, Morse does not say. Had Bolton-Bart any premonition that his number was up? There is no evidence to show it. Apparently even the sight of the familiar Wells, Fargo sign did not disturb him. Says Morse, "We went upstairs to the Superintendent's office and I introduced him to Mr. Hume who asked him to sit down." Bart sat, and the act brought him to the end of the long chain of circumstances that had begun to work toward his capture the moment he had unwittingly noted its first link—the presence of that extra man, the unknown, on the driver's box beside Reason McConnell as the Sonora-Milton stage toiled up Funk Hill. There had been seven fat years, during which Black Bart was known far and wide as the debonair, chivalrous, fearless poet-bandit who could not be caught. Now the seven lean years were beginning. Some hint of it must have come to the little man then, for Morse said that as he sat there waiting to learn what they wanted of him, "great drops of perspiration stood out on his forehead."

Hume lost no time. Mr. Bolton was a mining man. Where, then, was his mine? Bolton replied that it was in Nevada, on the California line. Pressed to describe its location more closely, he became confused, finally admitting that he was unable to give a more definite locality. What was the name of his mine? His answer was a pathetic effort to assert his dignity. "I am a gentleman," Morse says he replied, "and I don't know who you are. I want to know what this inquiry is all about!" Both Hume and Morse were careful and patient. They answered that if Mr. Bolton would please answer just a few questions satisfactorily they would then tell their reasons for asking them.

For three hours the quizzing continued. Morse noticed that Mr. Bolton's right hand had a piece of skin knocked off the knuckle; about the size of a ten-cent piece it was. That set him thinking about the bundle of blood-stained papers at the scene of the robbery, and he drew Hume's attention to it. How, asked Hume, had Mr. Bolton hurt his hand? Bart had an answer for that; he had done it, he said, getting off the train on a recent trip to Truckee. What had he been doing in Truckee? He had been on the way to his mine. What mine, and where? Again Bart grew indignant. It was the first time in his life, he said, that his character had ever been called into question. He was a gentleman, and should not be questioned in this manner. Hume and Morse did not feel that being a gentleman had anything to do with it. Even a gentleman should know the name of his mine, if he owned one, and should be able to locate it at least roughly. They went on with their questions. Where, for instance, was he born? How old was he? When had he come to California? And about that mine, now—what was the name of it again? Finally Bart grew stubborn. He would answer no more questions, he said, no matter what they were.

If Bart thought the session had ended in a stalemate, he was quickly disillusioned. The inquiry had merely reached its second stage. Summoning Captain Stone from the City Prison, Hume and Morse called a hack and drove their man to the Webb House. Doubtless there would be evidence in the room "Mr. Bolton" occupied there.

Even the detectives could hardly have expected the quantity of clues they found. There were, to begin with, a large trunk and three valises. These yielded several interesting articles. In the trunk, for example, were three or four suits of clothes, one of them answering the description of that worn by the robber McConnell had fired at. In one of the valises was a letter partly finished, and the detectives were certain that it was written in the same hand as the doggerel verses Bart had twice left behind him. Concerning this piece of evidence they were depending upon what was no more than snap judgment, to be sure. After all, the lines of verse had been written in several styles—a different slant and manner for each line. Still, the letter was relatively unimportant. What finished Bart was his haberdashery. For in a bundle in the trunk, Morse and Hume found what they had been looking for all along. Wrapped up ready to take to Mr. Ware were cuffs, collars, and another handkerchief. And all of them bore the laundry mark, F.X.O.7. Morse, who occasionally enjoyed a romantic touch, notes, "The handkerchief was perfumed with the same perfume." Evidence or not, the dash of scent contributes its bit to the picture of mining-man Bolton, alter ego of the stage-robber.

Nine out of ten men would have given up there and then, but not Bart. It was his special gift always to be able to think of something—not necessarily something sensible, but something. When they asked him about the laundry mark he had an answer, even two answers. "What of that?" he replied. "I am not the only one whose things bear this mark. Others have their washing done at the same place!" That might have done, at least for a while. But Bart could never let well enough alone. Immediately he thought of something else. "Why," he went on, without realizing what he was saying, "somebody may have stolen the handkerchief from me. Or I may have lost it and someone else found it!" Hume and Morse nodded their agreement. Yes, that could very well have happened. Indeed, it had happened. Only, as Mr. Bolton would please note, it had been lost and found in a very odd place; the precise spot, in fact, at which the Sonora-Milton stage had been robbed ten days before.

Bart saw then what he had said and, as before, his last refuge was his dignity. Morse notes that he spoke calmly and with a smile, though his voice was low and a trifle hollow. "What!" he said. "Do you take me for a stage-robber? I have never harmed anybody in all my life, and this is the first time my character has ever been brought into question!" Neither Hume nor Morse took the trouble to point out that the stage-robber in whom they were interested—one Black Bart—was well known for not "harming" anyone. They had found something else to interest them. Stuck into a Bible that Morse picked up was a loose page which proved to be the flyleaf, torn out and then slipped into the volume at random. "On it," Morse reports, "was some writing in pencil, rather indistinct and portions quite illegible. As near as could be made out, the writing read 'This precious Bible is presented to Charles E. Boles, First Sergeant, Company B, 116th Illinois Volunteer Infantry, by his wife as a New Year's gift. God gives us hearts to which His . . . faith to believe. Decatur, Illinois, 1865.' "

Bart-Bolton-Boles. They were getting somewhere. Since there was nothing else in the room that could be used as evidence, they were willing to call it a day. Bart, being a hopeful little man, may have thought that now these unpleasant fellows would just go away and leave him in peace. But the trap once sprung had to snap shut. Morse closes the episode in a single sentence: "We then told Black Bart that he was suspected of having committed the stage-robbery on the third of this month, and took him to the City Prison."

Yet it was Bart, unpredictable, imaginative, his scurrying little mind always cooking up something unexpected, who supplied the curtain line for Act One. When they took him to Central Station, the desk-sergeant asked him his name, as a matter of routine. Bart was ready for him.

"T. Z. Spaulding!" he said firmly.

The name had never appeared in the case before. It never appeared again. Thinking fast—he loved to think fast—Bart had just pulled it out of the hat, for any reason or no reason. But they couldn't make him change it. As "T. Z. Spaulding" he was booked, a prisoner at last.

4

No curious crowds jammed the city prison that night to look at Bart, as they did a week later when he was lodged there on his way to San Quentin. Morse and Hume were confident they had the right man, but preferred to keep quiet about it. When some of the up-country witnesses had had a look at Boles-Bolton-Bart it would be time enough to make the news public. The newspapers were told nothing, which is the reason for the discrepancies in different versions of the Bart story when the reporters finally got hold of it some days later, and invented details to fill in the gaps, each according to his fancy.

With no public hullabaloo to disturb him, the chances are that Bart slept well. He may even have believed, in his curiously involved little mind, that he would wiggle out of it yet. After all, he was a gentleman—he insisted on that—and gentlemen simply weren't arrested for banditry. At any rate, he was in a pleasant mood when they told him next morning to get ready to go up to Stockton on the seven o'clock river boat. Captain Stone of the city police was officially in charge of the prisoner, but Mr.

Hume of Wells, Fargo went along as far as Clinton Station, across the Bay in Alameda County. There Harry Morse and John Thacker met them, and Mr. Hume, whose presence was urgently required in Bakersfield on other business, went back to San Francisco, leaving his two assistants to take care of the Express Company's interests. Morse had wired Sheriff Thorn to meet the boat at Stockton and to bring with him old Martin, the hunter. Martin had said he was sure he would recognize the man who had asked him all those questions about going to Jackson without passing through Angels Camp, and his identification would be an important bit of evidence.

The hours on the river were spent pleasantly. Bart was not ironed and showed no disposition to attempt an escape. Perhaps he couldn't swim, though there is no record that the officers thought to inquire. At all events, Morse is authority for the statement that the waggish tendencies so often noted in Bart were well in evidence. "The prisoner," he notes conscientiously, "seemed full of fun all the way up on the boat." It may have been during the trip that they got him to try on the derby hat that had fallen from the head of the robber as McConnell and Jimmy Rolleri fired at him. Whether this took place then or at some other stage in the proceedings, Bart's response has been preserved by an anonymous reporter writing the story of the capture and conviction a week later. The derby was a perfect fit, of course, and as this reporter tells it, the detectives looked sharply at Bart to see how he would take it. If they had known their man better, they would have realized that so small a matter would never disturb him. Bart settled the derby on his head, removed it, and looked it over carefully, then put it back again at precisely the right angle. "Why, gentlemen," he said, "it fits very well, doesn't it? And it is a very good hat. Perhaps you would allow me to buy it from you!" It has been suggested that the incident is no more than pure reportorial invention, but it has the ring of truth. It is so exactly what Bart would have said, so completely the kind of defense his agile, childlike mind would have produced.

Up in the Valley there was none of the fine reticence about the prisoner that Hume had chosen to observe in San Francisco. It may have been Sheriff Thorn who let the word get out, or it may have been Sheriff Cunningham of San Joaquin or Sheriff McQuade of Tuolumne. However the news was spread, people knew what was up, and a large crowd had gathered at the wharf in Stockton to meet the boat.

Sheriff Thorn was clever about the identification. He had kept the hunter, Martin, away from the gangplank, and it was not until Morse, Captain Stone, Detective Thacker, and Bart were off the boat and well mixed in with the crowd that he brought the old fellow over and told him to see if he could find the man he had met in the woods that day of the stage-robbery. It didn't take long. As Morse puts it, "Old Martin took one look and said, 'That's the man! That's him!' picking him out of a crowd of about a hundred people who had gathered to see the noted prisoner."

Bart made no jokes then. He must have seen that his chances were growing slim indeed. For when Thorn told Morse he had made arrangements to have the prisoner photographed, Bart objected violently. "You have no right to do this," he cried. "You have no right! I have done nothing!" He may have mentioned once more that a gentleman should not be treated so; if he did, his protests were useless. But when he was taken to the studio and seated before the camera his curious sense of humor returned. As he sat in the chair and watched the photographer dive under the black hood and swing the lens toward him, he pretended to dodge. "Will that thing go off?" he asked, and added plaintively, "I would like to go off myself!" They gave him no chance to go off anywhere. He was photographed seated, moustache and imperial neatly brushed, pepper-and-salt jacket buttoned high but not too high to show the wide wing collar, dark silk scarf and diamond stickpin, handkerchief just peeping (as a gentleman's should) from his breast pocket. He was photographed again, this time standing, overcoat on, its silk-faced lapels open, the derby hat set stylishly down on his head, cane in hand, left foot thrust forward, the very picture of a reasonably prosperous, decently self-respecting business man with a mild dash of the dude about him. Then they took him away to the Stockton jail and locked him up for the night.

Next morning they were up early again, and drove on to Milton, into the rolling foothills that mark the beginning of the gold-country. The news had got about that little town too, and the crowd of gapers was large enough to attract Bart's attention. He seemed rather pleased than otherwise. "The whole town has turned out to meet me!" he said. "I guess they'll know me when they see me again!" The detectives had not taken him to Milton for the crowd's sake. McConnell, the stage-driver, was waiting for them there and they brought him over for the all-important question. Was this the man who had held him up? McConnell looked narrowly at Bart and finally said he did not know. The robber had been disguised in a flour sack, and it was hard to tell if this was actually the man. Shrewdly, the detectives gave the two a chance to talk for a few moments, then took McConnell aside. How about the voice, they asked? Was that the same? McConnell was certain of it. That was enough for the moment. They hired a team and drove on into the hills twenty-two miles to San Andreas, county seat of Calaveras. There the crowd that had gathered made an odd mistake. For the first minute or two, they mistook Morse for the culprit and took the well-dressed prisoner for the San Francisco detective. There should have been a twinkle in Bart's deep-set blue eyes then. It was so thoroughly the kind of joke he enjoyed. Morse, however, is content to record the error and let it go at that. He had a good many other things to think of. He was determined that this time he would put Bart through a real questioning. If patience and persistence could break the prisoner down, then he would get a confession before he was through. He saw Bart locked into a cell and went to eat his dinner.

At seven o'clock that evening, Morse was back in the jail, closeted with his man in the jailer's private quarters.

Over his dinner he had methodically prepared a list of all the facts that had been gathered: the matter of that laundry mark, F.X.O.7, the derby hat that fitted so well, old Martin's identification, McConnell's certainty that the voice was the same. He jotted down carefully, too, the things about which he wanted to remind the prisoner: his unusual diffidence about the location of his supposed mine, for instance, and his inability to account satisfac-

torily for his time on the day of the robbery; the fact that
Mrs. Crawford of Angels Camp had told Sheriff Thorn
that she remembered the stranger who had bought the
crackers and granulated sugar that were found at the
scene of the robbery; the story of "Doc" Sylvester who
recalled so clearly the appearance of the stranger who
had asked him for directions on that day of the holdup.
Here, too, Morse had set down what Mrs. McCreary's
daughter had told Mr. Hume about the man with the
bright blue eyes and the wedges of baldness at the temples, the man who had refused tobacco and alcohol but
had conversed so long and so amusingly with her and her
mother. On the list were such other points as the handwriting of the letter found in the prisoner's room, which
was so remarkably like that of the verses signed "Black
Bart, the PO8," some years ago. Wells, Fargo & Company had those verses still, and could produce them.
There was that business also of the skinned knuckle and
the blood on the bundle of papers. And of course Jimmy
Rolleri and his sisters at the inn at Reynolds Ferry remembered the stranger who had asked for a key to his
room. Morse went over the list aloud, pointing out to
Bart what bearing each piece of evidence would have at
the trial. Because there was going to be a trial. The prisoner—Boles or Bolton or Spaulding or whatever he called
himself—could be quite sure of that.

The quiz lasted for five hours and a half. Bart was
restless, nervous, sometimes excited and at other times
apathetic, apparently hearing nothing that was said to
him. On occasion he would discuss the evidence logically
with Morse. Then he would break off and talk of other
things, describing his exploits in the Civil War and ex-

plaining with gestures just how he had been wounded in battle. Frequently he switched the subject to Bible matters, on which, Morse notes, he seemed well posted. Once, just as the detective thought he was beginning to get somewhere, Bart asked him out of a clear sky whether he didn't think that Moses had pluck to reprove the Lord for his harsh dealings with the Children of Israel. Morse said yes, he did; but where had Bart been at seven o'clock on the morning of November third?

Then suddenly in the middle of the interview, Bart had a question of his own. "Mind you," he said, "I do not admit that I committed this robbery. But what benefit would it be to the man who did to acknowledge it?"

Morse was wise enough to give no sign that he was pleased at this evidence of weakening. He explained patiently that if the case went to trial, "it would show what sort of man the prisoner had been, and that he had committed numerous robberies, and it would naturally prejudice his case; while if he made restitution and should go into court and plead guilty, it would save the county the great expense of a trial, and would no doubt be taken into consideration by the court." When Bart wanted to know just how the court would show its consideration in such a case, Morse answered him in old-fashioned roundabout polysyllabics. It would, he said, "effect a mitigation of his sentence." The suggestion gave Bart one last ray of hope and he seized it eagerly. "Supposing," he asked, "that the man who did commit the robbery should do this, would it not be possible for him to get clear altogether?" Morse's tactics were perfect. "No," he answered, "but if such a man did go to trial, and if all the robberies were proved, he would stand a good chance of being sentenced for life!" That fetched Bart. He flushed violently and came as near shouting as his mild temperament would let him. "I want you to understand," he cried, "that I am not going to San Quentin Prison! I'll die first!"

Morse did not point out to Bart that in his emotion he had forgotten all about his hypothetical robber and had spoken out in the first person. Instead, he went back over the ground and stressed two points—restitution, and the number of robberies believed to have been committed by Black Bart. If he could make his prisoner see that this last holdup could be proved his crime without the shadow of a doubt, though the others might be a trifle harder to lay at his door, and if he could get him to understand that restitution of the loot would go a long way toward making it easier for him, then perhaps he would get somewhere. He dinned these things into his prisoner's ears. Sooner or later, Bart would see the point.

It took another hour. At first, Bart tried to debate the justice of convicting a man merely on the say-so of witnesses. "These men," he argued, "may all come up and testify just as you say. Men are apt to commit perjury, and courts are apt to be prejudiced, and whether a man is guilty or not he has to suffer the consequences!"

Since Morse did not appear to be sensibly affected by this view of it, Bart elaborated. He knew of a case, he said, in which a man was arrested for a stage-robbery and all the witnesses "swore against him." Yet the man was innocent. "I know of my own knowledge," Bart said, "that he didn't do it!" In a despairing effort to give the fantastic tale the appearance of truth, he added, "I wonder what ever became of him?" Morse showed quite plainly that he was not interested in what became of the unhappy figment of his prisoner's imagination. Stolidly he brought up the question of the amalgam from the Sonora-Milton stage. Where had Bart hidden it? How did it happen that the handkerchief with his own private laundry mark on it had been found just where a stage was robbed? And if Bart was a mining man, where was his mine?

From the moment Bart had cried, "I am not going to San Quentin! I'll die first!" Morse had been sure he would eventually confess. By midnight, he felt that a confession was not far off. By twelve-thirty, he judged the time had come to play his trump card. Going to the door, he called in Captain Stone and Sheriff Thorn and told them that the prisoner had something to say to them. When they asked innocently what it could be, Morse said it had to do with the loot from the Sonora-Milton stage; that Bart had indicated his willingness to show them where it was.

The maneuver was perfectly timed. Bart had had a chance to reason it all out. He had tried all the dodges he could think of, but the detective had ignored them and kept boring in. Now he could see that his best chance lay in confessing to this robbery, restoring the treasure from the Wells, Fargo chest, and taking his chance with the court. After all, there wasn't much to connect him with any other crimes. Handwriting, identifications by people who had not seen him for some years, testimony from drivers who might say they recognized his voice—all this would take a deal of proving. If he admitted this one crime and led his captors to the loot, he might get off fairly lightly. His mind made up, he rose to his feet. "Well," he said, "let's go after it!" This was what the detectives had been waiting for. Within half an hour they had roused a stableman, hired a team, and started on their twenty-mile drive to Funk Hill.

It was bright moonlight, Morse notes, and easy driving. Bart, too, was in a mood to talk. He explained that it was a great relief to him to get rid of the strain he had been under, and added that now, for the first time, he had "the opportunity to tell someone about this thing." Since Morse had been urging him to confess for something like three days, it is to be presumed that he took the statement with a grain of salt. Nevertheless he and the other officers listened while their prisoner talked.

Bart had plenty to say. He always relished a chance to brag a little; the testimony of acquaintances later brought out the fact that in speaking of his Civil War experiences he used to refer to himself as "The Captain" —a mild and harmless vanity, to be sure, but none the less an indication of his general temperament. And here he was on safe ground. The robbery once confessed, he could do himself no harm by making sure his captors appreciated his astuteness of method.

His first move, he told them, had been to make friends in Tuttletown, the site of the Patterson Mine, and to learn through them the date of the shipment of amalgam and the time the stage would pick it up. Then he had walked most of the route, following the stage-road in order to determine the most likely place for his venture. It was on this tour of inspection that he had first stayed at Reynolds Ferry and forgotten that travelers accustomed to country inns do not ask for keys to their rooms. After looking over the whole route from Tuttletown to Copperopolis, he had made up his mind that Funk Hill was just the spot, and he had established what he called a "sleeping camp" high on the mountain. There he had cut grass and made a soft bed on which to spread his blankets, and thence he had scanned the countryside with his field glasses, watching the stage for several mornings to be sure of its schedule. He didn't eat much, he said. Now and then he would have some crackers and make coffee, always extinguishing the fire before daylight so that there would be no smoke to attract notice. Water? He got that from down in the canyon, a walk of about a mile. Sometimes he went all the way to the river, a good two miles.

When he had the lie of the countryside well in mind, he went on, he spent several mornings at a second "camp" nearer the road, from which he could examine the stage at close quarters, observe the location of the treasure-chest, size up the driver, and check the time he arrived at the exact point he had chosen for the holdup. It was in this connection, Morse reports, that he had an anecdote to tell, an incomplete, fragmentary thing but interesting as far as it goes.

About three mornings before the robbery, Bart said, he was watching the stage as it came up the winding hill when he saw a man step from the brush into the road, a handkerchief or scarf round his face. Bart said he had never seen the man before, but from his actions concluded he was going to hold up the stage. Surprised, he had said to himself, "Well, here's a go! Here's opposition! This fellow is going to take in the stage; here's another agent in the business!" And on the heels of that thought, he had an idea. Why not let the unknown put on his holdup and then, after he got the plunder, capture him and take the booty? Bart repeated the joke to the officers, chuckling a long time over the humor of it. When the detectives failed to respond as heartily as he thought they should, he explained it all over again. Didn't they see how funny it was? Why, the first robber might even be captured and sent to San Quentin while he, Black Bart, had got away with the treasure! "Also," he continued, "if the fellow had not got much from the stage, I could have turned him over to Wells, Fargo and got the reward, for nobody knew Black Bart!" Morse does not record that he and his fellow-officers laughed, even at this exquisitely humorous notion. Perhaps, under the circumstances, they did not consider it tactful of Bart to make a point of Wells, Fargo's failure to catch up with him for so long. Morse says nothing, either, about the rest of the story. Apparently the strange man with a scarf round his face was no robber after all. Certainly there was no holdup until three days later, when Bart put his own plan into effect.

Once started, however, Bart was not to be stopped. The urge to confess is a strong one, and Bart was firmly in its grip. There was the matter of his name, for instance. One of the officers—Morse's record does not say which—wondered how he had come to call himself "Black Bart." Would he mind telling them how he had chosen that swashbuckling pseudonym? No, he would be very glad to explain. It had come out of a story; perhaps the officers had heard that he was a great reader? At any rate, he was. He had read this story, "The Case of Summerfield," by a San Francisco lawyer named William H. Rhodes, who wrote under the name of "Caxton," just a short time before he had decided to go on the road, and when he was casting about for a name to sign to his first bit of poetry, it had just popped into his head. If the other gentlemen remembered the tale, they would recall that a character in it was named Bartholomew Graham, but was commonly known as "Black Bart." The gentlemen did remember; the yarn—one of those pseudo-scientific affairs which had a vogue during the latter half of the century—had caused a great stir in California when it was published in the Sacramento *Union* in May, 1871.

About the poetry—well, of course it would hardly become the poet to comment upon his own work. But he had always liked versifying, and it gave him pleasure to leave a clue at once so plain and so baffling. As a matter of fact, he had had another poem ready to leave at the scene of this last robbery, but was unable to do so since he had been compelled to leave so quickly. No one seems to have asked him to recite it, though unquestionably Bart would have obliged.

As the reader of today follows the course of that night's conversation in the moonlight, it becomes increasingly evident that what Bart had to say does not jibe with the statements Morse and Hume made afterward to the press when they were accused of having made a deal with Bart in order to recover the treasure.

The San Francisco *Examiner* made the point publicly a few days later. Had or had not, the *Examiner* wanted to know, Hume and Morse promised their prisoner that if he restored the loot from this last robbery and made full confession they would not press further charges? Did or did not Hume and Morse guarantee to Mr. Charles E. Bolton that if he would get them back their treasure and save the county the expense of a trial, they would say nothing about his being Black Bart and having committed twenty-seven other robberies? The questions were purely rhetorical, for the editor followed them with the ringing declaration that Hume and Morse had done just these things, and that they had so conspired to defeat the proper ends of justice in order to recover the gold Bart had taken and save themselves the money loss. With righteous indignation, the editor concluded, "What is the result of this perversion of justice? A few detectives divide a few thousand dollars, and instil into the dime-novel charged heads of ten thousand youths of this city the idea that one has but to be a bold and successful robber to be able to force the united detective talent of the Coast to intercede with the judges to obtain light sentences and to get two-column notices in the newspapers!" As though this were not enough, the *Examiner* made its meaning even more clear. Said the editor, "Whether the Charles Bolton who was sentenced is Black Bart remains to be proved. If he is, then the law has been tampered with. . . . The only tenable explanation of such a miscarriage of justice is that Bart's prosecutors made a bargain with him whereby he received a light sentence and they the $4,000 which he had hid in the woods near Copperopolis."

To this, Messrs. Morse and Hume replied, through the press, that it was a flat falsehood; that Bart had been made no promises; and that there had never been any question of a "deal" in any form. Morse admitted he had told Bart that "confessions" regarding robberies committed before 1880, three years earlier, were "outlawed," whatever he meant by that. The *Examiner* did not think much of the detectives' reply, making the point that according to Morse's own account he had talked to Bart for five and

a half hours with the sole purpose of persuading him to
reveal where he had hidden the treasure, and that at the
end of that time Bart had said, "Well, let's go after it!"
Plainly, the *Examiner* noted, the detectives were after
"it." And the editor adds, "Some stolen amalgam was the
main object of this inquisition, and Bart finally agreed to
restore it, expecting thereby to receive a more lenient
sentence. He was not disappointed."

From the viewpoint of today's student endeavoring to
reconstruct the case, honors here rest with the *Examiner*.
For Bart, having freely confessed his identity to the detectives on that long night-ride through the moonlit
gulches and over the pine-clad hills, went on to tell much
more about his past performances.

The whole affair, he said, reminded him of his first
robbery, because it had been committed at the same spot.
That was in July, 1875, and when he sat watching Mc-
Connell's stage crawl up the hill he had said to himself,
"This was where I committed my first robbery. I wonder
if this will be my last!" It is from Bart's yarn about this
early crime, by the way, that those who have written about
him for the last fifty years got their favorite tale of the
bandit's chivalry in the matter of ladies. Bart himself
told it as he explained the details. "I had two shotguns
that time," he said, "and when I told them to throw down
the box one lady passenger became excited and threw me
her purse full of money. I picked it up and returned it
to her, saying that I did not wish her money, only boxes."
Two shotguns seem like a good deal to handle, but when
Bart explained that after extracting what the box contained he had left one of the shotguns at the scene, Morse
nodded in agreement. That shotgun had been found, he

admitted, but until now no one had known to whom it belonged.

Nor were Bart's reminiscences entirely concerned with his stage-robbing exploits. He was quite as proud of having lived in San Francisco, almost under the noses of the police, without anyone suspecting his true business. In fact, he said, it had been his custom to take breakfast regularly at William Pike's New York Bakery on Kearny near Clay Street, less than a block away from the Central Station in the old City Hall and a favorite eating-place of the force. Had he made the acquaintance of any of the officers, the detectives wanted to know? Why, yes; he had. He knew Dave Scannell, for example, and he was "a devilish nice fellow, too!" Had he ever had any business with any of them? His answer was not what the detectives were looking for, but it was enlightening just the same. Yes, he had had some business with the police. That was a year or two before, when he had gone over to the Station and got two detectives to hunt up a fine overcoat that had been stolen from his room at the Commercial Hotel where he was then living. They had recovered the coat and he had tipped them for their trouble. Morse asked if he hadn't been afraid to take the chance when he was wanted for so many crimes. Bart looked surprised. "Why, no," he said, "they didn't know who I was. I never associated with any but good people, and none of them ever dreamed what my business was!" Morse does not say so, but this lack of tact on the part of a captured bandit must have been hard to swallow. At least, now that they had run him down, Bart might have given them credit or else let them know outright that he thought them only simpletons who had stumbled on his trail by enormous good luck. Either attitude would have been easier to bear than this naïve simplicity which made it clear that he had just never thought about detectives much.

The ride over and through the hills lasted the rest of the night. A little after sunrise—Morse records it as 6:45 A.M.—they arrived at the scene of the robbery, tied the horses, and told Bart to reconstruct the crime from the beginning and then show them where he had hidden the gold. Bart was quite pleased, and made a dramatic account of it, faltering in his narrative only when the Sonora-Milton stage came by on its regular run, McConnell on the box again. Morse writes, "The driver had a sharp look at Black Bart as he went past." It seems reasonable that McConnell might have had as many as two or three sharp looks.

The detectives allowed Bart to tell the whole story. All of it checked with what McConnell and Jimmy Rolleri had seen. Their story, though, had ended when their quarry disappeared in the brush. They had fired three times. Bart agreed to that. (Unaccountably, Morse neglected to ask Bart if he had been hit by that last shot and if so where. Perhaps he took it for granted that the barked knuckle he and Hume had noticed was from that final bullet.) But what had Bart done after he had scuttled into the scrub?

Bart was glad to explain. In the first place, he had been dog-tired after his wrestle with the refractory treasure-chest. The sack of treasure must have weighed a full fifteen pounds as he estimated it, and he hadn't run very far, changing direction two or three times, before he was exhausted. "A ten-year-old could have captured me," he said. He had gone maybe a quarter of a mile when he decided he could run no farther without a rest. His first precaution was to throw the sack into the end of a rotten log and cover it up with dirt and leaves. Then, when his breath came back to him, he went down the ravine and up the other side, heading in the direction of Angels Camp. He did not go into the town there, but passed well to the east of it. It was at this point that he made up his mind he would carry his gun no farther, and with it he threw away everything else he was carrying except the cash he had taken from the Wells, Fargo box. The robbery had taken place on Saturday, November 3. By Monday night he had walked almost to Sacramento, a matter of a hundred miles in three days, over much rough country. On the way he had found a "fairly respectable hat" in a cabin and put it on to replace the derby lost in his flight. Tuesday morning he walked into Sacramento, got shaved, and went into a tailor shop and ordered a suit of clothes. Then he wandered about town until the eastbound train came in, when he bought a ticket for Reno. He had stayed there a day or two, writing to his landlady at the Webb House in San Francisco that he would be back in a few days, and to Mr. Ware, his laundry agent, telling him the same thing. On Friday he took the train from Reno back to Sacramento, got his new clothes from the tailor, and next day returned to San Francisco where he slept in a waterfront lodging house for one night and then went back to his regular lodgings on Second Street and "pursued his regular habits." He did not pursue them long, since it was on Monday, November 12, that Tobacconist Ware had said, "Mr. Bolton, this is Mr. Hamilton who wants to consult you on a mining matter," and brought his career to an end.

There was one thing more—the gold amalgam. Morse suggested that they finish the story by going and getting it. Bart led them through the brush around the side of the hill and down a short distance into the ravine. There it was, in the hollow log, just as he had told them; all 228 ounces of it, some forty-two hundred dollars' worth, the largest haul Black Bart had made in all his long years as a highwayman. They took it back to the wagon, dumped it under the seat, and drove the three or four miles on into Copperopolis where Morse and Captain Stone would begin their journey back to San Francisco. Bart was Sheriff Thorn's prisoner now, and the place for him was the county jail in San Andreas. Thorn lost no time. By early afternoon, Bart was in his cell. As for Detective Morse, what he needed was sleep, but there was a wire he had to send. He sought the telegraph office and wrote it out. It read:

Mr. Leonard F. Rowell, Division Superintendent
Wells, Fargo Express Company, San Francisco.

Black Bart throws up the sponge. Stone, Thorn and myself have recovered all the stolen treasure. Inform Thacker.

HARRY N. MORSE.

Ten days before, when Hume had handed him a handkerchief with the symbols F.X.O.7 marked in the corner, he had taken on a job. Now the job was done.

Next day, November 16, Bart appeared before Justice P. H. Kean in San Andreas, heard Ben Thorn give his testimony, waived counsel, said that he wished to plead guilty, and that he did not desire bail fixed. Justice Kean held him to answer and recommitted him to the care of the sheriff.

On November 17th—they lost no time in those days—Bart was brought before Judge C. V. Gottschalk of the Superior Court, entered his plea of guilty, waived trial, and asked the Court to pronounce judgment. There is a story that he had recovered sufficient spirit to make a speech before the Court. Authority for this is the Calaveras *Weekly Citizen*, which reports: "The prisoner appeared to be a little hard of hearing, and that he might thoroughly understand everything that was said, he stepped around to the Judge's stand, and stood within a few feet of His Honor, Judge Gottschalk. In reply to the question, 'Have you anything to say?' he made a long, rambling statement, emphatically denying that he was Black Bart and repeating the assertion several times that this was his first robbery and he hoped it would be his last. The speech seemed to have no effect whatever upon the Judge, and was considered rather weak by the lookers-on." The minutes of that day's proceedings, however, show no record of such a speech. They read, quite simply: "Whereas the said C. E. Bolton has been duly convicted of robbery by his own confession, it is therefore ordered Adjudged and Decreed that the said C. E. Bolton be punished by imprisonment in the State Prison of California for the term of six years." As footnote to this, the editor of the *Citizen* adds, "He seemed rather pleased with the sentence."

As a matter of fact, Bart had reason to be pleased. He had committed twenty-eight robberies, so Wells, Fargo's records later showed; he had confessed to one and been sentenced on the basis of that one. True, he had never been known to inflict physical injury upon anybody. He had

never been known to fire a shot. He had robbed no passengers; the Wells, Fargo box and the United States mail
were all he had ever touched. Yet, after all, treasure-chests
broken open, mail-sacks slit with his own peculiar T-cut
and the contents rifled—these were serious crimes. Six
years was little enough, especially since, under the recently
passed Goodwin Act, the six really came down to four and
a half, with additional time off for good behavior. If
there had been a bargain, Bart did not do so badly. And
in spite of the angry denials issued by Hume and Morse, a
bargain is what it looks like.

The six-year term began almost immediately. Sheriff
Thorn waited another day before he took the prisoner
down to the Bay. Bart was lodged in the San Francisco
city prison once more—not as "T. Z. Spaulding" this
time, but as Charles E. Bolton, since he persisted in denying that the name "Boles" on the torn flyleaf of the Bible
in his room had anything to do with him. In the Central
Station on the night of November 20, he held a sort of
impromptu court; the San Francisco newspapers had the
story now, and they were making as close to a three-ring
circus of it as the temper of the 1880s allowed. One reporter, sent to get a story on the crowds that pressed into
the prison to look at Bart, went so far as to write that
his mistress had come to see him in his cell. Perhaps this
was thought to add color to the account; at any rate, it
was printed. There is no evidence that there was a shred
of truth in the statement.

But the soiree was soon over. On the 21st, Bart was
taken across the Bay to San Quentin Prison and committed
as prisoner Number 11,046. Though he stuck to his story
that his name was Bolton and that his business was mining,

he provided the officials with a few new bits of information. He was fifty years old, he said, and was born in Jefferson County, New York. On the commitment form, he is described as five feet, eight inches tall and of light complexion. There is the additional note that his moustache and imperial were nearly white, and that his shoe size was Number Six. He did not use tobacco in any form, drink intoxicating liquors, or take opium, he told them, and he weighed 160 pounds. Mere cold facts, these; but the true Bart touch is discernible in his answer when they came to the blank space opposite the question, "Education?" Waving aside such inconsequential details as the number of school grades he had passed, he answered them in one inclusive word. "Liberal!" he said, grandly. Once more Bart had made the curtain speech.

## 5

In San Francisco the papers were busy remaking the Black Bart legend.

For years Bart had been a dim, horrific figure, his name a byword for determination, boldness, and success. Other highwaymen might try Bart's trick, and some did. But they were simple robbers, no more. Bart was different, a towering predatory terror, head and shoulders above his fraternity. He was here one day, and a hundred miles away the next. No stage-driver in the mines but had imagined himself hearing that deep voice, looking down the muzzle of that shotgun, obeying the hollow command, "Throw down the box!" The newspapers had helped along the legend, tended and watered it, taken care that it did not wither, a kind of husbandry which is the peculiar privilege of the Fourth Estate.

Now they were faced with a fact. Their legend had shriveled and died. Instead of a dashing, picturesque bandit, ur even one of the cold, grim sort, they had on their hands just Charley Boles, an ordinary, everyday kind of man who neither smoked nor drank liquor though he admitted to a fondness for coffee, whose conversation was of the intellectual order, and who prided himself on being a great reader. There was nothing to do but make the best of it. A dozen reporters turned to the task of inventing a new Black Bart.

Some of them tried hard to salvage at least a few twigs from their original tall tree of fancy. "Bart," wrote one, "is a man who might himself be a minister of Draconian justice or a gray-eyed Man of Destiny." The classical allusion was quite in the journalistic tradition of the time, though the latter reference is not so sound; it is a trifle difficult to reconcile the evocation of William Walker with the incontrovertible record of Bart's eyes of brilliant blue. The *Call's* reporter referred to him as "The Black Prince." Wrote another, "His face bears lines of intelligence and resolution," going on to note the high forehead, the well-shaped features, the gray hair, and moustache of the "popular hero." But it was not possible to hold the note of dignity indefinitely, and after another sentence or two this reporter came down to earth again and admitted that Bart was, after all, a robber. "His long hands," he adds, somewhat spitefully, "are indicative of cupidity and are too soft ever to have been much employed in honest toil." It may not have occurred to him that Bart could have said the same thing of him; even in the eighties the labor of writing pieces for the paper did not run to calluses.

Most of the gentlemen of the press, however, saved their faces by the convenient newspaper trick of ignoring all that had theretofore been printed and approaching their subject from a fresh angle. They vied with each other in producing new names for Bart. Some spelled "Boles" as "Bolles," others as "Bowles." One busy scribe set it down that Bart had been "known to intimates" (unspecified) as "Charley Barlow." Another announced that Boles had been called "Barton" by his friends. From somewhere the name "Fleming" appeared briefly. No one, evidently, thought to examine hotel registers in the mining towns. If they had, they might have found one authentic pseudonym to add to the list. But it was another fifty years before anyone discovered that on the books of the old Sperry Hotel, later the Mitcheler, in Murphy's near Angels Camp, Bart had once signed himself "Carlos Bolton." Perhaps he had drunk an extra cup or two of coffee that day. Surely he must have had one small private moment of delight when he meditated upon that fine romantic fillip to his own plain "Charles."

The punsters had their innings too. "He has at least this in his favor," one such wrote of Bart, "that he is strictly temperate and eschews the weed which his less erratic fellowship chews!" It may have been the copydesk that worried about whether the paper's readers were quite up to these linguistic acrobatics. At all events, the next sentence clears up any lingering doubts. "In other words," it reads, "Bart does not use tobacco in any form." Another newspaperman made much of Bart's supposed talents with a pen. "He is an expert," vowed this enthusiast, "executing schoolboy scrawls or the flourishes of a $1500 bookkeeper with equal facility." Nor was his verse forgotten. "He robbed his victims," said one shrewd critic, "and then harrowed their souls with rhyme!"

It was during these days of scrambling for a "new angle" on Bart that some minor mathematical genius conceived the idea of exaggerating the reward for Bart, making something really big of it. He did it by simple multiplication. As far as the papers then knew, Bart's robberies totaled twenty-three; it was not until the appearance of a definitive Wells, Fargo circular a week later that the number was known to be twenty-eight. What this reportorial idea-man did was to take the reward of eight hundred dollars offered jointly by Wells, Fargo, the State of California, and the United States Government, and multiply it by the number of robberies then laid at Bart's door. Twenty-three robberies at eight hundred dollars each come to $18,400, and this angle-seeking newsman was satisfied to get his one-day sensation out of it. He could hardly have known that to this day writers interested in Black Bart would quote that figure solemnly, in the belief that it represents the reward actually collected by those concerned in the capture.

The truth is that the total of Bart's stage-robbing gains over the eight-year period from July 26, 1875, to November 3, 1883, probably did not amount to anything like this sum. His last haul was not quite five thousand dollars; it was his largest, and the gold was recovered. The reader will recall the details of other robberies: "$379 in coin, one diamond ring [said to be worth $200], and one silver watch valued at $25," and "A package of gold specimens valued at $50 and a silver watch." The day of fabulously rich shipments had passed. Unless there were payrolls or some particular treasure in transit, the Wells, Fargo boxes were not the bonanzas they had been twenty years earlier. It is true, of course, that the amount of a reward does not depend upon the amount stolen. But in this case the correct figures are given for anyone willing to take the pains to trace them. The San Francisco *Call* went to the trouble of ascertaining the official disposition of the reward money, and printed the facts in its issue of November 16, 1883. Wells, Fargo's Mr. Hume naturally did not share; he was hired by the Company for the specific purpose of protecting its interests in just this way. But Morse was not then in Wells, Fargo's employ; he was an outside agent, working for Hume on this one case. The *Call's* story, then, is the answer: "Morse and his assistants will receive one-fourth of the recovered treasure, and rewards aggregating $800 in addition, namely $300 from Wells, Fargo & Co., $300 from the State, and $200 which the Government offers for the arrest of mail robbers." Unquestionably the fine large sum of $18,400 does sound better. It merely happens to be no more than the result of two minutes' figuring by a harassed reporter trying to please his editor who wanted something new on the bandit everybody was talking about.

There was one newspaper that did not join in this cheerful game of creating a new Black Bart for the public's pleasure. That was the San Francisco *Examiner*. Its editor was thoroughly irritated by the whole affair, though he took pains to conceal the true source of his annoyance. What he said in print was that detectives Hume and Morse had woefully mishandled the entire business; that in order to get more credit than they deserved, they had deliberately injected "mystery and glamour" into the capture and conviction of the robber, when the truth was that there had simply been a "deal" by which Bart had been promised a light sentence if he would confess and return the proceeds of the Sonora-Milton stage holdup. This, said the *Examiner*, taking a high moral tone, was contrary to the general good, and besides it was likely to put notions into the heads of San Francisco's impressionable youth who might be persuaded, now that they saw the punishment to be so light, to take up banditry as a career.

The matter of a possible bargain between Bart and his captors has already been discussed in this narrative, and the point made that to this extent the *Examiner* may well have cut close to the truth. It is hard to see any other reason for Morse's ignoring Bart's telltale chatter on the night-long drive through the moonlight to Funk Hill, or for his saying no more about the handwriting clues found in his prisoner's room. Unless there was an understanding, there should have been some attempt to establish in court that Bart was the author of the doggerel verses left at the scene of the earlier robberies, some effort to demonstrate his connection with the holdups he had so freely admitted that night to Morse, Thorn, and Stone. Morse did answer the *Examiner's* accusation the next day, pointing out very sensibly that if any "mystery and glamour" had been injected into the affair it was the newspapers that had done it and not the detectives. As for the alleged bargain, he said: "No inducements were held out for Bart to confess. He was simply told that a confession and restitution would likely be taken into con-

sideration by the court and go in mitigation of sentence."
The reader will agree that Morse scores on the mystery-
glamour point, but that in the matter of the "deal" his
defense is feeble. As the *Examiner* might have asked, what
would a bandit consider an "inducement" anyway? Most
students of the case will be satisfied that the *Examiner*
had the detectives there.

But it is also clear that this was not the true reason for
the paper's annoyance. For all its protestations, the *Examiner* was not worried about the city's youth, nor yet
about the length of the sentence Bart would serve. What
had rubbed its editor the wrong way was that Hume and
Morse had not let him in on the case at the beginning.
They had caught and questioned a robber, found clues
in his room, and then taken him down and secretly cast
him into clink. Cried the *Examiner* indignantly, "The
criminal should have been *openly* lodged in the City
Prison!" That was where the shoe pinched. By "openly,"
the editor meant that his paper ought to have been informed. Further, the detectives had spirited their man
away to Stockton where they let some hunter or other
look at him, and then allowed the truth to leak out in
the remote county seat of San Andreas where the city
reporters had no chance to get at the prisoner. Worst of
all, when the information was finally released, it was the
*Morning Call* that carried the full story. That was not
playing the game as the *Examiner* understood it. That
Hume and Morse had conducted their case in the only
safe way, that they had painstakingly made sure and
doubly sure of their man before letting the news get about
—all this did not matter. The *Examiner* was The Press,
and it should have been told. It is not the first time, nor

the last, that The Press has confused itself with The Almighty.

It is this chastisement of Hume and Morse in the *Examiner*, by the way, which is responsible for much of the confusion that has arisen among writers who have tried to retell the story of Black Bart. For its editor, bitterly angry at the two detectives, resorted to one of the least pleasant of journalistic tricks—the deliberate obfuscation (including flat misstatement of fact) of the whole case in order to put Hume and Morse in a bad light and, if possible, discredit the *Call*. Says the *Examiner*, for example, "The long-winded and romantic version of Morse's story put forth by the *Call* of Saturday has already become laughable." It continues: "The credit of capture and conviction would seem to belong to Thorn and Thacker instead of to Hume and Morse, and doubtless both men are sorry they trusted the latter to the extent of letting them have the handkerchief by which they gained so much advertising."

Both statements are typical of the *Examiner's* disingenuous tactics. How had the Morse story in the *Call* "become laughable"? The *Examiner* does not explain; it merely makes the statement. Thorn and Thacker may have been "sorry they trusted Hume and Morse to the extent of letting them have the handkerchief," but if they were it can only have been because if they had retained it they, instead of Morse, might have caught Bart. Certainly credit is due Thorn; he found the handkerchief, and it was his thorough scouring of the countryside that uncovered Martin, the hunter, whose identification played such an important part in persuading Bart to confess. But Morse gave Thorn full credit on both counts. So did the *Call*, in that story on which the *Examiner* was so hopelessly scooped. No, there is nothing in the *Examiner's* angry attack that will hold water—nothing, that is to say, excepting the suggestion of a "deal." And if, as the *Examiner* claimed, it was Sheriff Thorn, rather than Morse, who actually obtained the confession from Bart, then it must have been Thorn who made the reprehensible "deal" for which the *Examiner* was so righteously scolding Hume and Morse.

However, the *Examiner* had other fish to fry. It eventually forgot its grudge (only temporarily, as will appear) and dried the crocodile tears it had shed over the dangers to which San Francisco's tender youth had been exposed. The other papers tapered off, too, as the story grew colder and imaginations flagged. For a while, enterprising peddlers did a land-office business with prints of the two photographs for which Bart had had to pose. The *Call* telegraphed to Decatur, Illinois, for information, but received only the statement that Charles E. Boles had lived there twenty years before and had been a sergeant in the 116th Illinois Volunteer Infantry during the Civil War. The dispatch added that he had "served with great bravery for three years." Aside from its pleasant corroboration of Bart's own tales of his military prowess, this did no more than confirm the writing on the flyleaf of the Bible that had been found in his room. Another paper learned (or said it had) that Bart had mined in California in the 1850s, returned to Illinois for his War service, and after his discharge had left his wife and three small daughters to work in the mines in Montana. His family heard from him for some time, this story continued, finally receiving a letter in which he hinted that he had something really

good on the fire and would send for them soon. That was
the last message of any kind from the erring husband and
father. After some years without further word, they concluded he had been killed by Indians. Still another report
was printed, quoting an unidentified source as authority
for the statement that Bart had once taught school in the
northern part of California, and that his fondness for
gambling had cost him his job. In support of this, it was
said that Bart's friends had spoken of his participation in
horse-racing pools and of his fondness for mining stocks.

How much of it was true and how much sheer invention
it is impossible to tell now. All of it has been thoroughly
interwoven with the Black Bart story as it survives today;
that much is certain. The student of the case may be
thankful that the stories soon ceased to be printed. Black
Bart was in prison; the excitement faded; the newspapers
forgot him and so did the public. He was no longer news.
He was serving his time.

Apparently Bart settled into prison routine with very
little trouble. A quiet, reserved man, he would naturally
keep much to himself. There is evidence that he did make
one friend in San Quentin, a highwayman called Dorsey.
He was not Bart's sort of robber; he was the violent kind
that does not stop at murder. He had served three previous
terms for various offenses, but this time he was in for life;
he and a companion had killed William F. Cummings, a
Nevada City banker, in 1879. Perhaps Bart and Dorsey
were drawn together through their common understanding
of the road-agent's trade, perhaps merely because they
happened to get along well with each other. At all events,
the record notes their friendship for what it is worth.

With time on his hands, too, Bart again took up his pen. His first recorded letter was to Reason McConnell, driver of the Sonora-Milton stage on that unhappy day when Bart's plans went all wrong. It is one of the few that have been preserved, and because it shows that at least the first six weeks in San Quentin had not dampened Bart's curious sense of humor, it is worth quoting. Wrote Bart, on January 10, 1884:

> Mr. McConnell, Dear Sir:—You will please pardon me for this long delay in acknowledging your "kind compliments" so hastily sent me on the 3rd of November last, but rest fully assured, my dear sir, that you are remembered, and with nothing but the most friendly feelings as a man having done your whole duty to your employer, yourself and to the community at large. I have often admired your fine qualities as a driver, and only regret that I am unable to compliment you on your marksmanship. I would like to hear from you, however, if consistent with your wishes, and, my dear sir, you have my best wishes for an unmolested, prosperous and happy drive through life.
>
> I am, dear sir, yours in haste,
>
> **B. B.**

There was a postscript; one of Bart's failings, as has been noted, was always to think of something else he might have said, and if possible say it. In this case his afterthought was only another gentle effort at humor. It read: "P.S.—But not quite in so much of a hurry as on a former occasion!"

McConnell may have replied, but if he did the letter has not turned up.

Jimmy Rolleri's sisters also believe that Bart wrote to their brother, addressing him, they recall, as "Young Jimmy," waggishly complimenting him on his shooting which Bart said was better than McConnell's (evidence that it was really Jimmy's shot that drew blood that day?), and assuring him that Black Bart held no grudge. But again if there were such letters they cannot be found now. There is no proof that Jimmy replied, nor has anyone any idea of what he said to Bart if he did.

Much later, after Bart was discharged from prison, the San Francisco papers printed an interview with Mr. Hume in which they quoted him as referring to a certain letter "written by Bart to his son-in-law," as being violently abusive in tone. That letter was explained (by the *Examiner*) in a fantastic "interview" with Bart himself, months after he had disappeared from public view. Mr. Hume called the "interview" a tissue of lies and let it go at that, though it will appear in its proper place in this narrative and the reader may make up his own mind about it. As part of his reply, Mr. Hume said also that he would not comment on the *Examiner's* "explanation" that the letter was written, not to a son-in-law but to a brother-in-law, and was well justified since that relative had defrauded Mrs. Boles of some money. When Hume was asked about this, he said merely that his information had come from Captain Aull and Warden Shirley of San Quentin, and that he would say nothing more about it. The reporters took what comfort they could from that meager answer. Apparently none of them thought it worth the trip across the Bay to ask Warden Shirley what he could add to the story.

As for any further information on Bart in San Quentin, the records show nothing. Chumming quietly with murderer Dorsey, going about his prison duties, he put in his time, a model prisoner for all evidence to the contrary.

Only one reference to his feelings during the four years and two months of his term has ever appeared: a paragraph from a letter to his wife written immediately after his discharge, while he was temporarily lodged in San Francisco wondering what to do next. Free once more, he was not yet adjusted to the world "outside," and his few sentences clearly show his unsettled mind.

"Dear Family," he wrote, "I am completely demoralized and feel like getting entirely out of reach of everybody for a few months and see what effect that will have. Oh my dear family, how little you know of the terrible ordeal I have passed through, and how few of what the world calls good men are worth the giant powder it would take to blow them into eternity. Thousands that under your every-day life you would call good, *nice* men are, until the circumstances change to give them a chance to show their real character. I have reference now to those that have charge of our Public Institutions. For instance, you might go about them as a visitor and meet men there that you would think the very essence of official purity. But go into the Hospital and there see what they are doing for those that need their care and you will find 99, yes 99, in every 100 that would not turn his hand over to save a prisoner's life!"

What, one wonders, had Warden Shirley done to Bart, if anything? Had Aull been harsh, or had the prison doctor perhaps turned an unsympathetic ear and prescribed ipecac and Glauber's salts? No one can know, of course. But at least this much of a glimpse remains to show the curious what Bart thought of California's treatment of those who had broken its laws. For the rest, there is only the flat official statement on the books. Charles E. Bolton was released from San Quentin, his term completed, the law satisfied, on January 21, 1888.

As a matter of course, the reporters met the boat that brought Bart over to the San Francisco shore and, in the prying manner of The Press, asked him whatever questions they could think up. Had prison life hurt him, for example? No, Bart replied, he felt very well. He was four years older, to be sure, and he had found that he needed glasses now for reading. He seemed to be getting slightly deaf, too, he thought. Otherwise he was in good health, as they might see for themselves. Someone started him on his past, and he brightened a little as he told some of his better Civil War yarns. It is interesting here to observe that life in San Quentin had made Bart a trifle more conservative. His old-time friends had reported that he used to tell them he had been a Captain in the 116th Illinois Volunteer Infantry. The Bible found in his room had made it clear, the reader will recall, that its owner was "Sergeant" Charles E. Boles. Conditioned by his confinement, Bart was now willing to split the difference. The reporters wrote that he told them tales of how he was wounded "as a Lieutenant in the Civil War." Did he intend to rob stages again, now that he was free? Bart shook his head vigorously and answered that he would never rob again, stages or anything else. But it was not long before the barrage of questions tired him. "It is no use asking more of me," he said to the newspapermen, "I will say nothing further." One reporter, however, had thought of something else, and chanced the query. How about poetry, he wanted to know. Had Bart any more verses up his sleeve? For a moment the old waggish gleam shone in Bart's bright blue eye. "Young man," he replied, "didn't you hear me say I would commit no more crimes?"

The Sunday papers next day printed substantially the same accounts of the interview under such heads as "Black Bart Out of Prison," and then dropped the subject. A week later, Ambrose Bierce, hard put to it to fill his long "Prattle" column in the *Examiner*, contributed his bit to the Bart Saga by publishing a long poem of his own on Bart's release. It is second-rate Bierce, and not worth quoting here save for one stanza. Wrote Bierce, most ungenerously when it is remembered that one journeyman poet was addressing another:

> *"What's that?—you 'ne'er again will rob a stage'?*
> *What! did you so? Faith, I didn't know it.*
> *Was that what threw poor Themis in a rage?*
> *I thought you were convicted as a poet!"*

It was said at the time that during Bart's term of imprisonment the police, penitentiary officials, and Wells, Fargo detectives had all received letters from Mrs. Boles telling them her Charles had been a good husband and pleading with them to send him back to her when his sentence was served. A story in the *Chronicle*, after Bart was released and had disappeared, goes so far as to say that his wife asked the prison authorities whether it might not be a good idea for her to come to San Francisco and take Bart back with her to Hannibal, Missouri, where she was living with a married daughter. If the story is true, they assured her, Bart concurring, this was not necessary, since to join his family was precisely what he planned to do.

Perhaps it was his intention. If so, he failed to carry

it out. He wrote letters that were unfailingly affectionate, letters in which he expressed the most unexceptionable sentiments in the high-flown language of the day, but letters which were invariably vague as to his plans. One of them, sent by Mrs. Boles to Mr. Hume and printed in the San Francisco papers, is interesting because, to the outsider reading between the lines, it shows so plainly that in spite of its author's expressions cf devotion he had not the slightest intention of coming home, at least not immediately.

"Oh, my constant loving Mary and my children," wrote Bart, "I did hope and had good reason for hoping to be able to come to you and end all this terrible uncertainty but it seems it will end only in my life. Although I am 'Free' and in fair health, I am most miserable. My dear family, I wish you would give me up forever and be happy, for I feel I shall be a burthen to you as I live no matter where I am. My loving family, I would willingly sacrifice my life to enjoy your loving company for a single week as I once was. I fear you will blame me for not coming but Heaven knows it is an utter impossibility. I love you but I fear you will not believe me & I know the world will scoff at the idea."

The sensible reader will not scoff. Bart was sincere enough. He held his wife and his family in the highest esteem. As a wife and family they were the best in the world, he was sure. They might blame him; Heaven knew they would be unhappy. They wanted him to come to them; he knew that. He was free, his time served, and his health reasonably good. But they'd better give him up, because he was not coming home. He could hardly have said it more plainly.

Mrs. Boles had snipped this bit from a longer epistle, her purpose being to show Mr. Hume that any suggestion that her husband did not love his family was a gross libel. Unfortunately, since it was so amputated from the body of the letter, there is no indication of where it was written or when. The chances are that Bart wrote it from San Francisco soon after he was set free. For something is known, though very little, of his movements for a short time after he left San Quentin Prison.

It was natural for the police to keep an eye on so noted a character as Bart, even after he had paid his debt to the State. They did not want him, but they did want to have some idea where he was and what he was doing. It is to the police that we are indebted for the knowledge that for two or three weeks Bart stayed inconspicuously in San Francisco, rooming at the Nevada House, shunning his old friends. Someone was looking for him, though, and perhaps found him.

On Monday, January 23, 1888, the *Examiner* printed the following paid notice in its "Personals" column: "Black Bart will hear something to his advantage by sending his address to M. R., Box 29, this office." The notice appeared only once.

Who was it that tried to get in touch with Bart? Was it—a guess, no more—the "mistress" to whom the *Call's* reporter had referred four years before? There is no evidence that Bart ever had such a mistress, but the question is still open. Could it have been someone who had an idea for exploiting Bart's notoriety? It might have been. One of Bart's letters to his wife, printed in a Hannibal newspaper in the year of his release, declares that "the manager of the Oakwood Theater and Dietz Opera House"

had approached him with "a chance to make some coin,"
but that he had refused. Wrote Bart, in startlingly modern-
sounding phraseology, "I cannot, of course, lend myself
to any dime-museum racket." Or perhaps had this modest
advertisement been inserted by a sister of Bart's? In this
same letter to his wife, Bart makes the only reference in
the entire case to this relative, but the possibility remains.
After telling Mrs. Boles how much he appreciated her
"wonderful constancy and affection" (as well he might),
he adds, "All other relations are as 'ropes of sand': Only
think of a once-loving sister, only a few miles away, and
never bestowed a line or likely a thought on her once-loved
brother simply because he was in trouble and in need of a
sister's sympathy." Bart, with his lively little mind, might
easily have invented a sister, or for that matter a whole
family Bibleful of relatives, but manifestly he would not
have tried to put over a non-existent sister on his wife
who would know the facts. Who was the sister, and where
did she live? Again there is no further record, though it
may have been she who had, after all, bestowed a thought
and as much as four lines of agate type on her brother
Charles. There is no need to pursue the speculation further.
Since it appeared only on that day, the "Personal" probably found its mark.

Why, however, didn't Bart join his wife? He might
have answered that question, but it is evident that he was
not telling. One can only be sure he never meant to do
so. "Oh, my dear," he writes in another letter, "how I do
hope you may retain your health until I can come to you.
. . . I hope you will not think or attribute my not coming home to any lack of desire on my part, or lack of
affection for any of you." But he made it very plain in-

deed that he was not coming. "I do regret," he writes, "not being able to come to you. The clouds look dark and gloomy and the real struggle of life is at hand, and I must meet it and fight it out." What dark clouds? What struggle? The reader had better try not to care. It is Charley Boles writing, and Charley Boles-Bolton-Bart was at heart always a romantic with a weakness for a rhetorical flourish. "Let come what will," he concludes this letter (the reader will remember the phrase from Bart's early PO8ry), "I must see my own loved Mary and our loving children once more. When that time comes—then, and not until then, can I expect the first ray of sunlight to enter my poor bleeding, desolate heart. . . . Direct as before to San Francisco. Good night. Charles." When would that ray of sunlight enter his desolate and bleeding heart? He was vague about it, mysterious, hopeful for some dim, unspecified future. One of these days, next month, next year, some time. But not now. Only a fond and loving wife could have failed to see that, whatever her husband was planning, it was not a trip to Hannibal, Missouri.

Then suddenly one day, Bart was not seen in San Francisco. Apparently he had headed southward, for he was reported in Modesto, Merced, Madera, and Visalia. There the trail ended. No more Wells, Fargo agents sent in reports on him. No peace officers wired Mr. Hume that he had passed their way. He was gone as completely as a stone cast into a pond. Yet, like the stone, his passing left a ripple that eventually reached the shore. Early in March, 1888, Mr. Hume got a heavy bundle, sent him via Wells, Fargo Express from a hotelkeeper in Visalia.

That wide-awake gentleman also sent along a note explaining that he thought Mr. Hume might be interested in a certain "Mr. M. Moore" who had registered with him on February 28, left a valise for which he said he would call, and had then vanished. What had made the hotel man suspect that Mr. Hume would care to see the valise was something he did not explain; he merely said here it was. Mr. Hume opened the bundle. In the valise he found two pairs of cuffs bearing the laundry mark, F.X.O.7, two neckties, small paper packages of crackers, sugar and pickles, a pound of coffee, a can each of corned beef and tongue, and (perhaps the most touching memento Bart left behind him in all his career) a glass of currant jelly. There is no good proof that anybody anywhere ever saw Black Bart again.

## 6

One of the most interesting things about Bart is the confusion he left behind him when he disappeared.

For the mere fact that he had vanished did not mean that he was forgotten, least of all by Wells, Fargo. On July 27, the stage from Bieber to Redding was held up by one man, and the treasure-box and mail robbed. On November 8, the stage from Downieville to Nevada City was stopped on Ditch Hill near Nigger Tent by one man who rifled three mail bags and obtained from the Wells, Fargo chest a small amount in coin and a gold bar valued at $2,200. The bar had the name "H. Scammon" stamped on the bottom and across each corner. Mr. Hume went up into the hills to investigate.

He came back quite sure, so he said, that both robberies were the work of Black Bart. In fact he was sufficiently convinced to issue a brand-new circular on which was printed a full description of Bart along with his picture. "We have reason to believe," said the circular, "that the robberies described above were committed by C. E. Boles, *alias* C. E. Bolton, *alias* Black Bart, the PO8." But Mr. Hume was not certain enough of his facts to suggest to his agents that if they saw the man they should apprehend him forthwith. Instead, he counseled caution. "We have not sufficient evidence," reads the circular, "to warrant a conviction or arrest, but are desirous of locating this man. Make careful inquiries, get your local officers interested. *Do not arrest*, but wire any information obtained at once to the undersigned." The circular was dated November 14, 1888.

Two weeks later the stage from Eureka to Ukiah was robbed by a lone bandit who got almost seven hundred dollars in coin and whatever there was of value in eleven mail sacks. Mr. Hume's agents had seen no one like Black Bart, nor had anyone else, but the newspapers began asking questions. "Is Black Bart on the Road Again?" they inquired in various sizes and styles of type. Bart was back on the front page.

In spite of the attempt to whip up the excitement, nothing much came of it. Interviewed by the reporters, Mr. Hume said yes, he was quite certain that these robberies had been committed by Bart. He recognized his style, though in neither case were there any verses to confirm his belief. As though to supply this lack, a newspaper up in the mines triumphantly produced a poem said to have been found at the scene of a minor holdup.

*"So here I've stood while wind and rain*
*Have set the trees a-sobbin'*
*And risked my life for that damned stage*
*That wasn't worth the robbin'."*
                    BLACK BART, THE PO8.

Is that verse genuine? It is plaintive in tone, pervaded by a characteristic gentle melancholy; so far, it does resemble the PO8's earlier work. Yet there is something specious about it. This business of "a-sobbin'" and "worth the robbin'" does not, after all, seem quite like Bart. When the PO8 wanted a rhyme he went out and got it, even if he had to twist his tenses and commit any sort of orthographic crime. "But on my corns too long you've tred"; the reader will remember that one. There is something a touch too literary about "a-sobbin'," let alone the reference to the wind and the rain. For the matter of that, the whole quatrain trips along too patly; it is too neat—not much too neat, but a little. Besides, Mr. Hume had his own reasons for doubting the poem's authenticity. Ignoring the literary niceties involved, he said simply that the handwriting was not Bart's. If the verse was a reporter-poetaster's hoax, it fell flat. Mr. Hume continued to supply his agents with copies of the new Bart circular, urging them to keep their eyes open and if possible bring the subject in for questioning.

It is interesting to note that in this persistence of Mr. Hume lies the best evidence to refute one of the liveliest of all the rumors that still cling round the case of Black Bart, the PO8.

Some time later—there is no way to tell just when— it began to be whispered that Wells, Fargo & Company had subsidized Bart. They were paying him a fine big

salary, so the story went (and still goes), not to rob their
stages any more. Every responsible individual connected
with the case denied the story, not once but many times.
Hume himself issued statement after statement branding
it as a lie. Yet, in the manner of such stories, this one
would not be downed. Today, most people who have
heard anything at all of Black Bart will finish their account of his career by saying, "Of course, Wells, Fargo &
Company had to pay him a salary for the rest of his life,
or none of their stages would have been safe!" There are
even those who assert that they once knew a Wells, Fargo
agent who told them the story was true. John Wilkes Booth
was not killed; Rudolf did not die at Mayerling; Czar
Alexander I was not in the coffin that was buried; Bart
was hired by Wells, Fargo—there is something about
such tales that has nothing to do with evidence. The will-
to-believe is a curious thing.

Yet at least one piece of fairly good evidence to the
contrary is this very circular. Why, if Wells, Fargo was
paying Bart a salary to be good, did Mr. Hume spend his
Company's money on printing an elaborate notice for
his agents, complete with Bart's picture? Where, for the
matter of that, was Bart? Unless he kept himself locked
within doors, who could tell at what moment a Wells,
Fargo man or local peace officer somewhere might spot
him and turn him in, as the circular instructed? Or if the
circular was merely a blind—that point has been made—
why was any blind necessary?

The fact is that the whole story of a Bart subsidy, flatly
denied by everyone who was in a position to know, has
no solid foundation whatever. It started no one knew

where. It grew as such tales do; it took root and has become
firmly fixed as part of the Black Bart legend. But it dies
harder than any of the hundreds of false statements that
have been made about Bart. There is nothing people hate
so much as having their fairy tales taken away from them.

The robbery of the Eureka-Ukiah stage, however, was
to have a far more spectacular result than the mild effort
of the newspaper editor to imitate Black Bart's poetry.
It put ideas into the head of the managing editor of the
San Francisco *Examiner*. That newspaper liked Mr. J. B.
Hume no better than it had five years earlier, and here
was a chance to discredit him and at the same time to produce a circulation feature that really had something. The
idea was to print an interview with the actual mystery
man, Black Bart himself.

Whether the editor or one of his staff cooked up the
scheme is not important. On December 2, 1888, it burst
upon the surprised citizens of San Francisco, who were
still not quite hardened to the shocks that this young sprig,
William Randolph Hearst, was beginning to hand them.
Two purported telegrams introduced the fantastic story:

―― November 30, 1888

*To Managing Editor, Examiner: San Francisco:* Have seen
the man of whom I spoke. Am under absolute obligation to
conceal whereabouts. Will send interview if you guarantee
strict compliance with conditions. As wires may leak, will forward under cover to ―― by Wells, Fargo.

MARTIN

No one explained who "Martin" was, nor anything else
about him. But immediately beneath this "telegram" was
the answer:

San Francisco, November 30, 1888

*To* ——: Guarantee given. Send story as soon as possible. Hire courier to catch train at —— if necessary. Don't spare expense to save time.

W. R. HEARST

Then followed the story:

The above telegrams passed between the editor of the *Examiner* and a special correspondent at a point which, for reasons that will appear, cannot be named. The correspondent had declared his belief that by going to a certain place he could get information about Black Bart, who, the detectives say, has been robbing Wells, Fargo & Co.'s stages with his customary diligence and skill in the northern part of the State. He was not at liberty to say upon what he founded that belief, and in response to a suggestion that he might find it somewhat embarrssing to interview a gentleman who carried a shotgun and would have particular objections to being found, he replied that he did not believe Bart had taken to the road again, and as he was not going in search of him in the role of a detective, he was ready to take all the chances.

The telegram at the head of this column was the next that was heard of the correspondent, and it indicates the result of his trip. Following is his detailed account of the affair.

The entire interview, if it was one, is too long to reprint here, but it simmers down to this:

The writer of the story went to the point where he had said he had reason to believe Bart might be, and found him. He handed Bart, he said, a batch of clippings in which were printed the remarks Mr. Hume had been reported as making to the press at various times since Bart's release. Bart, the interviewer wrote, declared that most of what Hume said was untrue. He was not robbing stages any more. He was not a "pusillanimous wretch." (There is no record that Hume ever said he was; this is merely a typical *Examiner* tactic against Hume.) Further, wrote the correspondent, Bart declared that he was not as black as he had been painted, that he had never gained any man's confidence to betray it, had never swindled anyone, never plundered working people but only Wells, Fargo & Company. (Here, of course, is the start of the legend that Bart was a Robin Hood, who stole from the rich and gave to the poor. Note again that no one had accused Bart of any of the things the reporter says he denied.)

The correspondent then said he asked Bart about his past. Bart, he wrote, said that Mr. Hume was in error there too. He had not "gone to Montana" and left his family, but had joined them in Iowa and tried farming until he saw that it only meant starvation, when he had decided to go West. He had sent money, though what he sent with his last letter had never arrived, as he subsequently learned. He had disappeared because he knew that if he was thought to be dead, his father would look out for his widow. His father had done this until his death, when he left Mrs. Boles well provided for. It was this money which had led her own brother to try to swindle her while Bart was in prison, and it was because of this vile deed that Bart had written the brother a severe letter which was returned to Warden Shirley, who gave it to Captain Aull and thus earned Bart a rebuke. (Mr. Hume's story was not widely different from this in the first place, and it is a point of no importance in any case.)

The correspondent, so the story continued, then asked Bart about his purported confession. Bart, he said, replied that he did admit one other robbery to Hume, but then told him that if he wanted to "clear his books" that was his affair, and that he, Bart, would tell him nothing more.

Hume, he went on, had been quite friendly and had suggested that Bart write an account of his exploits in which he would "crack up the detectives as the greatest that ever lived." Bart, the reporter said, told him that he had refused indignantly to do this, and that the detectives were not so friendly after that.

From this, the *Examiner* went on to accuse Hume indirectly and through the mouths of this unidentified "correspondent" and the purported Bart, of trying to steal Bart's diamonds while he was in prison. In this connection the reporter has Bart minimizing the part that Hume had played in his capture. Unfortunately, the *Examiner* quite forgot to check up on its story of five years earlier; perhaps it didn't bother to try, since editors know how little the public remembers. Wrote the correspondent, "Bart said it was just an accident that put the clue into the hands of Hume and his associates, and then they had to get Harry Morse to follow it up and catch Black Bart for them." But what about the *Examiner's* contention, in 1883, that Morse had had nothing to do with it, that Thorn and Thacker were the men who had done the job? Perhaps the *Examiner* wasn't angry at Morse any more.

Then comes a part of the "interview" which has been widely quoted as fact, even in accounts which ignore the rest of this story as pure fabrication. It is Bart's supposed story of how he came to go on the road, the tale of his walking about the country looking for work, finally for food, and encountering a farmer who brought him "some scraps in a tin dish." At this point, says the correspondent, "Bart quietly took the dish and put it down in front of the dogs, saying, 'This is the first time I ever asked anybody to give me anything, and it will be the last. Hereafter when I want anything, I shall demand it and take it!'" It's a good yarn, to be sure. In fact, it is just the kind of yarn that a smart newspaperman would be likely to think up.

In this "interview," too, is to be found the tale about the time that Bart deceived everyone by going to his room in a country inn, cutting an inch off the bottom of his candle to make it seem that it had burned a long time, slipping out, and robbing a stage and then getting back to the inn before daylight, with the candle to prove that he had stayed awake in his room far past the time when the stage had been held up. The trick is a very old one, to be sure; perhaps the special correspondent hadn't time to invent a better one.

With a bit more mud flung at Mr. Hume, the story closes. The *Examiner* had produced another "feature."

Next day the paper followed it up with a half-column headed "Mr. Hume Gets Angry." If the reporter who called at Wells, Fargo & Company's office quoted Hume correctly, he said, "The interview is a falsehood, made up of distorted and villainous lies, and the man who wrote it is a low, malignant, contemptible cur." He added that the "interview" was the boldest of inventions and the man who invented it was too cowardly to sign his name. After cooling down a trifle, however, he made one good point. In the story about the candle which Bart was supposed to have cut down as an alibi, the correspondent had said that Bart rode a horse to get ahead of the stage, and after the holdup had ridden the beast back again to the hotel. Mr. Hume wanted to know how it happened that this new and strange robbery, the place of which was not specified, and the details of which fitted no unsolved robbery on record, was the only one in the commission of which Bart had used a horse. He had the *Examiner* there. Not that it made any difference. The editor knew very well that in his kind of journalism when you're caught up you need only change the subject and the reader will forget. The paper did not attempt to answer Mr. Hume's pertinent question. It merely went on to say that his language had been "diversified and denunciatory." The account concluded with a paragraph that the *Examiner* apparently thought would put Hume in a bad light. As a matter of fact, it should have won the sympathy of every reader, as it does that of the student today:

"Before you go," said Mr. Hume to the reporter, "I want to say again that the anonymous scoundrel who directed that attack against me is a vile miscreant, a cowardly, contemptible cur. I say it again, and I live at 1466 Eighth Street, Oakland, and my office is Room 28, over Wells, Fargo & Company's, and I'm always in!"

For a week or so the San Francisco newspapers printed follow-up stories on Bart. The *Examiner* recorded that "The man who loaned his rifle to the stage-driver to shoot at Bart got a gun which nearly blew his head off the first time he fired it." The idea, of course, was to say something disagreeable about Wells, Fargo and Mr. Hume, wherefore that story did not mention the second rifle that the Company had sent Jimmy Rolleri with its apologies. There was a third one-man holdup, this time in Mendocino County to the north, and the *Examiner* declared flatly that it was "Black Bart Again," though the *Call*, the *Alta*, and the *Chronicle* were sensibly content merely to raise the question. But the seven-day wonder petered out as the biggest newspaper sensation will. In this case, the *Chron-*

*icle* helped kill it by springing an interview—an actual one—with General John McComb, new warden at San Quentin Prison. McComb, perhaps, should not have spilled Mr. Hume's beans for him, but what he said made it plain that the *Examiner* had been barking up the wrong tree. To the *Chronicle* reporter McComb explained that Mr. Hume had recently come over to the prison to get some information about an ex-convict named Wright whom he believed to be responsible for the Mendocino robbery. While he was getting his facts, he had told McComb that now he was positive Black Bart had left California. He didn't say how he knew, only that he knew. It is worth noting here that if the *Examiner's* "special correspondent" had really interviewed Bart, naturally he knew where he was. If he knew where Bart was, he could have enabled his paper to discredit Hume and the *Chronicle* both at one time—an opportunity his editor would have jumped at. But it is not necessary to labor the point. Today's student of the case can conclude only that the "interview" was faked from beginning to end for the double purpose of creating a "feature" and taking out the old grudge against Hume.

There was never any more excitement about Black Bart. Now and then a lone bandit would rob a stage somewhere, and some reporter with a good memory would recall the exploits of the PO8 and speculate upon the possibility that Bart had returned to the road. He was said to have gone to Australia, to China, to various points unspecified in "the East." Once there was a rumor that he had been seen in Indian Territory during the land rush in the spring of 1889. On another occasion the sheriff of

Cripple Creek, Colorado, telegraphed Mr. Hume that a man answering Black Bart's description had been seen in his town. Hume replied that he did not want him; that there was nothing against Bart in California. By 1892 Mrs. Boles was appearing in the directory of Hannibal, Missouri, as "Widow of Charles E. Boles." Did she know that her husband had died? Or had she merely taken account of the conventionalities of the proper nineties and decided that a lone lady had a more regular status as a widow than as a woman whose husband was just away, no one knew where? It is impossible to tell now.

One of the most fantastic stories on record is a Sunday-supplement spread in the San Francisco *Chronicle* as late as 1909. It purports to be the true story of the adventures of one Francis Reno, described as "the noted detective," who relates that he had seen Black Bart in Mexico City only a few years earlier. He went under the name of "Jim Clarkson," Reno is reported as saying, and always worked with three associates. Reno described him as tall and rangy, of dark complexion and fierce-looking. He added that "Black Bart" had told him his first big venture was the holdup of "a stage running between Angels Camp and Milton," in California in 1886. Since in 1886 Bart was safely under Warden Shirley's care in San Quentin and had been there for two and a half years, it is hardly worth while to underline the other charming discrepancies in the yarn.

Another curious tale developed in Kansas, as late as 1897. In September of that year the police of the town of Olathe arrested a man known to them as "James Croombs," or "James Gordon," for the crime of stealing four hundred dollars' worth of general merchandise from the store of a certain Mr. M. S. Detar at Edgerton, Kansas. They took him down to the Chief of Police, who remembered his face. Ten years before, he had been arrested in Olathe for a robbery committed in California, and had been sent West to serve his sentence in that State.

It may have been the mention of California that put the idea into Croombs-Gordon's head. Whatever it was, he admitted that he had indeed been the robber the California authorities had taken back to the Coast a decade earlier. While he was at it, he admitted more. He was actually Black Bart, he said; certainly, the officers had heard of him, hadn't they? They had. It may have been their respect for Black Bart's name that led them to tell the judge who his prisoner was. At any rate the judge lectured his man severely before imposing a five-year sentence on him, and the newspapers reported lecture, sentence, and the presence in Kansas of the noted stage-robber and bandit. It was this report that brought Wells, Fargo operative, John Thacker, to Kansas to investigate.

Thacker needed no more than one look at the prisoner to explode his story. He was as much like the true Black Bart, said Thacker, "as a bird's nest is like a mile post." Moreover, Thacker knew who he was as well as who he wasn't. He was a small-time criminal named H. L. Gorton, who had served seven years of a ten-year sentence at Folsom, been released, and returned to Kansas. Thacker noted also that Wells, Fargo had kept an eye on his activities for a while, but that it hadn't been worth their time. After all, there were grades in crime, and there were some things in which Wells, Fargo simply weren't interested. Gorton had sunk too low for them; that was it. Wrote Thacker,

"He became a cheap-skate burglar and chicken-thief, and we dropped him."

However, it is for the last paragraph of his report that Thacker's trip to Kansas is interesting. For he went on to discuss the genuine Bart. He wrote:

"As for the original Black Bart, he is out of the country. He served his time, and it became my duty to look after him for a few weeks after he got out of San Quentin Prison. He went to Utah and then up to Montana and then to Hailey, Idaho. I think he had some business to settle there. Anyhow, he was as straight as a string. Finally he made a bee-line for Vancouver, and boarded the steamer, *Empress of China*, for Japan. He is in that country now."

Did Wells, Fargo,'s Detective Thacker know these things to be facts, or was he merely repeating some of the legends that had already begun to grow up about Black Bart? If Thacker had actually been detailed to "look after" Bart, and if he had done his job, why didn't he know that Bart had gone to Visalia and had left there the suitcase which the Visalia hotelkeeper had forwarded to Mr. Hume? The student may speculate; it is not possible to do more.

Nor is it to the point to record here the many other tales that have been told of Bart's latter years. It is still possible to find men who will swear that they have talked with people who saw Bart in Alaska during the Yukon days, in Los Angeles before World War I, in Panama, in Denver, in a dozen other places. None of these willing believers has any proof; they just choose to think it's so. Finally, there is an unsupported story that "A New York newspaper carried the account of the death of Charles

E. Boles in 1917." If it did, and if it was true, Bart was 87 when he died.

There is at least one grandchild living who has a sound point to make about her Grandfather Boles. She denies strenuously that he robbed the mails, though the Government regularly posted rewards and the Wells, Fargo circulars all took pains to describe the T-shaped slit Bart customarily cut in the sacks. She says further, "His quarrel was with Wells, Fargo & Company alone and it was their money he took and felt justified in taking," whatever that may be understood to mean. She says also that he "never carried a real gun," though it is hardly likely that twenty-eight stage-drivers and three police officers (Morse, Thorn, and Stone were all with Bart when he pointed out where he had hidden his gun after the Sonora-Milton stage-robbery) could have been deceived by a make-believe. True, Bart's gun may never have been loaded; there is no record that he ever fired a shot from it.

But when this grandchild writes: "To us he does not seem the ruthless robber he is made out to be in the various stories we see published about him," she is thoroughly justified. It is quite true that Bart was no ruthless robber. In spite of the Beadle Dime Library's tasty little item, written by W. H. Manning and bearing the sensational title of *The Gold Dragon, Or the California Bloodhound: A Story of PO8, the Lone Highwayman*, Bart was neither dragon nor hound. Quiet, polite, dapper in his dress, a waggish, mannerly, proper little man, he demonstrated to the Californians of his day that stage-robbing could be made a gentlemanly business, and that a man who knew the hills and was hardy enough to tackle the job could set at naught the forces of the law by sheer ability to get from place to place faster than anyone would believe it could be done. He served his time, a model prisoner, attended to his own affairs, and walked out of the world leaving behind him a satchelful of marked cuffs, old neckties, crackers, pickles, coffee, tinned meats, and a jar of currant jelly.

Yet a man like Black Bart never dies. He is the stuff of which folklore is made. Black Bart, the PO8! He immortalized himself in that horrid pun no less than in the rhymes he wrote to justify the title. Indeed, it is with one more poem, implausibly attributed to Bart by some anonymous joker that we may best bid him good-bye:

> *"I rob the rich to feed the poor,*
> *Which hardly is a sin;*
> *A widow ne'er knocked at my door*
> *But what I let her in.*
>
> *"So blame me not for what I've done,*
> *I don't deserve your curses,*
> *And if for any cause I'm hung,*
> *Let it be for my verses!"*

**O**NE WONDERS WHERE AND how Dick Fellows, perhaps the most unsuccessful bandit that ever roamed California's highways, acquired his passion for horses.

Horses played Dick false at every turn. It was because of a horse that he broke his leg at a crucial moment in his career, thus losing forever the opportunity to go down in history as one of California's really big-time road-agents. If it had not been for a horse, he might once have been nearly a quarter of a million dollars richer. Nobody ever gave Dick a horse he could ride, nor was he able to steal one. Very likely the horse that Dick could ride was never foaled; horses appeared to know him, and to realize the moment they saw him that here was one of those humans they could handle. Horses threw him, ran away with him and from him, led him into trouble and never out of it. Yet this curious bandit-on-horseback never seemed to learn. No matter what horses did to him, he came back for more. In the end it was through a horse that he was finally captured and given the long prison sentence that wound up his brave attempts to lead a life of crime.

It may have been a kind of pride in the man. Stocky and strong, with a luxuriant curly black beard, Dick Fellows may have felt that so fine a figure of a robber should not demean himself by traveling on foot. Perhaps it was sheer obstinacy. Once he made up his mind to anything, Dick never seemed to consider such small matters as whether or not he possessed the talents for accomplishing it. On several occasions in his career he advertised himself as "G. Brett Lytle, Professor of Languages," though there is no evidence that he owned to more than a smattering of Spanish. There is no evidence, either, that he got any pupils, though this did not seem to discourage him at all. Or it may have been that his fixation on horseflesh was a consequence of too romantic a temperament. In the literature of banditry, from the old plays and novels down to the latest penny-dreadfuls, a highwayman always had a horse; the beast was part of the picture, as essential an item as the pistol, blunderbuss, or shotgun with which the robber intimidated his victim. And Dick may simply have felt that in order to play his part properly, once he made up his mind to take to the road in earnest, he must use all the trappings of his trade.

At any rate, whatever the reason, this Captain Jinks of California emerges from the ranks of the small fry of his time almost solely because of his persistent error in believing he could ride. Horses were his ruin, but it is because of the part horses played in his curious history that his memory remains green. At least horses did that much for him.

One day some careful snapper-up of unconsidered trifles may discover in the old files of Los Angeles or Santa Barbara newspapers some details concerning Richard

Perkins, *alias* George Brett Lytle, *alias* Dick Fellows, earlier than the story of the crime that brought him for the first time into the northern part of California.

So far, it has been learned only that during the localized crime wave of late 1869, Dick had robbed a lone rider near Los Angeles, had then attempted unsuccessfully to hold up the Coast Line stage on the outskirts of Santa Barbara, and had promptly been caught, convicted of robbery and assault with intent to murder, and sent to San Quentin Prison on the 31st of January, 1870. How long Dick had been breaking the law, whether or not he had a jail record, why he took to violence in a time when it was relatively easy for a young and strong man to make his way by legitimate means—these details are shrouded in mystery. We know only the charge against him, and that he was entered on the Prison register as a native of Kentucky, twenty-four years of age. There is a legend that he was a graduate of Harvard, but no evidence has ever been offered in support of the story. Mr. J. B. Hume of the Wells, Fargo detective service, who knew him as well as anyone, says nothing about this in his long and circumstantial account of Dick's life. However, there is ground for belief that he had at least some education. Almost as soon as he got to San Quentin he was given a job in the library and became known for his long and wordy lectures to the convicts, who listened to him when they had nothing better to do.

His prison activities did not stop there. His next move was to organize a Sunday-school Bible class among the men. From his point of vantage as leader of this class he conducted the lesson each week with what an observer of the time described as "a vigor and eloquence that struck terror to the souls of the minions of Satan." The same reporter notes that "it was not long before Fellows was looked upon as the proper leader of the entire religious element of the prison." In fact his sanctity was so pronounced that even the frankly ungodly among prisoners and guards refrained from swearing in his presence. Before long, Dick Fellows was pointed out to visitors as one who had seen the error of his ways and come up out of great tribulation, an example of what a man can do when he makes up his mind to it. It was a matter of only two or three years until the Prison officials, convinced that Dick's change of heart was genuine, were suggesting that he be released. Some of them, apparently, carried weight at Sacramento. For on April 4, 1874, with less than half his sentence served, Dick found that Governor Newton Booth had granted him an unconditional pardon and restored him to citizenship. He shook hands with everyone, conducted an impromptu prayer-service over those convicts whose hearts were still so hardened that they had the temerity to hint at his possible lack of good faith, and walked out of San Quentin a free man. His reformation may or may not have been sincere. At least for a year and a half he kept out of the way of the law.

In 1875 the Southern Pacific Railway was busy digging and blasting its right of way through the rugged Tehachapi Mountains that divide the broad, hot valleys of northern California from the fertile orange groves of the south. Trains chuffed down from San Francisco as far as the little town of Caliente, at the foot of the range. Thence passengers and goods were transferred to stages for the twenty-three-hour ride over the hills to Los Angeles.

Like all rail-head towns, particularly during construction, Caliente was tough. Police, sheriffs of the various counties, even Wells, Fargo detectives had a habit of taking a look at Caliente now and then, just to see if any of the unsavory characters on their books had come temporarily to anchor there. Mr. Hume of Wells, Fargo may or may not have been surprised when it was reported to him by one of his agents that Dick Fellows had been seen in town. Hume had been long enough at his business to be skeptical of reformations. The chances are he merely made a notation that the psalm-singer of San Quentin had turned up once more. Perhaps he issued instructions to his men in Caliente that they would do well to keep an eye on Dick. Because, as Hume knew, there was something big in the wind that November. Wells, Fargo was getting ready to send an unusually heavy shipment of gold by train to the end of the line, and then by stage over the rough trail through the Tehachapis to Los Angeles. That city, shocked by the suspension of the private bank of Temple & Workman, had been informed that cessation of specie payments was only temporary. On December 6, the citizens were promised, cash would again be available at the bank's windows. It was this cash that Wells, Fargo was planning to send over the dangerous road from Caliente south, a matter of some $240,000 in good gold coin.

On the morning of December 3, Hume was already in Caliente waiting for word from his superiors in the home office. That afternoon the message came. A wire from Mr. S. D. Brastow, Division Superintendent for Wells, Fargo, ordered him to meet the train on the morning of the 4th. Stages left regularly at eight o'clock in the morning, and the train got in approximately at seven. There would be ample time for the transfer, and Hume was ready to see that nothing could happen to the gold. Nothing did. The train arrived punctually. With the shipment of gold were Mr. Brastow himself, and Jerome Meyers, Chief of Police of Stockton, who were making the trip straight through to Los Angeles. The three express boxes containing the treasure were carried to the stage and placed inside it, Mr. Brastow and Chief Meyers taking seats between the boxes and the other passengers. Mr. Hume, who had been told he was to accompany the shipment also, sat outside, on the box with the driver. All three of the officers wore pistols, though they did not display them, and Hume had beside him a case containing two double-barreled shotguns and two Winchester rifles. As far as he knew, no one in Caliente could have heard about the shipment, but it did not pay to take chances. Moreover, in the crowd that had gathered at the depot to meet the train, he had seen a man he recognized. He was quite certain that it was Dick Fellows. And when the transfer of the express boxes was taking place, Mr. Hume noticed that Dick and an ugly-looking companion had moved over toward the stage to watch what was going on. It might have been mere idle curiosity, to be sure. But again it might not. As the stage rolled out of town to begin the slow climb, eighteen miles to the summit, Mr. Hume opened up his little arsenal, laying one of the shotguns carefully across his knees, and the other close beside him. The rifles he left in the case within easy reach. Probably no one would think of trying to stop the stage, but if anyone did, Mr. Hume would be ready for him.

Back in Caliente, Dick Fellows and his friend talked things over. They had heard no rumors of any shipment of gold, nor had anyone else. But it was not difficult to guess that three express boxes, each heavy enough so that two men struggled under its weight, did not contain waste paper. They knew nothing of Mr. Brastow and Chief Meyers; as far as they were concerned, the men were two passengers. But Dick, at least, knew Hume. And the combination of three weighty express boxes inside a stage and Mr. Hume on top of it was something to make the most stupid ex-convict think twice. Dick thought to sufficiently good account so that he felt his ideas worth communicating to his friend. Together they hatched a plan, and the first of Dick's horses made its entrance into his career.

Whether this was Dick's initial departure from righteousness since he had left San Quentin is an open question. At any rate, he seems to have made a careful distinction between the various grades of theft. Neither he nor his companion had any idea what was in the express boxes, but it was quite certainly treasure, and in quantity. Dick was ready to commit the crime of highway robbery to get his hands on some of it. Yet he was not prepared to preface this major offense by a lesser one. His ugly companion had a horse. Very well; Dick would get one too. But he would not come down to horse-stealing, at least not too obviously. He would rent a horse; that was the way to do it. He knew of a livery stable close by, and he would pick out a likely animal, hire it for the morning, and meet his companion at a spot agreed upon: a bend in the road about a mile out of town. From there the two would ride across country, cutting ahead of the stage to intercept it in the hills. After they had robbed the stage— well, that was different. Naturally, Dick felt, he could hardly be expected to return the hired horse when it was plain that he needed the beast to make his escape. It was a fine point, perhaps, but it must have satisfied Dick. Arrangements were made that way, his fellow-highwayman-to-be rode out along the stage road, and Dick turned his steps toward the livery stable, an innocent citizen bent on recreation and exercise.

There is unfortunately no record of the kind of horse the livery-stable keeper rented Dick. Later events made it clear that it need not have been a "bronco or mustang," as one newspaper reported. The mildest, most gentle cob could have been Dick's undoing. Indeed, the chances are that this beast was tame enough, for Dick rode him out of town without undue trouble. But gradually the animal, whatever its temper, must have come to know that the man on its back did not understand horses. Long before they were within sight of the rendezvous, it decided that it had had enough. Half an hour later, the owner of the stable was surprised to see his horse trot into the corral, its saddle empty. As for Dick, he had been unfortunate enough to light on his head in the road. It was some time before he regained consciousness and sadly made his way back to town. He had enough money to pay the stableman; that was not what bothered him. What hurt was that he had failed to make good his promise. His companion would not dare to attack the stage alone. For that matter, he might not venture to come back to town, at least for some time. He would naturally suppose that Dick had been arrested, that somehow the law had got wind of their scheme, and he would be sure to keep out of sight. Dick was sensitive; he did not like to think of the ridicule that would descend upon him when the truth came out. And he would have to tell the story or else be thought a coward whose nerve had failed at the last moment. It was not a pleasant prospect. Dick's head hurt, too, as he spent the afternoon brooding on his ill luck.

Then he had an idea. The northbound stage was due in from Los Angeles between eight and nine o'clock that evening. He had no notion what might be in the Wells, Fargo box, but certainly there would be something. No one could call him a coward if he held up that stage alone. As the thought occurred to him he noticed a saddle-horse hitched in front of Sisson & Wallace's store. Perhaps he was still a little dizzy from the accident earlier in the day; maybe he simply felt that his trouble that morning had come from his ignorant selection of a particularly spirited mount. Other men swung carelessly into the saddle and just rode away. Why couldn't he? Acting on the thought, he unhitched the animal and started up the road. He would redeem himself or know the reason why.

This time things went better, at least at first. Dick had timed himself well. About a mile and a half out of town he saw the stage coming, drew his pistol, and posted himself by the side of the road. When he urged the horse forward, presented his weapon, and commanded Dugan, the driver, to stop, he was obeyed. When he ordered Dugan harshly to throw out the box, Dugan threw it out. It was all very gratifying. Dick flourished his pistol in the direction of Caliente and suggested that the stage be on its way. The driver lowered his hands, picked up the reins, cracked his whip and rattled down the road in a cloud of dust. It was all over so soon that it seemed like nothing. That was the way to conduct the business. Dick must have wished that his companion had been there to see how well he handled it. He dismounted to see what the treasure-box held.

For a few minutes luck had been with Dick. Now it left him again. In his impulsive dash out of town on a stolen horse, he had forgotten that a Wells, Fargo box took a bit of opening. Neither a pistol nor a clasp-knife was of much help; the proper bandit—Dick had read about it often in the papers—always equipped himself with at least an old axe to do that part of the job. Moreover, even if he had been able to crack the chest, he had brought along no sack for the booty. He must not stand here thinking about it, either. The stage would be in town any minute now, and officers would be riding out to find the man who had held it up. The thing to do was to take the box along and break it open somewhere off the road, up some hidden canyon in the hills. Perhaps he could balance it in front of the saddle somehow. He picked it up awkwardly and turned toward the horse.

It is not to be supposed that Dick's borrowed mount had any especial grudge against Wells, Fargo or its boxes. That would be taking too much for granted. But the most mild-mannered horse could hardly observe with equanimity the heavy square-cornered object that its rider was carrying in the direction of its back. When that strange, bulky object was in the hands of a stranger who had already demonstrated that his style of riding was, to say the least, not what a decent animal was accustomed to, even a quiet and tractable horse might become alarmed. Dick's stolen steed was sufficiently upset to turn and head for home on a dead run. Once more Dick was left afoot, this time with the worst kind of incriminating evidence in his possession.

Something had to be done about it, and quickly.

A short distance from the road the contractors for the Southern Pacific had begun a long series of tunnels and new grading to carry the railway through the mountains. Dick shouldered the chest and started off in the darkness toward what should be the workings. Until daylight he could hide in the confusion of earth and rock, perhaps find a tunnel into which he could crawl far enough to be out of sight. He was meditating upon his best move next morning when he walked straight off an eighteen-foot drop into the approach to Tunnel Five. His left leg was broken above the ankle, and the instep of the same foot was crushed by the falling box.

That would have been the end for most men. But Dick was of proper stuff, even if he could not get it through his head that he did not understand horses. After he had re-covered a bit from the shock, he made certain that the rest of his limbs were in order, rolled over on to his hands and knees and began to push the chest ahead of him. The important thing was to get out of sight somewhere before daylight came and he was found there by the workmen. It took several painful hours, but by the time the lights began to twinkle on in the tents of the Chinese laborers scattered up the hill, Dick had made his way to the thicket of brush that bordered Tehachapi Creek. As he crawled, he had passed close enough to one tent to snatch an axe, and with this he broke open the box. There was no big treasure inside it; merely some eighteen hundred dollars, though that was better than nothing. Dick scratched up the earth with his axe, buried the broken chest as well as he could, covered the place with leaves and twigs, and crawled into another part of the brush, where he spent the day. In the evening he cut a pair of willow-forks for crutches, took a few dollars, and hopped over to a Chinese tent, where he bought some food. So far, by great good fortune, no

one had found his hiding place. But sooner or later someone would stumble on it. He must get farther away, out
of that part of the country entirely. Fortified by the food,
he turned down the creek toward a farm he had seen about
a mile away, owned by a Mr. Fountain. His leg and foot
were paining him greatly, but anything was better than
going back to San Quentin. The reader will find it hard
to credit what was in Dick's mind, but the stubborn fact
remains to testify to his purpose. What Dick wanted on
Mr. Fountain's farm was no more and no less than a horse.

Mr. Hume had been pleased to reach Los Angeles safely
with the quarter of a million dollars for the relief of the
suspended bank and its depositors. But he had little time
for self-congratulation. Waiting for him was a telegram
with the bad news that the up-stage had been robbed
scarcely twelve hours after he and his precious freight had
passed. Chasing robbers was his job, and he took the next
stage north. With him went Meyers, who had to go back
to Stockton anyway, and who didn't mind helping Wells,
Fargo's man run a bandit down. After all, there was always the reward, and even a Chief of Police is human
enough to take account of an extra dollar or two legiti-
mately earned.

In Caliente, Hume and Meyers rented horses at the
livery stable and proceeded to the scene of the robbery,
where they cast about to find some clue. Dugan, the stage-
driver, had no idea who the robber might be, nor had he
been able to describe him very clearly. He was a man on a
horse and he had a pistol. More than that he couldn't say.
Hume and Meyers went on searching; as police officers
they both knew that clues were the result of careful, plod-

ding work. Something might turn up. They would comb
the ground on both sides of the highway and see what
came of it.

It was on one of their slow circlings that they encountered Mr. Fountain's son, Tommy. The boy was
doing a little circling of his own, his eyes fixed on the
ground, his head swinging anxiously from left to right and
back again as he rode.

Mr. Hume asked him what he had lost. Perhaps, he
suggested, the boy was also trying to pick up the robber's
trail in the hope of some of the reward. No, Tommy said,
that wasn't it. The night before someone had stolen a horse
from his father's barn, and he was trying to find it. Luckily
the thief had chosen, out of three horses in the stable, the
one that could most easily be traced. Mr. Hume wanted
to know how that was, and Tommy explained. Only a few
days earlier the missing animal had cast a shoe, and his
father had tacked on a mule-shoe to protect the hoof until
he could take him to the blacksmith. On this soft ground
it would be easy enough to follow a trail marked by three
horseshoes and one mule-shoe. The officers agreed that this
would be simple. All a man needed to do would be to
cross the trail once. They told Tommy that if they found
any such tracks they would send word to him. As an afterthought, Hume told the boy to let them know, too, in case
he came across the trail. There was no reason to connect
a stage-robber and a stolen horse, especially since the driver
had reported the bandit as a mounted man. Still, you
never knew. A horse-thief might be a robber too, and
Hume didn't mind picking up some minor criminal while
he was at it.

As it turned out, it was just this persistent interest in

his job that led Hume to the very man he was looking for. For young Tommy Fountain was a conscientious boy, and he kept at it until he was rewarded by striking the unmistakable track of a horse with one mule-shoe. He sent word to Mr. Hume and then rode into Bakersfield and got hold of the sheriff, who went out with him to track the thief down. By the time Hume and Meyers got to Bakersfield, Tommy and the sheriff had returned, with them a bearded figure supported on rough crutches, dragging a foot and leg so badly swollen that the jail doctor had trouble cutting the boot away. Hume recognized him immediately as Dick Fellows. He admitted stealing the horse but stoutly denied that he had any connection whatever with the robbery of the Los Angeles stage. Why, then, asked Mr. Hume, had the sheriff found on him the sum of $1,294? A man with that much money didn't need to steal horses. Dick stubbornly shook his head. His money was no concern of theirs. He had nothing to do with any stage-robbery. He would say no more.

Next morning, Hume and Meyers moved in with Dick and talked to him. If the sheriff had found only $1,294, there must be another five hundred dollars hidden somewhere. What had Dick done with that? Dick had done nothing with it, he said. How could he have hidden money that he had never seen? If this money about which Mr. Hume was talking so much had come from the Los Angeles stage, it was nothing that he, Dick, had anything to do with. He stuck to his story and after a while Hume and Meyers gave up their grilling. As Hume left the room, however, Dick made one significant remark. "Mr. Hume," he said, "things are not going just right for me. If I should send for you, will you come back from San Francisco?" Mr. Hume did not let the prisoner see that he was pleased with this turn of affairs. He replied merely that if Dick meant business he would be glad to come back and talk to him at any time. Dick was left to think that over while Hume caught the eleven o'clock evening train north.

Something had certainly gone very wrong, and Dick was pretty sure he knew what it was. After one day of thinking it over, he wrote Hume a note. The Wells, Fargo officer was waiting for it; he had smelled a rat too. The next train brought him back to Bakersfield. What, he wanted to know, did Dick have to say? This time Dick came out frankly with his story. Yes, he had robbed the stage. He had broken his leg trying to escape after his horse had left him, and he had made his way to Mr. Fountain's farm and stolen another horse, the one on which he was found. Those were the facts, and he was sure Mr. Hume had guessed most of them already.

But this was not what was on his mind. What had made him angry was something else. On the way back to town with the Bakersfield sheriff, Dick had made a bargain. The understanding was that the sheriff was to aid Dick to escape, in return for which he was to keep a share of the Wells, Fargo money. Instead, he had turned in some of the cash to Mr. Hume, kept out five hundred dollars for himself, and then refused to let Dick escape after all. This kind of treatment was more than Dick could stand. What he wanted now was revenge on the sheriff who had double-crossed him.

Mr. Hume was glad to oblige. The sheriff was called in and charged, in Dick's presence. He tried denials at first, but Mr. Hume persisted and at length the officer said that perhaps the money might have dropped from his pocket while he was bringing Dick in. He would go out and look over the ground, he said. He came in later with two hundred dollars which he said he had discovered on the trail, but he could not account for the rest. Mr. Hume saw to it that he was dismissed from the office of sheriff; Dick had that much satisfaction.

As for himself, he was indicted for highway robbery and put to bed until his leg could heal. Six months later he was found guilty, made a touching plea for mercy which did not sensibly affect the court, and was sentenced to eight years in State's Prison. It appeared that Dick, with his hymns and his horses, had at last come up against a stone wall.

Yet even this second phase of his criminal career was not quite over. Bakersfield had only recently been made the seat of Kern County, and until the new jail was built prisoners were housed in a plank building. After being sentenced, Dick was alone in this improvised prison, waiting to be transported to San Quentin. There was a guard on duty; Jailer Reed watched outside the building all night. But in the morning when he opened the door to take Dick his breakfast, he found the room empty. In one corner of the floor was a gaping hole through which Dick had fled, taking with him the fine new pair of crutches with which the county had supplied him.

It is not the fact of his recapture within four days that will startle the reader, but Dick's own story of what he had done while he was at large. For once again he had obstinately turned to his oldest and weakest trick to save himself. After two days and nights spent hiding in the swamps of Kern River, Dick had made his way to a ranch and once more stolen a horse. This time the animal was not saddled, and Dick had led it to another farmhouse, where he had hitched it to a post in the small corral while he went into the barn to find a saddle. He must have been a strange-looking figure as he came out of the barn, crutches under his arms, the ungainly saddle flopping in front of him—so strange, indeed, that the horse reared in a panic, broke the head-rope with which Dick had tied him and galloped for home.

Dick must have known then that he was done for. But he had spunk enough to take back the saddle and hide in the barn until the farmer hitched up and went to town. Then he made himself as neat as possible, put on his best manner, knocked at the farmhouse door, and turned the full force of his charm on the woman of the house. He was a traveler, he said, who had lost his way. Could the lady please direct him to Bakersfield? She could and did. Better, she suggested that he come in and have a bite to eat. Dick was only too glad. He ate heartily, made polite conversation, thanked his hostess, and went on his way. Unfortunately for him, the husband came back that noon full of the story he had heard in town, a fantastic tale of a stage-robber who had escaped from the jail, actually on crutches. His wife confessed sadly that she had given that very robber breakfast. This time they both rode into Bakersfield. By noon two posses were out and Dick was back in jail before evening. Two jailers watched him that night; next day the new sheriff took him north. On June 16 the gates of San Quentin Prison shut behind Dick Fellows for the second time.

2

The Bible-class trick might work once, but there was no use trying it again.

Dick contented himself with watching his behavior, breaking no rules, working hard at all the tasks set him. It was not long before they gave him back his old job in the prison library. There he had time to indulge his taste for reading and for writing letters. One specimen of his correspondence has been preserved, a long epistle in which he apologized to Mr. Hume of Wells, Fargo for taking so much of his time, deplored the folly of his escape from Bakersfield jail since it had accomplished nothing excepting to waste the county's money, and expressed his opinion of the crooked sheriff who had taken his bribe and then turned him over to the law.

He spoke his mind, too, about those who had finally captured him; a crowd of nincompoops he called them. "They even had the bad taste," he wrote, "to divert from their legitimate calling a group of sheepherders in order to add to the distress of an unfortunate fellow-being who was only endeavoring to flee the country. As they crowded around, each discussing his relative importance in effecting my capture, I could not help thinking (save the profane comparison) that unless shepherds had woefully degenerated since Oriental times, the infant Jesus himself would have met short shrift at their hands, if Herod had had the foresight to offer a suitable reward!"

Also he was anxious to reassure Hume regarding his activities when he should have served his sentence. "I do not think," he wrote, "that your Company should be too

hard on me. I have never directed against them particularly any matured scheme for plunder, or in fact against
anyone, and indeed I have had no definite idea in regard
to the matter, unless it was that I should try to live honestly within the pale of society, and if at any time compelled to trespass to supply my immediate wants, I would
aim at affluent corporations and never molest poor persons or private individuals. I do not say this complain-
ingly, but merely for the sake of a better understanding,
and think my whole record will attest to the truth of it."

It is hard to say whether Dick thought this disingenuous plea would move Mr. Hume to do something toward
getting him out of prison, or whether he was just talking
for the sake of making conversation. Nevertheless it is
interesting to note the old, familiar rationalization. Dick
would never rob the poor; not a bit of it. Good old Robin-
Hood-Perkins-Lytle-Fellows was just after the "affluent
corporations." If only Mr. Hume would realize this, perhaps it would lead to a "better understanding." How
Hume was expected to improve his understanding when
he already knew quite well that Dick robbed big corporations, Wells, Fargo included, is something that Dick himself could hardly have explained.

In any event, it was with such letter-writing and his
routine prison tasks that Dick occupied himself for the
five years he spent in San Quentin. There being no black
marks against him in prison, his term was up in May,
1881. Again Dick left State's Prison, presumably to "try
to live honestly within the pale of society," as he had
assured Mr. Hume he intended to do.

His endeavor lasted exactly two months, during which
he got a job as a solicitor on the *Daily Echo* in Santa

Cruz, taking part of his pay in advertising in which he announced that he was a teacher of Spanish and would be glad to have pupils. No one in Santa Cruz wanted to learn any more Spanish than he already knew, and Dick gave it up. On July 19 he held up the stage from San Luis Obispo to Soledad. He got only ten dollars for his pains, but he was back in the business.

All that summer and autumn stages were robbed with alarming frequency. Dick ranged far and wide, once traveling north all the way to the Russian River to stop a stage near Duncan's Mills at almost the precise spot where Black Bart had held it up four years earlier. He never bothered to go that far afield again, for in the box when he broke it open there was no money, no gold dust, no treasure of any sort, only one document which proved on examination to be a letter written in Chinese.

But his depredations between San Luis Obispo and the Santa Clara Valley became more and more bold. Stages were held up sometimes no more than a week apart. No one was quite sure who the robber was, but Mr. Hume was beginning to think it might be Dick, and sent one of his special officers, Captain Charles Aull, who was later an official at San Quentin, to see if he could not bring the daring highwayman to justice. Something had to be done if Wells, Fargo & Company were to continue doing business with the confidence of the public.

Captain Aull believed with Mr. Hume that the way to catch a criminal was by slow and patient staff-work. First he drew a map of the towns and villages in the valley north of Soledad. Then, armed with descriptive circulars, he proceeded to cover them all, one after another, interesting local officers and as many citizens as possible, leaving copies of his leaflet wherever he went. Sooner or later he would cross Dick's trail, he felt sure. In the meantime he was making it impossible for the bandit to hide in any of the towns through which he passed.

The first place in which Captain Aull found any hint of Dick was in Santa Cruz, to which he had returned, and where he had again attempted to find some pupils in Spanish. This was the occasion on which he christened himself "G. Brett Lytle," and perhaps this did indicate an honest desire to lead a respectable life. Nevertheless if this was the case, Dick had been a bit late in making up his mind. There were now a dozen or more robberies for which he was wanted, and neither Mr. Hume nor Captain Aull was the kind of man to let down, once a pursuit had definitely been started.

Dick himself must have come to the same conclusion, for he did not stay long in Santa Cruz. One morning he got up early, paid his bill, gave his landlord a carpetbag with instructions to ship it to Soledad, where he would call for it, and left town on foot, following the coast, as was later reported, toward Pescadero. The landlord had no notion who his guest might be, and took the satchel down to the Wells, Fargo office to ship it as he had been told. There Dick Thompson, the agent, remembered Captain Aull's visit and the instructions to be curious about strangers. He asked the hotel keeper about his guest, and decided that the stranger must be the man Aull was looking for. He wired the officer, and one more mesh of the net was closed to Dick.

After that, the denouement came quickly. It was plain that Dick was heading northward, making for San Francisco, where he might conceal himself far better than in the countryside. Captain Aull redoubled his efforts and with Hume's permission set more men to work disturbing circulars and questioning local officers and hotel men. Within a week the trap closed. Dick was caught between two groups of searchers and tried to hide on a ranch near Mayfield. The foreman, who was on the lookout, saw him slip into a barn, called two of his men and made Dick prisoner. If Constable Burke of Santa Clara had not been quite so vain, Dick's career would have been over there and then.

Burke was a good, hard-working officer as far as his talents went. He was capable enough so long as he had someone to give him orders, and there was never any question of his honesty. But under his own power he was not so reliable. His trouble was that he did not know his own weakness, which was an exceptional appetite for flattery. And Dick lost no time in taking advantage of this. When Burke searched him and found on him a watch that had been stolen from a stage-driver only the month before, Dick said he was willing to give up and confess. No one else, he explained, could have made him tell the facts; but Burke's brilliant discovery had showed him how hopeless it was to try to deceive him. Now he was willing to admit all the robberies. He gave Burke a list of his crimes and talked to him at length about the fabulous sums of money he had hidden, and the rewards to which Burke would be entitled, now that he knew where to find them. When they got off the evening train in San José, Dick explained to the gaping crowd that no one but Constable Burke could have run him down, adding that he had the greatest respect for Burke's abilities, and that he was the kind of man who would go far, perhaps even as a detective for Wells, Fargo up in San Francisco. When they finally left the depot, Burke could hardly refuse Dick's request that he join him in a parting drink at the IXL Saloon before turning him over to the officers who were waiting at the jail.

Burke should have known better. The fact remains that he did not. Dick's careful flattery had numbed what judgment he had, which was little enough. In the IXL Saloon, they had two drinks, Burke whispering to the bartender that his handcuffed companion was Dick Fellows, the famous stage-robber, and that he had captured him single-handed. That was poor Burke's last chance to boast. For as they left the bar and stepped out into the street, Dick raised his manacled wrists and brought them down hard on the back of Burke's neck. The constable measured his length on the sidewalk, and Dick was gone. Burke fired one hopeless shot into the dark and then turned unhappily toward where Captain Aull and his fellow-officers were waiting impatiently at the jail for him to bring in the prisoner.

There was nothing for it but to begin again. Now, however, there was no need to proceed quietly. Dick knew they were on his trail; the more generally his latest escape was known, the better. The officers routed out a printer and put him to work. Before morning they had distributed two thousand new circulars offering six hundred dollars' reward for Dick's delivery at the jail. It was only a question of time.

A few miles out of San José, not far from Santa Clara College, a certain Dr. Gunckel lived quietly on his little ranch, seeing such patients as came to him, caring for his few head of stock, tending his small vegetable garden. Early in the evening of the sixth day after Dick had fooled Constable Burke so badly, Dr. Gunckel went out to his barn to roll down a bale of hay. He was quite surprised, when he pulled it away from the others, to find a tramp sitting coolly behind it. He was still more astonished to note that on the floor beside the stranger was the remainder of a good meal, including some canned fruit that he recognized as coming from his own cellar and a half-bottle of what was most certainly his own special imported London Stout.

The tramp was Dick, of course. Somehow he had rid himself of the cuffs Officer Burke had snapped on him. And Dick could talk fast, while this was only a mild, unworldly little country doctor. Before he knew it, Dr. Gunckel found himself sympathizing with the unfortunate man who had allowed himself to drink too much and had been so harshly stoned by a group of small boys that he had had to take refuge in the Doctor's barn. He even gave the poor fellow an old hat he happened to have about the place and helped him brush up and tidy himself. He was beginning to offer a gentle word or two of counsel on the dangers of intemperance, when the tramp uncerermoniously took his leave. Only then did Dr. Gunckel remember the hue and cry about an escaped stage-robber. He gave the alarm, but it was too late. Dick had vanished, apparently into thin air.

But with the countryside aroused as it was by this new report, no one could have hoped to remain hidden for long. Next day word came to the officers that a man answering Dick's description had been seen in the hills near Los Gatos. Chief Dan Haskell of San José and one of his officers named Juan Edson set out in pursuit. At the Mountain Dale House in that village they learned that their man had stopped for a short time and read a copy of the San José *Mercury* in which was printed a long story of the escape of Dick Fellows, together with a detailed description of the robber. He had put down the paper, the innkeeper said, and walked out of the hotel and up the road.

All afternoon, Haskell and Edson tramped the vicinity, asking questions. And early in the evening their patience had its inevitable result. Up a narrow lane that led into one of the hundreds of little canyons of the Coast Range hills, they saw a lighted cabin window and went to investigate. As a precautionary measure, they looked in at the window before knocking. At a table in the center of the room sat Dick, waiting for his innocent host to bring him his supper. The officers did not knock. While Edson covered Dick through the window, Chief Haskell walked in and put handcuffs on Dick's wrists once more. They took him to the San José jail, but this time they gave him no chance to play any tricks. While they waited for Mr. Hume to come down from San Francisco, three shifts of wakeful guards watched Dick every minute. So did some seven hundred citizens of San José, who were curious to see the noted bandit whose deeds had had the town in an uproar for weeks. The *Mercury* reporter wrote that he "seemed not at all displeased at this evidence of his notoriety." However he felt about it, he treated everyone with courtesy, discussing his case with all who chose to speak to him and conducting himself, as even his guards admitted, altogether in the manner of a gentleman.

Nor did Mr. Hume take any risks with his slippery

prisoner. The sheriff of Santa Barbara was on his way north to receive Dick, who was to be tried in that county for a robbery committed there. Since he was coming that far, Mr. Hume reasoned, he might as well come on up to San Francisco, in whose sturdy jail Dick would be far safer. The journey was not tiresome. Dick entertained Mr. Hume all the way with a detailed narrative of his crimes. Now that he was caught, confessing, he said, gave him actual pleasure. When the sheriff of Santa Barbara arrived, he found Dick safe and sound. In his custody, Dick made the trip to Santa Barbara no less safely. There he was tried, found guilty on all counts, and sentenced to Folsom Prison for the term of his natural life.

By all rules the story of Dick Perkins, *alias* Lytle, *alias* Fellows, should end here. And if the Santa Barbara officials had realized just how resourceful a man they had in their jail, it would have been the end. But they failed to appreciate Dick. Perhaps they were not to blame; after all, it was the northern counties that knew him, northern officers and citizens who had learned to their cost how quickly Dick could think and act. Constable Burke could have told them a few things; so could Mr. Hume, or Bakersfield's bribe-taking and double-crossing sheriff, or Mr. Fountain's boy Tommy, or Dr. Gunckel. Nobody warned them. Wherefore Dick had one more chance to get together with a horse.

On April 2, 1882, when they were almost ready to take him up to Folsom Prison, Dick struck down his jailer, leaping to his shoulders from a shelf in his cell and bearing him to the floor. "It is life or death for me," Dick was reported as saying to the guard, "and I am going to get your revolver." He got it and fled. Two blocks from the jail there was a horse staked out to graze. There was neither saddle nor bridle, but this was no time to be choosy. Dick pulled up the stake, looped the long rope into a kind of coil, scrambled on to the bony back, and dug his heels into the animal's ribs. For the last time he was trusting himself to a horse.

Neither Dick nor anyone else could have known it, of course, but the horse had been staked where it was for a very good reason. Its owner had almost lost the beast through its mistaken nibbling of loco-weed the week before. It had made a partial recovery, but some of its narcotic nightmares must have lingered. Because Dick had covered scarcely a hundred yards before his mount suddenly went into a fit. Dick had no chance at all. Even his arms flung round the horse's neck saved him for only half a minute. Early risers in Santa Barbara that morning were treated to the spectacle of the famous stage-robber ignominiously rolled in the dust of the public square. Pistol or no pistol, it was no trouble to catch him after that.

Dick had time to write one letter before they took him under heavy guard to Folsom. He addressed it to the editor of the Santa Barbara *Press*, and in it he made it plain that he had come to certain conclusions about the profession of highwayman. "Dear Sir," he wrote, "I have just noticed your article in reference to my recent attempt at escape and also your editorial in regard to my past career entitled 'It Don't Pay.' After thanking you for your kindly notices, I have to say that both are in the main correct, and I most heartily concur in what you have to say in the last named. I would add only that the same may be said of any unlawful calling. My unfortunate experience has thrown me into the society of thousands of law-breakers in all walks of life, and in every instance the result is the same sad story. 'It Don't Pay,' in any sense. I learn that the boat will leave here in a few minutes, and I bid you and the people of Santa Barbara good-bye.                              DICK FELLOWS"

It will be noted that Dick did not mention horses. No one could call it anything but the merest coincidence that one sentence of his polite note reads, "My unfortunate experience has thrown me. . . ." But from the tone of his letter it is quite clear that he had already begun to lay plans for the manner in which he would serve his sentence. Only the hardest-hearted reader can deny at least a momentary glow of pleasure at learning that within the year Dick Fellows was made a teacher in the Department of Moral Instruction at Folsom Prison.

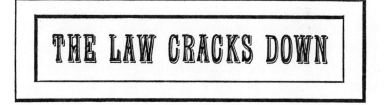

# THE LAW CRACKS DOWN

**M**OST CRIMINALS TRY IN ONE
way or another to rationalize their careers of crime. It
seems to be a characteristic of the human mind, or perhaps the human conscience, to try to achieve some kind
of balance. Hence the familiar urge of the man who has
done wrong to find a "reason" for his anti-social doings,
someone or something to blame. The reader will remember, for instance, Dick Fellows' curious letterful of *non
sequiturs* to Wells, Fargo's Detective Hume (the last man
in the world to whom his excuses could appear valid),
explaining that he, Dick, had "only aimed at affluent corporations and never molested poor people or private individuals." Black Bart, after his capture, made vague references to a "wrong" he had suffered at the hands of the
Express Company; the implication, of course, was that
his stage-robberies were thus somehow justified. The brutal
Tom Bell knew and made clear, in the letter they allowed
him to write just before they strung him up, precisely how
and why he had engaged in his career of robbery and murder; as the reader will recall, it was the fault of those
wicked men who had taught him to drink and to gamble

when he was young. Rattlesnake Dick had twice been falsely accused of theft wherefore he turned against the society that injured him. It is an old and commonplace story.

Sometimes, to be sure, there is some logic at the bottom of such rationalizing. And in the matter of California's early-day bandits racial prejudice played a significant role. The "Joaquins" of whom Murieta was one, had at least the kernel of a justified grudge against the community on which they preyed. Consider what happened in those earliest days when Americans were pouring into the mining country by the thousands.

Because they were closer and because after all California had been a Mexican province up to the moment of the gold discovery at Sutter's Mill, almost the first to arrive in the gold fields were Mexicans, and after them Argonauts from Chile and Peru. These were men most of whom had mining experience; time and time again it was a Mexican who showed the greenhorn from Massachusetts or New York how to use his "bowl" or pan, how to get water in order to wash the gold-bearing earth of the "dry diggings" during the long months when there was no rain in California. Further, for some time, especially in the Southern Mines, the Latin-American miners outnumbered the Yankees.

But there was one thing that the American remembered, one obstinate fact to which he held. The United States had won the Mexican War. And Mexicans, including Chileans and Peruvians—well, they were all part of a conquered race. They were "foreigners." So were the Chinese, but they had learned the trick of subservience: they bowed and grinned and moved on when they were

told; they were content to work over the tailings and
dumps, save their gold, and go into small businesses. It
was the Latin-American, even though the odds were he
had been in California long before the Yankee came,
against whom the American miner directed his spleen.

The thing began very early. Under pressure, the first
session of the California Legislature in the spring of 1850
passed a frankly illiberal and hurtful statute, the "Foreign
Miners' Tax Law" which set up a tax system purposely
designed to make it impossible for any excepting "native
or natural-born citizens of the United States" to mine
gold in California. The law provided what amounted to a
confiscatory tax; it stipulated that "foreigners" must buy
a license to mine which must be renewed, with another
payment, each thirty days; still further that if the "foreign" miner refused or neglected to take out his license
each month, the sheriff should summon a "posse of American citizens" and drive him off. If this occurred, all further
mining by such a "foreigner" should be deemed a mis-
demeanor punishable by a heavy fine and imprisonment.
As the historian, Hittell, noted, it was an outrageous and
oppressive law, rendered even more outrageous by the fact
that tax collectors were to be appointed at the pleasure
of the governor, and that their wages should be retained
by them out of the taxes they collected. No more effective
way could have been devised to put a premium upon per-
secution of "foreigners," and upon graft and corruption of
every sort.

At first the "foreign" miners tried to fight the law.
Meetings were called, petitions were drawn up; there were
riots and mass demonstrations and some outright pitched
battles. But the end could have been foreseen. With

Americans flooding the mining region as fast as overland caravans and ships could bring them, with every kind of "white" frequently blanketed in as an "American," including the hundreds fresh from Australian convict settlements, the "foreigner," which meant principally the Hispano-Californian and Mexican, had no chance. Many went home; there was a large-scale exodus of Latin-Americans from the mines in 1850, most of them Chileans and Peruvians who had formed companies to seek their fortunes exactly as so many Americans had done. But thousands stayed, chiefly the Hispano-Californians whose home it was, after all. It was not surprising that a good many of these should take to outlawry when it was made so plain to them that they could not look for fair treatment from the *gringo*. Nor is it surprising that such outlaws were aided under cover by their sympathetic countrymen everywhere throughout California.

There is a good chance that rough treatment by the Americans was what drove the "five Joaquins" to their trade of plunder and murder. As the reader has seen, John Ridge who, in his fiction-yarn, set the pattern for the entire Murieta story as it has been told ever since, made great play with the vicious treatment his hero received from American miners. Dame Shirley, whose *Letters* are one of the best sources for the color and atmosphere of early mining days, reports whippings and hangings of Mexicans on the slightest pretext. Other objective writers of the day, especially visiting Englishmen, tell the same story; most of them were frankly shocked by the injustices done to Mexicans and the callousness with which American miners ignored and even tacitly approved it all. Perhaps even this kind of treatment did not justify banditry, but it goes a long way to explain at least some of it.

There was another factor involved, too. During what has been called the Pastoral Age of California, the great *ranchos* supported among them thousands of hangers-on; it was the Mexican habit to cluster in family groups, and every large ranch had attached to it hundreds of ostensible "workers"—men who had little to do but whose keep, with cattle multiplying uncounted on the hills and corn and beans producing several crops a year in the mild climate, amounted to very little. By the time the gold rush began, however, the era of the great ranches was over. The enormous land-grants were beginning to break up; the free and easy days were gone. And these thousands of vaguely employed Mexicans found themselves with nowhere to go, displaced persons without quite understanding what had happened to them. Some could adjust, though in the cities and towns of the new American California a Mexican could rarely find anything to do but the most menial work. Others simply took what they needed as they could find it, and if this meant living off a society which, as it seemed to them, had refused them support, why that was the way it was. Against this background, it is not difficult to see how patriotism came to be wrapped up in the same package with outlawry. Through the operation of economic and social forces of which they had not the faintest awareness, such men were suddenly cut adrift. Manifestly it was some more of the *gringo's* work, and it was entirely reasonable to hate him for it. Moreover, this hatred was encouraged and strengthened by hundreds who had fought the Yankee in the war just past and who, when the war was lost, wandered north into Cali-

fornia to join the native in his bitter struggle against the
American who had done him down. This injection of patriotism into the business makes it quite clear why even
the Mexican who remained honest, somehow found work
to do, and was peaceably inclined, was still secretly
friendly to the outlaws, gave them information, did his
best to mislead their pursuers whenever possible and altogether helped in his way to oppose strategy to superior
strength. Nor is it hard to see why, even after the decapitation of Murieta (if the exhibited head was actually his),
the hills and valleys of California did not suddenly become safe. An important gang had been broken up by the
band of rangers assembled for that specific purpose. But
the rangers had then been dissolved, and the dozens of
smaller fry at the bandits' game saw that they could remain active with impunity.

They remained active for about two decades. In the
mining camps, lynch law and the fact that, by and large,
the mines were a tough region whose citizens had learned
to take care of themselves, made it good sense if you were
an outlaw to steal your cattle and cut your throats in less
well-policed parts of the State. Wherefore during the
latter Fifties and early Sixties it was the San Joaquin
Valley and the general area of the Coast Range that became the last stamping-ground of such bandit gangs as
remained. The "five Joaquins" had used unexplored parts
of the coastal mountains as their stronghold; now the in-
heritors of their tradition made good use of the same
trick. As the Sixties opened, Californians were disturbed
about the new wave of cattle-stealing, highway-robbery,
and sudden death. New names were on everyone's tongue
—Procopio, Pancho Ruiz, Juan Soto, Escalante, Bartolo

Sepulveda, and others who sometimes gave themselves vainglorious names such as "José California," or Eduardo Gallego, "The Cock." Once more something had to be done. Newspapers printed impassioned editorials demanding that State and county officials get busy. California was a law-abiding community, wasn't it? Well then, let the officers of the law do something about protecting the property and lives of the citizens who had put them in office.

A man turned up to do the job. He was Harry N. Morse, the same whose shrewd, careful detective work was to bring to book the great stage-robber Black Bart in the early Eighties. It took Morse several years, but he broke up the Mexican gangs for good. The last of them, led by Tiburcio Vasquez, was given its *coup de grace* by other men, but it was Harry Morse who did the tedious and difficult spade-work that made it possible.

Harry Morse came to California in 1849, an ambitious, hard-working boy of fifteen. He mined for a short time but the life did not suit him. He was not one of the fortunate ones; he made no sudden rich finds, and it seemed foolish to live a life that was one continual gamble with the cards stacked against you. Much as the average man might earn by back-breaking labor in the placers, and even if he was wise enough to stay away from liquor, the fandango halls, and the monte-tables, he had to spend all he made for the fantastically high-priced necessities of life. And, barring the lucky discovery of a rich claim, he might go on doing this for years. Morse, like many another sensible man, saw the point. He came down to Oakland on the shore of San Francisco Bay and got a job as a butcher boy. In a year or two he bettered himself, find-ing employment as an expressman. People apparently liked the quiet, reliable-seeming young fellow, for before long he was on the fringes of local politics. When he was still in his twenties he became deputy provost-marshal of Alameda County, of which Oakland was soon to be county seat. At twenty-eight he was elected sheriff and served in that capacity for the next fourteen years.

A writer of the time describes Morse as "calm, cautious and persistent," says that his best quality was "a patient skill and sagacity in pursuing his purpose," and adds that "he never shrank from conflict." The description fits him admirably as his career demonstrates.

The first thing Sheriff Morse did was to spend the bet-ter part of a year riding up and down the hills and ravines of the little-explored Coast Range, learning the topog-raphy of half a dozen counties beside his own, and finding out whom he could trust. At the end of this period he knew the country as well as the shrewdest of the outlaws that infested it. They did not know him, however; to those with whom he chatted now and then he was simply a beardless young fellow sizing up the region with a view to running stock there. He never asked questions about outlaws; he merely kept his eyes and ears open and ab-sorbed all he could about the names and histories and habits of the men who hid out in those hills, piecing and patching bits of conversation until he had put together in his mind the fragments of the puzzle. When he had learned enough he would act.

Characteristically, his first moves were cautious and well planned. Working quietly and carefully he secured warrants against one after another of the lesser outlaws whose names and descriptions he had noted. Then he went out, often alone, and served the warrants—at fandangos, at wedding celebrations, in the hidden camps in the hills he had scoured so thoroughly. "He lived in the saddle," says a contemporary reporter, "with the same freedom the bandits themselves possessed." One by one he ran down and arrested these smaller fry. Then he began to move against the bigger gangs and tougher characters. When Narciso Bojorques, a peculiarly bad egg who killed everyone he robbed (it was reported that he took special pleasure in the act of murder), boasted that he would shoot Morse on sight, the young sheriff took the first chance to meet him, riding the forty miles down to Mission San José where Bojorques had been seen. That outlaw had just committed a particularly atrocious crime, descending on the cabin of a rancher named Golding, tying up the *vaquero* outside, then shooting Golding, his wife, and his child, systematically looting the house and setting fire to it, and finishing off by hanging the *vaquero*, tied as he was, to a tree in front of the blazing dwelling. The outlaw had been seen and identified, and Morse had no trouble getting his warrant, but when he arrived at the Mission Bojorques had left. Morse rode after him, and an hour later caught up with a Mexican horseman. It was the outlaw, and the two men recognized each other immediately, drawing pistols at the same instant. Bojorques' weapon missed fire, and since Morse's quick shot had glanced off the outlaw's ribs, the latter was able to slip from the saddle and escape into the brush. Five months later he was shot to death by a small-time American bad man named One-Eyed Jack in a saloon brawl in Copperopolis on the border of the gold region. But after his encounter with Morse many of the superstitious Mexicans believed that the sheriff carried a charm against bullets.

Next on Morse's list was Narrato Ponce, a Chileño horse-thief who had deliberately shot and killed an old man named Jay in the little settlement of Hayward. This was Morse's own territory and he dropped all other business to get the murderer. Ponce, bad as he was, had courage and a certain dash to him; he had done the killing in a *cantina* and, with the old man dead on the floor, had walked up to the bar, ordered a drink, inquired politely if anybody else wanted anything—he did not specify whether he meant whiskey or lead—and, when no one replied, drank his drink and rode away. It took Morse three weeks to find Ponce, but he was tipped off one dark night that the man he wanted had just ridden out of Livermore toward the flank of Mount Diablo. Morse and a deputy were on Ponce's heels as the bandit turned off the road into a field of straw-stacks, and all three men emptied their pistols in a running gunfight, firing at the flashes in the pitchy darkness. Neither Morse nor his deputy was hit, and the two ran from stack to stack, setting fire to them all. The blaze lit up the entire countryside but Ponce had somehow got away. In the morning, behind a burned stack, the officers found a blood-soaked coat and hat, but that was all. Some months later Morse got another tip, and with two deputies this time rode up to Pinole where Ponce had been reported. An informer there told them that the outlaw had gone up Pinole Canyon, and Morse and his men moved slowly up toward its dead end, examining the Mexicans' adobes as they went. Finally Morse saw a man come out of a hut ahead of him and dodge into the scrub on the hill-side. He went after him, and at the same moment another man ran from the house in the opposite direction. The second one was Ponce; the first had been a decoy. Morse raised his rifle and called to him to surrender, and Ponce stopped and turned, threw down his *sarape*, rested his re-volver carefully on his left arm, and took aim. Morse fired first and Ponce fell dead. When the three officers exam-ined his body they found that their shooting on that dark night among the straw-stacks had not been too bad; Ponce had received thirteen buckshot in his body and three pistol wounds.

As the 1860s wore on, Morse continued steadily in his pursuit of the thinning bands of thieves and murderers that remained in the hills of the Coast Range. One named Procopio—he had chosen the name as more mellifluous than his own which was Tomaso Redondo—had been associated with Bojorques and was rumored to be a cousin of Murieta. Perhaps he was; at any rate his six-foot frame and gallant manner fitted nicely into the picture, since the legend of the handsome, dashing Murieta was by this time widely spread. Procopio, in spite of his gallant style, was something less than the menace the stories at the time made him, for he had once surrendered meekly enough to a citizens' posse and had served time in State's Prison for stealing horses. He had been discharged a year or so before and had gone back to his old tricks, even sticking up a stage or two when he and his companions had found no horses or cattle handy. Morse understood his man and how to handle him. He followed him into San Francisco and to a Mexican dance hall, walked straight up to him as he was dancing, took him by the throat with one hand and pressed a pistol firmly to his temple. It is recorded that Morse said just "Procopio, you're my man!" The outlaw put up no resistance nor did any of his friends make a move, and Morse marched him out. This time Procopio went to San Quentin for a nine-year term. There is no further record of him; evidently if he remained in California he stayed clear of the law.

With the same kind of directness Morse pursued Jesus Tejada, as vicious a wholesale murderer as California ever saw. Tejada and two of his men had shocked the State into violent revulsion by entering a small Italian general store on the old Mokelumne Road about twenty miles from Stockton, and at pistols' point tying up and gagging the storekeeper, his clerk, and two Mexicans and a Negro who happened to be there. Then the outlaws had deliberately shot the five men to death; a reporter of the time wrote that the bodies were "stacked up like cordwood." Morse followed Tejada's trail for a year, eventually getting a trustworthy report that he and some of his followers were camped on Los Baños Creek in Merced County. On this occasion Morse disguised himself, took along two deputies, rode up to the group of shacks in which the gang was living, and captured the lot of them alive. The reader will scarcely credit the disguise Morse had chosen; the description reads for all the world like something out of a mail-order course in *How to Be a Detective in Ten Easy Lessons*, and it is difficult to believe that it could have deceived even the least observant bandit that ever lived. Yet the authority is Morse himself. "I wore an old pair of ragged pants," he wrote, "a gray woolen shirt, a great broad-brimmed hat that flopped about my ears like a dilapidated umbrella in a rainstorm. A pair of dark green goggles covered my eyes, and the lower part of my face was hidden by a long shaggy beard." Fantastic as the get-up seems, it was enough to allow Morse to get past the lookout man—one wonders just what he took Morse for—and to the door of the shack, where his pistol was all that was needed to bring Tejada and his men to time.

So Morse's work went on. Concerning some of the other less important figures accounts are charmingly vague—as in the case of one Alejandro Morales who had the gall to attempt theft on the grand scale, driving off some six hundred sheep from the vicinity of San Leandro. It is clear merely that neither Morales nor the sheep moved fast enough to escape the Alameda Sheriff. But on the elimination of the highly dangerous Juan Soto the details are precise and the language of the contemporary reporters is eloquent. There is little question that this exploit was, for sheer intrepidity, Morse's greatest.

Juan Soto has been described by many writers of the time, and all agree that he was the most fearsome figure of an outlaw that ever roamed California's hills.

Soto, three-quarters Indian, stood six feet two inches in height, weighed more than two hundred pounds, yet was as powerful and as agile as a wildcat. One surviving photograph shows him to have been singularly unpleasant in appearance, with a thick underlip, a narrow forehead, long coarse black hair, heavy brows beetling over violently crossed eyes, and a general expression of animal ferocity. His followers were said to be in abject fear of his outbreaks of wild fury and, as events proved, even those peaceful Mexican settlers who were always so close-mouthed when it came to helping officers capture others of their countrymen were willing, provided protection was promised, to report on Soto when they were asked. It was perfectly clear that here was a man so near to the brute that everyone joined in wishing him out of the way.

Throughout the latter 1860's, however, Soto and his men managed to stay hidden in the hills, making quick sorties to kill and burn and rob, retreating to the dark canyons and the rough and broken hills of the Coast Range about which very little was known. Then, in January of 1871, Soto and two of his band made their most daring raid and brought Harry Morse into the picture. Coming as far north as Sunol, they entered the store of Thomas Scott, ex-Assemblyman from Morse's own county, shot and killed Scott's clerk, ransacked the store, and then out of sheer savagery fired several rounds apiece through the flimsy wall into the room at the back where Scott's wife and children were hiding. As it happened, no one was hit and the terrified woman and her children ran across the small valley to neighbors and escaped. Soto and his party, with what cash they got from the till and several sacks of groceries, rode off and disappeared. The few neighbors had wisely stayed indoors during the raid, but Morse, who reached Sunol next morning, pieced together enough evidence to convince him that two of the men had been a rascal named Bartolo Sepulveda and Soto himself.

It was general knowledge that Soto and his band hid out in a valley called Saucelito from the profusion of willows growing there, a spot in the Panoche mountains about fifty miles below Gilroy and the area, more or less, in which the "five Joaquins" had been accustomed to lie low almost two decades earlier. This was country Morse knew; it was the very region over which, in his first year as sheriff, he had ridden so thoroughly, working out in his painstaking mind just what he would do and where he would go if he chanced to be an outlaw in those parts. He got together three of his men, persuaded Sheriff Harris of Santa Clara and some of his deputies to join with them, and headed for the wild area east of Pacheco Pass and up toward the headwaters of Los Baños Creek. There were no roads; the region was inhabited only by scattered sheepherders, most of them Mexicans. But Morse knew where he was going, and he directed the disposal of his party in a wide skirmish-line, combing the country thoroughly as he moved southward.

On the third day they found a Mexican whose acquaintance Morse had made on his original scouting trip, and the man agreed to show them the easiest route into Saucelito Valley where, he admitted, Soto and his men were camped. He made only one condition; as Morse put it later, "The officers must allow him to retire before the bandits could see him." Morse agreed, and the sheepherder took the party to a spot where, as they came over a small ridge, they looked directly down upon the little valley and its willow-bordered creek. There were three adobe huts across the stream, almost directly below them, and the Mexican explained that they were outposts; Soto's actual stronghold, he said, was farther up the canyon. The man was frightened half out of his wits, and Morse let him go back to his sheep, bringing the posse together out of sight behind the ridge to discuss their course of action.

Morse and Harris drew up a simple plan. They would divide into three groups. Morse and one deputy named Winchell would capture the nearest adobe and secure whatever lookout might be there. Sheriff Harris would divide the rest of the men into two squads and surround the other huts. The whole maneuver was to be executed quietly, with no firing unless it was absolutely necessary. The outposts captured, they would meet and work out their method of attack on the main camp.

According to plan, Morse and Winchell then rode over the ridge and down across the creek to the corral beside the nearest adobe. There was a Mexican there with some horses, and Morse asked if he and his friend might have a drink of water. The man replied that there was water in the house, and Morse and Winchell dismounted and followed him. Winchell carried a double-barreled shotgun. Morse took only his pistol, leaving his rifle hanging to his saddle. Neither expected any opposition; the adobe, they thought, was probably empty.

The wide, low room into which they stepped was far from empty. Directly opposite the door was a large table occupying a good half of the space. Grouped about it were a dozen Mexicans, men and women, as bad-looking a lot as Morse had ever laid eyes on. And at the far side of the table, facing the door, was Juan Soto himself.

As has been noted, Harry Morse was a careful, patient, logical sort of man. But, as circumstances showed, he was also a split-second thinker when the occasion demanded fast thinking. Now he saw instantly that the only way to save himself and his deputy was to take the initiative. He moved forward one long step, covered Soto with his revolver, and ordered the giant outlaw to put up his hands. Winchell, at his left and slightly behind him, held his shotgun aimed at Soto's breast.

Reading Morse's own account of the tableau, the scene comes through with the horrid vividness of a nightmare—the small, shadowy room, the Mexicans and their women, Soto himself glaring from under his heavy brows, his brutish countenance flushed with rage, all of them frozen in position, knowing that the least movement might bring the deadly shot from the sheriff's revolver, the blast from his deputy's shotgun. As in a nightmare, too, the tension was drawn still finer by Soto's continued immobility and Morse's insistent repetition of his command, "Soto! Put up your hands!" Perhaps if the deputy had been of the same hard stuff as Morse that would have been the end of it. For when Soto ignored Morse's second command, the sheriff pulled a pair of handcuffs from his pocket with his left hand, threw them clattering on the table, and said, "Winchell, put them on him!"

You can pick up a pair of cuffs and continue to hold a revolver steady with the other hand. But a shotgun is another matter. Winchell stepped around the end of the table, took up the cuffs, and leaned toward Soto. But to do it he had to hold his shotgun in the crook of his arm, his finger no longer ready on the trigger. And when Soto turned his head and Winchell found that furious glare focussed on him at short range, the deputy hesitated. The moment's hesitation gave him time to think, and in such a situation the moment thought takes the place of action the thread is broken. Morse's account says simply, "The next second Winchell backed out and ran away."

Now the tableau dissolved with frantic speed. One of the Mexican women—Morse said she was "a muscular

Amazon"—jumped the sheriff from behind as he leaned across the table, seizing his pistol arm. Instantly one of the men took Morse by the other wrist. Soto moved as quickly, leaping from his chair, drawing two pistols, and shouting to his men to stand by while he killed Morse.

In that dimly lit room the whole affair must have been more than ever like a bad dream. Morse, knowing that he was now fighting for his life, managed to wrest himself free and jumped backward through the door, firing as he went. Soto had launched himself straight across the table, and the bullet took off his hat.

One of the curious things about what followed is that no one interfered. Perhaps Soto's band felt that their leader would resent any attempt to rob him of the pleasure of finishing off Morse; they knew Soto was a fine shot, and they had heard him swear on many occasions that he and nobody else would be the one to prove that Morse's supposed immunity to bullets was a fable. The chances are that they thought they had only Morse and his fleeing deputy to deal with; there had been no sound from the other members of the party. Or it may have been that events moved just too rapidly for them to decide what to do. At any rate, what came next was a straight-out duel between the sheriff and the outlaw.

Morse had a purpose in mind; he wanted to reach his Henry rifle where it hung from his saddle, and as he fired he kept backing, step by step, toward his horse.

Soto fired four shots altogether, and the story of what happened comes from Sheriff Harris who, with his party, had now ridden into sight. Incredible as it sounds, Morse dodged all four bullets, dropping to the ground at exactly the right moment each time the outlaw fired. Each time, Sheriff Harris reported, he was sure Morse had been hit. Each time Morse rose and fired once more at Soto. And his fifth shot took effect, striking Soto's pistol and jamming the cylinder. At this, Soto turned and sprang back into the adobe while Morse ran at top speed for his rifle.

The duel had taken place in a matter of seconds, and the ensuing action was as fast. In the hut, Soto threw off his blue coat and seized three pistols, sticking one into his belt and carrying the other two as he ran from the back door toward a horse which stood saddled under a tree. One of his men slipped on the coat and ran away from the corral and down the canyon, evidently with the purpose of misleading Sheriff Harris and his party, now coming up fast. (The reader will recall that Narrato Ponce had tried the same trick on Morse at Pinole some years earlier.) If Soto had reached his horse it might have been another story, but his headlong approach frightened the animal which broke away and headed at a gallop in the same direction the blue-coated outlaw had taken. Soto did not hesitate, but ran for a second horse. Morse, who had now reached his rifle, called to him, "Throw down your pistols, Juan! There has been enough shooting!" The outlaw continued to run, and Morse raised his rifle. The bullet struck Soto's shoulder, the shock turning him around, and Sheriff Harris said afterward that he would never forget how the giant Indian looked as he came rushing back down the slope, evidently abandoning his hope of escape and determined to kill Morse as his last act. For a moment the outlaw vanished; his way led through the adobe and he took advantage of the brief shelter. Then, said Harris, "He emerged from the house on a

dead run, bareheaded, his long black hair streaming behind him, a cocked revolver in each hand." Morse brought
up his rifle steadily and shot him through the head.

After that the two sheriffs and their men rounded up
Soto's companions, rode on up the canyon, and arrested
half a dozen more at the headquarters. The man in Soto's
coat had caught the frightened horse and got away.

A year and a half later Morse arrested him near San
Jose. He was the same Bartolo Sepulveda who had helped
Soto shoot the unarmed clerk in Scott's store.

This was very nearly the end of the Mexican outlaw
gangs. Working almost single-handed, Harry Morse had
wiped them out, his patience never failing, his methodical, careful police work bringing one after another within
his reach, his courage and cool willingness to meet any
bandit on the latter's terms and even on his own ground
proving at last too much for even the most dangerous.
Other sheriffs had done their jobs too—Ben Thorn of
Calaveras, Tom Cunningham of San Joaquin, Harris of
Santa Clara, and many more. But Morse, as the record
proves, was the best of them. Indeed, he was so good at
tracking down outlaws that he was the man actually responsible for the eventual capture of the single bandit-
leader of any account now left in the State. The man was
Tiburcio Vasquez, and he came the closest of any of the
Mexican gang leaders to being what the legend had made
Murieta seem. Like the rest, Vasquez came at last to an
ignominious end, and it was Morse who did the plodding
detail work that paid off in the moment of drama when
the capture was made. But when Vasquez was caught,
Morse was not among those present. He should have been.

He would have been, but for the desire of another sheriff to take the credit.

It is best, however, to keep this chapter at least roughly chronological. And it was to be another three years before Tiburcio Vasquez was run to earth and the Coast Range was finally cleared of its Mexican cattle-thieves and murderers. Meantime, up in the Sierra foothills and down in Southern California a fine and varied assortment of stickup men, stage-robbers, and desperadoes had been keeping peace officers, Wells, Fargo's shotgun messengers, and citizens' posses busier than any of them wanted to be.

2

The reader has already made the acquaintance of the two men, Tom Bell and Rattlesnake Dick, who were easily the outstanding outlaws of the mining region during the Fifties after the five Joaquins and their gang had been dispersed. Outside the gold-mining country, however, and some four hundred miles to the southward in the general area of Santa Barbara and Los Angeles where the rough Tehachapi mountain range offered ideal cover for bandits, the citizens were having their troubles too.

Southern California had its gang-pattern ready made, the chief early exponent being one Salomon Pico who was said to collect the ears of *gringo* victims, speaking of them affectionately as "My pearls!" and stringing them in grisly festoons about his saddle-horn. (The reader will perhaps remember the San Francisco *Call's* lady reporter who helped confuse the Murieta legend so thoroughly, and her attribution of this ropes-of-ears habit to Joaquin— a macabre borrowing which doubtless seemed useful when she was casting about for still another sensation to bring fresh color to the Murieta fantasy.) Pico vanished into Mexico eventually, his most notable contribution to California history being the private and personal murder of his colleague in banditry, Andres Fontes, the last of the instigators of the Flores "revolution." This affair, actually, came close to being just that, and for a short time Southern Californians trembled at the thought that a full-scale uprising of the Mexicans in their part of the State might result in a general slaughter of the *gringo* south of the Tehachapis.

Flores' career began like that of many another outlaw of his time; he was caught stealing horses and sentenced in Los Angeles to a term in San Quentin Prison. Ranger Horace Bell, who had seen him, described Flores in his memoirs as being "young, lithe and graceful, and a beautiful figure in the *fandango*." It was his eyes that Bell remembered best, however; he writes that they were "neither black, gray nor blue, but something of each, resembling those of the owl—always moving, watchful and wary, the most cruel and vindictive eyes ever set in human head." Barring the vagueness as to color, the description is a purely subjective one, of course, but Major Bell had had enough to do with bad men in his time so that his reaction is worth mentioning, for it is plain that Flores impressed him more than most.

At San Quentin, Flores participated in an attempted prison break which failed, and he and almost a hundred others were put under special discipline. The authorities evidently underestimated their man. Chumming up with a vicious robber from Shasta County known as "Red Horse" Webster, Flores proceeded to plan more successfully, and in the autumn of 1856 he and Webster led a large group of convicts in an assault upon a ship while it was unloading brick at the prison wharf. Though the guards opened fire with pistols and rifles, and even manned the prison battery on the point, pouring heavy fire into the brig from one six-pounder and a twelve-pound howitzer, Flores and "Red Horse" managed to overpower the ship's officers and crew, set sail, and escaped across the Bay to Contra Costa County. They moved quickly southward toward country they knew, in San Luis Obispo picking up Andres Fontes who had sworn to kill Los Angeles' Sheriff Barton and was therefore happy to join them. If Fontes' claim is to be believed, Barton had sent him to prison at eighteen on a trumped-up charge because the boy had interfered with the sheriff's beating of a Mexican woman. Whatever the truth of it, Fontes was delighted to go along with Flores, and the latter must have felt that here was a useful if young recruit.

For Flores now had a definite scheme afoot. With such of his fellow-Mexicans as he could gather, he would stage a general revolt against the *gringo*, making his headquarters in San Juan Capistrano near the coast—an ideal central point from which to control Southern California settlements as they were then distributed. At first, too, the plan seemed to go well. Flores gathered new adherents every day. Further, his scheme to make the *gringo* finance the rebellion actually worked for a time, Flores and his men making the rounds of the *ranchos* in the region and robbing them one after another at pistols' point. One German rancher who refused to pay was formally taken to the plaza in San Juan Capistrano and shot for "treason."

Flores had another scheme, moreover, this one a plot to
help Fontes get his revenge on the sheriff of Los Angeles.
They would send a false message to Barton that Flores
and a very few men were in hiding at a ranch nearby,
thus drawing the sheriff out to ambush and death. It
might not have worked if Barton had listened to Ranger
Lyon who flatly refused to join any posse for this purpose
unless it numbered fifty or more. But Barton thought a
dozen men would be plenty and rode into the trap. Flores
had set it neatly; members of the posse were shot down
one by one before they knew what was happening. Two
of them escaped by hard riding, but Barton did not. He
was lying wounded where he had fallen from his horse,
when Andres Fontes approached, took slow and deliberate
aim and shot him dead. It is of record that Sheriff Barton's last act was to raise himself on one elbow and hurl
his empty pistol at Fontes' head. The revolutionaries took
the equipment and horses of the ten dead and rode back
triumphantly to San Juan.

The sheriff's failure and the massacre of so many of
his men stirred Southern California profoundly. As a
writer of the period put it, "All *gringos* held their breaths
in the intensity of their alarm," though he does not say
for how long. He did not exaggerate, however, when he
added, "Men looked at each other and asked 'Where will
this end?'" They did; and their very terror turned the
trick, for when a call was issued for volunteers practically
every able-bodied man in the countryside reported with
his rifle. They were organized rapidly into companies,
officers were chosen, and the little army set out. On its
small scale it was something very like a war, with the
Flores gang retreating in good order into the hills, the

ranchers disposing their forces so as to cut off all passes, and the pursuit being conducted generally with the careful staff-work of an organized campaign. The upshot of it was that the outlaws—or insurgents as one pleases—were isolated in small bands of ten or a dozen at a time and killed or captured according to the degree of resistance they put up. What with executions and long prison terms the "revolution" was brought to a sharp and bloody end. One important figure got away. That was Fontes. He had joined Juan Flores only for the purpose of making good his promise to kill Sheriff Barton. That done, he left the others before the citizens' army was formed and escaped to Baja California. It was there that he had his falling out with Salomon Pico and came to his death. In the end, Flores' attempt at revolution, if it was actually that, proved only the firm determination of the more solid *Californios*—men like General Andres Pico and Don Tomás Sanchez and many others who helped lead the little army against Flores—that it was time Californians of every sort got together to stamp out crime, even when it made its bid under the banners of "patriotism" and "revolution."

Organized outlawry of this kind could be met with overwhelming force and taken care of, and in the turbulent years from 1849 to the 1870s this was the rule. The man who conducted his criminal career chiefly on his own and operated with the connivance of the politicians and venal courts—well, he was something else. Such a man was Jack Powers who, during the early Fifties, came close to having the lovely village of Santa Barbara in the hollow of his hand.

Powers had come to California with his brother Ed in 1847 with Colonel Jonathan D. Stevenson's regiment of New York Volunteers; on the records of the regiment both brothers appear as "Power," Jack with the grade of sergeant. Company F, in which they were enrolled, had been stationed at Santa Barbara on temporary garrison duty, the Mexican war being over by the time it arrived, and Barbareños considered the men a particularly rough lot. Perhaps some of them were; the Stevenson Regiment had all kinds in it, and Company F was probably pretty much of a cross-section. The roughness of its men, however, when it comes to specific cases, seems to have consisted mostly in playing in the town streets what the Barbareños considered an outlandish game with a ball which the soldiers pursued with loud shouts and oaths across the private property of quiet and respectable citizens.

Whatever their degree of roughness, the men of Company F were in due course mustered out, and most of them disappeared from Santa Barbara's streets, making their way like everybody else up into the foothills of northern California to search for gold. Ed Power died that year; the contemporary historian who notes the fact does not say how. As for Jack, now known as "Powers," he evidently considered that Los Angeles offered more scope for his special talents, for the record picks him up in that city doing very well indeed as a professional gambler. A newspaper writer of the time sets it down that in Los Angeles Powers "made many friends among the sporting men and politicians" and adds with a touch of asperity, "The reader may wonder that these two classes are thus mentioned together, but he may feel assured that

the moral worth of either class is nothing to speak of."
There was talk that Jack was the most successful of all
the city's gamblers in those early years; a rumor credits
him with having possessed at one time the sum of a quarter of a million dollars in gold. It is evident that Jack
made good use of what money he had, for he came to be
accepted by many honorable men of the town as an upright and solid character. He had a way with him, no
doubt of it; Major Horace Bell who knew him, says in
his *Reminiscences* that in Los Angeles Jack carried himself "like a lion walking among rats." Bell, in fact, never
got over the impression Powers made on him; the man's
boldness and dash, his fine carriage and handsome appearance seem to have won the Major over completely.
Perhaps Jack's extraordinarily fine horsemanship had
something to do with it. There is a well-authenticated
story that he once wagered he could ride one hundred and
fifty miles in eight hours and won his bet, using twenty-
five horses altogether and covering the distance in six
hours, forty-three minutes and thirty-one seconds, including two rests of seven minutes each and an extra mile at
the end which he insisted on riding just to show how fresh
he was.

His knowledge of horses, at any rate, gave Powers his
best cover, for after some difficulty in Los Angeles he
went to work for the honored de la Guerra family in
Santa Barbara as chief horse-wrangler. He gambled on
the side to be sure, but gambling was, as now, officially
frowned upon and privately condoned. And Jack knew
everybody who was anybody, from William Dana of the
great *Rancho Nipomo*, to the Governor of the State.
More, he spent his money with a flourish, and took care

to make the flourishes count. There was the time, for example, that Powers attended the sentencing of one Zavaleta, a murderer, and heard the man say that since he was to be hanged he would at least like to go to his death in a decent suit of clothes. Jack stepped forward and declared that his tailor would give the condemned man any kind of suit he wanted, and Zavaleta was duly swung off in handsome navy-blue broadcloth at Jack's expense. On another occasion, when an Indian named Alisal was sentenced to death, there was some doubt about his guilt and a petition had gone to the Governor for commutation of the sentence. The day for the execution arrived, no word had come from the Governor, and the man was about to be hanged when Jack Powers boldly climbed halfway up the gallows steps and made an impassioned speech, moving for stay of execution on the ground that the Governor's commutation was probably on the steamer then overdue. So well did Jack put the case that the spectators demanded a vote be taken, and the hanging was postponed. As Jack had guessed, the commutation was on the steamer, which arrived next day; but the reaction to his arbitrary act was so strong that Los Angeles' Sheriff Twist, who had permitted the unconventional postponement, was forced to resign.

It was this talent for the dramatic gesture that kept Powers out of serious trouble for several years, even though it was widely known that his influence with the courts was far more powerful than that of any honest man. It had been strong enough, on one occasion, so that nothing happened to Jack even when he went so far as to defy the law to eject him from a ranch he had leased from Don Nicolas Den and then tried to steal, claiming it as government land, when the lease expired. The thing had blown up into a full-scale siege, with Jack and fifteen of his adherents defending their fort in the Arroyo Burro and the sheriff assembling an army of some two hundred men, equipped with a small cannon, to capture Powers and his crowd. Powers had laid in a good supply of food and fine wines, invited to his headquarters an assortment of willing ladies, and hired several musicians to keep everybody in good spirits, but in spite of these comic-opera touches, the affair might have been a very nasty one; in fact there was one sharp brush which did end in bloodshed, when three of Jack's men rode drunkenly down the *arroyo* in an attempt to lasso the sheriff's cannon and drag it away. Two of the three were killed, and the sheriff suffered a knife-thrust which persuaded him to withdraw his forces for the moment. Then cooler heads took charge, and the greatly respected Don Pablo de la Guerra himself rode up to the Powers fort under a flag of truce. Jack listened to the old man—perhaps he felt that he had had his fun—and submitted to the law. The sheriff got well and, what with Jack's influential connections and some judicious dispensing of bribes, the incident blew over.

But men of Powers' stamp inevitably go too far. Jack continued in his lawless ways, growing bolder and more careless. People began to whisper, then openly to attribute to him and his men the thefts, the holdups, the killings that were growing so numerous in the region between Santa Barbara and San Luis Obispo. And there were signs that in spite of his personal charm and good friends in high places the citizens were getting tired of his high-handedness. There was the case, for example, of the ruffian named Dunn.

Dunn was known to be close to Jack, and for a year or so he did much as he pleased in Santa Barbara, his specialty being to drink himself into a frenzy and then start shooting. For a time, Barbareños contented themselves with vanishing around corners whenever the word went out that the big Irishman was on one of his rampages. But one day Dunn overdid it. This time he stopped a stranger who was peacefully strolling in the plaza across from the de la Guerra house, and said to him roughly, "That's a damn fine hat you have!" The stranger replied mildly that he didn't know his hat was any of Dunn's business. Dunn persisted, "Say, I'd like that hat!" There was only one thing for the stranger to do. He reached for his revolver, saying "You can have it if you can take it!" Dunn was a shade quicker on the draw, and shot the man dead before he could fire. He was arrested and tried, but witnesses begged off and the jurors listened to Dunn's plea of self-defense. At least, some of them listened closely enough so that the jury could not agree. Dunn was tried again, this time in Los Angeles with similar results, and went free. But word went around that both judge and district attorney had received anonymous warnings that they would be killed if Dunn were found guilty, and people generally said that certain jurors had been bribed. When Dunn continued in his violent habit, attempting to shoot still another man—this time he used a shotgun which happily missed fire—it was just too much. He was sentenced to State's Prison, and though Powers let it be known that he would rescue the prisoner when he was being transferred from the jail to the San Francisco steamer, the new sheriff swore in twenty-five deputies and issued firm instructions that they were to concentrate their fire on two persons, Dunn and Powers, the moment anyone made a move that looked suspicious. Powers was there on the beach on steamer day with thirty of his friends, but if they had made any plans they thought better of them. Dunn, in irons, was marched between armed deputies to the boat and put aboard without Powers or his men making any move.

Jack's time was running out; that was the truth of it. He made one more dramatic gesture, taking under his wing a disreputable character, a venal judge named Edward McGowan who had fled San Francisco just in time to escape the angry Vigilance Committee of 1856. Jack probably saved McGowan's life; certainly the Judge thought so at the time, though in his memoirs he writes with some indignation about the hours he was forced to spend inside the flea-infested carpet in which Powers had been inspired to roll him while he and his men led the Vigilante pursuers hallooing down alleys and around corners until they were worn out and abandoned the chase. The whole of Southern California laughed; a dishonest judge from San Francisco was nothing much to them, and Jack had turned an amusing trick.

But the Powers luck had changed. In 1858 he and his gang planned a big coup, a holdup of two well-to-do Basque cattlemen who were known to have bought a large herd in Ventura County and would be driving their cattle northward past Santa Barbara. Usually Powers laid out his strategy in such affairs so that things went off smoothly, but in this case everything went wrong. The Basque brothers did not obey Powers' injunction to surrender, even though it was obvious that they were outnumbered; instead, both began shooting. Powers and his gang had either to run or kill the pair of them, and they chose the latter course. The Frenchmen had time to put a bullet into Jack's horse, which belonged to one of the de la Guerra family, and to wound Jack severely in the leg. This was what finished Powers, for although friends hid him, sending privately for Doctor Brinkerhoff to dress the wound, the honest doctor reported the incident. Perhaps he may have been a trifle irritated by Jack's bland assumption that he would be a party to crime; at any rate he remarked afterward, "Powers said he had a neglected boil, painfully irritated by riding. He must think I know very little of my profession to mistake a gunshot wound for a boil!" The result was the spontaneous formation of a company of fifty vigilantes in San Luis Obispo County. Handsomely caparisoned in red flannel shirts and white straw hats—the description comes from a contemporary newspaper report—but fully determined to hunt down the murderers, this unofficial posse descended on Santa Barbara and Jack at last concluded his number was up. Friends helped him once more, and he made his escape to Mexico. California never saw him again. A few years later a final report on him came from Sonora. The dashing, handsome Jack Powers had got into a drunken brawl with some of his men on the ranch where he had settled, and one of them had shot him. His body had been found some time later, half devoured by the starving hogs in the corral into which the killer had thrown it.

While Southern California was having its peculiar troubles, first with revolution-cum-robbery and then with organized gangsterism such as Powers', the mining country to the northward began to realize that the work of Harry Love's Rangers in removing the threat of the "five Joaquins" had not put an end to trouble. In the gold region, however, the pattern was quite different from that set in the south by Salomon Pico, Flores, and Powers. After the rangers dissolved there had been a few group attempts to terrorize the mines; the reader has already seen how Tom Bell for one and Rattlesnake Dick for another had tried to apply the gang principle to their operations. But Bell was hunted down quickly, and Dick discovered that he simply had not the capacity for leadership needed to hold together a band of outlaws. What now disturbed the foothill area was a series of individual stickup men, all interested almost exclusively in one thing —the Wells, Fargo treasure-box. Now and then these robbers would work in twos and threes, but such alliances were temporary; there were no successful gangs in the mines after the middle Fifties. The next two decades in the gold country were the years of the lone highwayman.

The greatest of these—the greatest, so many believe, of all holdup men that ever worked the roads—was Black Bart, whose career the reader has already followed in this book. But there were many others, unimportant by comparison with Bart but nevertheless a thorn in the side of Wells, Fargo and the rest of the express and freighting companies that did business in the hills. In 1885, Wells, Fargo's Detectives James B. Hume and John N. Thacker compiled for their employers a *Robber's Record*, which catalogues the men the authors succeeded in sending to prison for stage-robberies in the years from 1875 to 1883. The list runs to more than two hundred names. Seven of these were eventually hanged. During the period only eleven bandits were killed. Stage-drivers and passengers were more fortunate; only four of each met death in that time, though many more were wounded in holdups.

In most cases, the road-agents were an ordinary lot; frequently they were captured after their first try. Often they failed entirely to stop the stage; drivers and shotgun messengers were alert and courageous, and men like George Hackett (one of whose bullets carried away Bart's hat in the only stage-robbery, excepting his last, when he was fired upon), were not easily intimidated. Now and then a pleasant oddity turns up in the old files. Such an affair was one in which the same George Hackett was involved—the holdup of a stage between Forest City and Marysville which remains a highlight of some sort in the annals of stage-robbery in California because the two men who perpetrated it had decided, for reasons best known to themselves, to do the job clad only in long underwear and their handkerchief-masks. They had reckoned without the shotgun messenger. At the shout, "Halt, and throw down the box!" Hackett raised his gun and took aim. The two men turned and ran before he could fire, and Hackett jumped down and went after them, shotgun in hand. The men had vanished, but in the brush he found their clothes and a valise in which there was six hundred and twenty dollars that had been taken the day before from the Forbestown-Marysville stage. In one pair of pants, moreover, there was two hundred and fifty-six dollars in gold coin. Hackett gathered up valise and trousers, took them back to the stage and tossed them up to the driver, suggesting that he move stage and passengers half a mile or so farther on, to a clearing where no surprise was possible. Then he went back to the place where he had found the robbers' loot. One of the men was there; it was plain that he was looking for his pants. Hackett arrested him promptly and a court gave him fifteen years in the penitentiary. No one learned what became of the second robber. Nor had anyone thought to ask the prisoner why he and his partner had chosen to do the job trouserless.

There was the ghost-robber of Nevada City, too, a flesh-and-blood shade with a wry sense of humor.

It was no ghost, of course, but a man; a bad egg who had taken to the road and adopted as his alias the name of "Jack Williams." There had been a Jack Williams thereabouts, earlier hanged for assuming too great a degree of freedom with his own pistols and other men's pokes, wherefore when the new Williams announced himself he was immediately dubbed "Jack Williams' Ghost." Nevada City's town marshal, Steven Venard, disposed of him eventually, but before the marshal had shown that he could shoot faster and better than the ectoplasmic bandit, the latter had committed one wholesale robbery as cheerfully bizarre as any in the long California record.

Jack Williams' Ghost, like many another stickup man (one remembers Jack Shepard on Hounslow Heath and Robin Hood in Sherwood Forest), had a regular beat. This was the short stretch of road that connected the adjacent camps of Nevada City and Grass Valley. After the ghost-robber had held up a dozen or so travelers on that particular highway, a local citizen named Hilton boasted that he could and would traverse the ghost-patrolled stretch—at night, moreover, and afoot—and arrive in Grass Valley, hide and purse intact. He was quite firm about it; no ghost, or robber calling himself a ghost, would get very far with him. Word of the brag came to Jack Williams' Ghost who accepted the challenge.

As things fell out, traffic between Nevada City and Grass Valley was exceptionally heavy on the evening that Hilton set out to make his boast good. Five time altogether, the Ghost stepped out of the darkness, issued his order to halt, frisked his victim, and ordered him to stand at the side of the road, hands folded on his head, while the Ghost waited for Hilton to come along. All five did as they were told. Then Hilton walked around a turn, and the robber stepped out for the sixth time. He must have been at least mildly surprised that the braggart made no attempt to resist, but he relieved him of sixty dollars and his pistol, stood him up beside the others, warned them all that if they stirred a step he would fire on them from behind, and faded into the night. It was ten minutes before Hilton dared move, to discover that the Ghost was long gone and that the six of them were alone, foolishly standing in a row beside an empty road. On the way back, Hilton explained very carefully to his fellow-victims how the thing had happened. In the dark, he said, he had taken them for members of the Ghost's gang. It was a perfectly natural mistake. No man in his right mind would attempt resistance against half a dozen armed bandits, would he? Of course not. Anyone could see that. There is no record of what the other five replied.

El Dorado County's most famous robbery, the holdup at Bullion Bend, also had its curious angles. This was in the Sixties, and the stage was loaded with Comstock wealth and the Comstock wealthy, but that was not what made the affair interesting. The really unique features of the event were three. The leader of the robber-gang turned out to be an ex-officer of the law; his men were, or claimed to be, Confederate soldiers; and one of them who styled himself "Captain Ingram" not only wrote out a proper receipt for the eight heavy sacks of silver he took from under the driver's seat, but had the consummate gall—and the oratorical genius—to talk the passengers into passing a hat so that the sacred cause of the South might gain a few extra dollars over and above Wells, Fargo & Company's contribution. At the scene of the holdup things went off neatly enough, but in the subsequent pursuit several men were killed before the fire-eaters from Dixie were caught some two hundred miles away near San José where they had designs on the payroll of the New Almaden quicksilver mine. Most of the loot was recovered, though nobody ever found a way to redeem "Captain Ingram's" receipt.

For the most part, however, robberies in the gold country in the Sixties and Seventies were fairly humdrum affairs and the robbers a colorless lot. There were the exceptions this book has noted in some of its earlier chapters. There were a few lesser lights with originality enough about them, in name or deed, so that they are remembered.

In Placerville one Richard Crone, a notorious gambler suspected of robbery, known as Irish Dick and also as New Orleans Dick, stabbed and killed a miner in an argument about a debt, figuring that he and his fellow-gamblers were strong enough in the camp so that no one would dare to punish him. Two thousand miners gathered in town that night to prove him wrong. Sheriff Rogers and Judge Humphries did their best to keep the thing legal, but the mob did not approve and Dick was hanged there and then. Over toward Coloma Sam Brown, a known thief and bully, was luckier for a time when the law stepped in and saved him from the rope after he had wantonly killed a bystander in a saloon on the Hangtown road. Brown had a lawyer who knew how to take advantage of technicalities, and he served only three years for that crime. But he chose to shift base to the new Comstock camp of Virginia City, and found he had tackled something too big for him. When he celebrated his arrival in that wide-open camp by shooting an inoffensive drunk in a saloon, the proprietor quietly lifted from behind the bar a short-barreled shotgun filled with lead slugs and blew Mr. Brown out of Washoe County for good. A town never disposed to suffer outlaws gladly was Marysville, home of Stephen J. Field who was a brother of Cyrus the ocean cable-layer and great-uncle of Rachel Field, whose *All This and Heaven Too* contributed its bit to the literature of high crime as most readers will remember. Judge Field, later Chief Justice of the U. S. Supreme Court, may have had something to do with Marysville's insistence upon summary treatment of criminals on the one hand and complete fairness on the other. At any rate, when an innkeeper named Dunbar unaccountably disappeared, and his cook, a young man from Lowell, Massachusetts, took over the hotel, Marysville peace officers decided they'd better look into things. They found Dunbar; he was tidily inhumed in the far corner of his own corral. They found the young cook, too, though he had skipped after questioning; he was in San Francisco, just about to embark for Panama. They also found two men holed up in a cabin on Rabbit Creek, not

far from the late Mr. Dunbar's hotel. The cook accused
the Rabbit Creek pair; they retaliated by swearing that
he and no other had murdered Dunbar. Marysville was
confused, but not for long. A rope was brought and the
two friends were swung off together, cursing the cook
with their last breath. Certain hotheads were certain
from this that the cook was guilty too, and a noose was
settled about his neck when a Marysville citizen stepped
upon a box and made a plea for democratic justice. "This
kind of thing," he concluded, "calls for a vote. All in
favor of hanging this man step downhill! All opposed
step uphill!" It looked as though the cook would get off;
the uphill move was clearly greater, and two of the crowd
made a quick count and struggled through to inform the
prisoner of his good fortune. No one, however, had
thought to suggest that the rope be left slack. When the
messengers of mercy reached the cook they found he had
been strangled to death in the excitement. But Marysville had retained its reputation for impartiality and fair
dealing.

These small-time criminals were hardly holdup men,
of course, though those mentioned had done their bit at
armed robbery too. There were others, such men as Big-
Foot Andrus, or John M. Brannan who rejoiced in the
sobriquet of Johnny-Behind-the-Rocks (recalling Ari-
zona's tinhorn gambler, Johnny-Behind-the-Deuce, a decade later), or James Harrington who called himself "The
Emigrant Boy" and served five terms in San Quentin for
highway-robbery before he saw the error of his ways,
or "Liverpool" Norton (Wells, Fargo's George Hackett
caught him too), or the man Pratt who stuck up six
stages, served six sentences and finally died in prison

under the name of "Charlie the Shoemaker," or the Wisconsin bad man named Wilson who chose the unlikely pseudonym of "Otto Schwartzwalter." These and a few more flashed briefly across the consciousness of the mining-camp region and were forgotten as Detective Hume and his men ran them down and put them away. Of the lot, only one has spark enough to make him worth more than brief mention. He was the last of the notable gold-region bandits with the single exception of the remarkable Black Bart, who outshone him in every way. (Tiburcio Vasquez, of course, was still to get his come-uppance, but his depredations were committed in the Coast Range country and not in the gold region.) We shall close this chronicle with the story of Vasquez. Meantime, a quick look at a final item of California Baroque in the bandit line—a tattooed, sandy-haired, dapper New Yorker soberly named John Allen but more widely known in his time by the singular nickname of "Sheet-Iron Jack."

The trouble with John Allen was that he knew too much about horses and too little about other people's ideas of honesty.

There was a rumor that he was a minister's son; from all reports he had been well educated for his time. He was a smallish man, though for some reason contemporary newspaper writers invariably describe him as "tall and handsome"; the San Quentin records show him to have been five feet six and one-half inches. At any rate he had a good deal of charm, as his escapades demonstrated; and his gray eyes and reddish-brown hair, the red-and-blue flags and undressed ladies with which his forearms were tattooed, his innocently fair complexion and his gallant manner of speech all made him well liked in Shasta County at the tail-end of the Sixties.

Jack Allen was in his middle twenties when he practiced the barber's trade in the prosperous camps of the region. Men made allowances for his drinking habits which were perhaps somewhat more extravagant than most men's, even for the time and place, and enjoyed his rambling talk as he trimmed their hair and shaved them in the small shop where he worked. The girls (it is of record) said he "danced like an angel." But it was not long before people began to wonder about him. John Allen had too much money to spend; it didn't seem as though it could all come out of his wages. Still, he had a nice knack at the guitar, he had picked up enough Spanish to sing the sentimental Mexican airs in a languishing baritone, and there was no denying he was excellent company. A certain amount of whispering went on, but for a year or two no one said anything specific about Jack, although more horses than ever before were stolen in the northern valleys overlooked by the peaks of Mount Shasta, Yolla Bally, and Lassen.

Then suddenly the news was out. Jack Allen had been caught redhanded, slipping into the hills with three horses about whose proper ownership there could be no possible doubt. He had spurred his own mount, yelled back surprisingly violent imprecations at the five men who had unexpectedly come upon him in their search for the animals, and disappeared into the rough brush undisturbed by the fact that two of the party, known to be good shots, had fired both barrels of their shotguns after him. The little group rode back to town with the two horses Jack had abandoned and reported that what people had been wondering about the barber was true. One of the men was quite definite about another matter. When he and his companion had fired at Jack he had distinctly heard the shot "strike hard," though the fleeing man had not faltered. It sounded, he said, as though he had shot at a bird on a tin roof. From that moment John Allen had his nickname; he was Sheet-Iron Jack.

Now the sheriffs of the northern counties were on the lookout for Jack and he had his chance to show his mettle. He had also the opportunity to indulge the love of the spotlight which must have been very near the surface in the loquacious, guitar-playing little barber who danced so angelically and sang romantic songs. Shortly after he took to outlawry, the sheriff of Tehama County was out after him for another horse-stealing. Jack took advantage of the fact that this particular peace officer had never laid eyes on him, innocently joined the party, charmed them all with song and anecdote and, when they stopped for the night at a lonely roadhouse, bunked with the sheriff himself at the latter's invitation. Before daylight Jack slipped quietly out of the room—remembering to drive his knife firmly into the doorpost outside to hold the sheriff prisoner in case he awoke—and tiptoed down to the corral. There he unerringly chose the best horse, transferred his own saddle to the animal, and departed, leading two more of the posse's mounts. It was still dark when he stopped at a settler's cabin a mile or two away, begged a candle, and by its light wrote a pleasant letter of thanks to the sheriff. The settler directed the posse as well as he could when its members arrived some hours later. The best they could do was to trace Jack and their stolen mounts to where his trail disappeared into the wilds of the Trinities.

Jack went on with his successful thefts. Horses were his specialty, but now and then he held up a lone traveler. All victims reported that he did not bother to disguise himself, even to the extent of a mask, and that his discourse while relieving them of their valuables was both elevating and amusing. Once, when some angry ranchers were no more than an hour behind him, he stopped at a Saturday night dance, chose the prettiest girl there and stepped up to her partner, announcing that he was Sheet-Iron Jack and that he would do himself the honor of dancing with the young lady. He repeated this with half a dozen of the girls present (though he wore a revolver, the testimony is that he did not draw it), then looked at his watch and remarked to the company that he was sorry but some acquaintances of his would interrupt his pleasure if he remained longer. In the doorway he turned and added that it was a pity the young men were not as brave as the young ladies were handsome, mounted his horse, and clattered off into the night. Twenty minutes later the searchers arrived and listened to the story. One member reported that it was the girls from whom they got the details; the men seemed to prefer to remain silent.

On another occasion, Jack made a firm friend by what appeared to be a wholly disinterested good deed, though in the end it turned out that he had combined profit with kindness.

The incident took place in Tehama County where Jack encountered a young German greenhorn sitting disconsolately by the side of the road, his shoes off and his expression woebegone. Asked what he was doing afoot in such country, the boy told Jack his story. He had started on his journey mounted, but his horse had gone lame, and while he was wondering what to do a mountaineer had met him, looked the horse over, declared that the lameness would be a year in the curing, and offered him thirty dollars for the beast, take it or leave it. The tenderfoot, not knowing what else to do, had accepted the thirty dollars and started to walk to the nearest stage-station, a matter of some eighteen mountain miles. Jack quizzed him further and learned that the young man's horse had been shod the same morning in one of the valley towns; the beast's lameness, plainly, was due to careless shoeing. Without doubt the mountaineer, whom Jack recognized from the young German's description, had swindled the boy thoroughly. Jack told him so, adding, "But this is my beat, and nobody has any business doing any swindling here but me!" Telling the lad to wait where he was, Jack rode off, found the mountaineer—a man named Phillips—forced him at gunpoint to identify the greenhorn's horse and told him that as for the thirty dollars, he, Jack, would take that as his "lawyer's fee." Phillips objected, and Jack said grimly, "If you'd kept your mouth shut you'd have been better off!" adding, "I should have remembered that a lawyer always takes all his client has got!" Phillips surrendered his gun and some six hundred dollars more. Jack rode back to where the German boy was waiting, returned the horse, and told him to keep the thirty dollars, explaining why the animal had gone lame and how to watch a blacksmith to make sure he did not shoe a horse too tightly. Then he sent the boy on his way with the advice not to come back, since now Jack would consider him fair game and next time would most certainly take his horse and anything else he had. The boy told the story to the marshal in Redding, but stoutly maintained that Sheet-Iron Jack was a good man and his friend.

Perhaps if he had been less gregarious Jack would have managed to keep clear of the law. But there is no use in being a good talker, after all, unless you can now and then count on an audience, and singing or playing a guitar to one's self can become a dull affair. So one evening Jack concluded he would like a little company, and rode down into Shasta, walking into a bar and ordering a drink with all the nonchalance of a man who had never so much as thought that anybody was looking for him. Even then he might have got away with it, but he drank too much and got into a row in the saloon of his choice. Words led to action, and though Jack's shot inflicted only a slight flesh wound on his victim, the crowd at the bar disapproved in principle. They grabbed him and turned him over to the town constable. He was sentenced to two years in San Quentin. Riding handcuffed in the down stage, a deputy by his side, he had another chance at the spotlight and took it. Just outside the town the passengers heard a shout and then the roar of a gun and the rattle of buckshot on the stage. It was an attempted holdup which cost the driver, Jerry Culverhouse, the sight of one eye and retired him from the road. After firing their single shot, the two robbers had thought better of it and were retreating when Jack stuck his head from the window. Wrote the editor of the Shasta *Courier* next day: "Sheet-Iron Jack cussed the robbers until the very air smelled like brimstone, and small streaks of lightning flashed from his mouth and played in fiery circles around his head. He said that it was an unmitigated outrage that a man could not be permitted to travel over Shasta County territory, especially when he was on his way to work for the interest of the State, without having his life endangered by shots fired by murderous highwaymen."

One wonders whether this attempted robbery may not have set Jack thinking. His stay in San Quentin was short, for his lawyer found a way to have the sentence set aside on technical grounds, and after only five months in prison Jack was sent back to be tried again. This time his jailers must have been careless; within a week Jack had escaped. And now his ideas had taken a new turn. With two ex-convicts named Toney and Chapman he did a little careful planning. Then, three times within a week, the partners held up the stages out of Redding—two headed for Shasta, on November 6 and again on November 8, 1876, and one going north to Yreka on November 11. But Jack had always done better working alone. After the third holdup the sheriff caught Toney and Chapman, and from them learned first that their fellow-bandit had been Sheet-Iron Jack and then where he was hiding. All three were tried, convicted, and sentenced for the robberies in less than a month, and early in December Jack was on his way to San Quentin once more; this time his sentence was twenty-four years. Even this did not dampen his spirits entirely. When a passer-by recognized him in the stage as it paused in Red Bluff and called out to ask where he was going, Jack replied with dignity, "I am going where I can get some sea breeze. This northern climate does not agree with my health, and I find I must make a change."

Jack stayed in prison for six years. Then, in 1882, Governor Perkins was prevailed upon to review his case, and came to the conclusion that he had been convicted on insufficient evidence. What with this and the fact that prison officials said his conduct had been "uniformly good," the Governor decided to commute his sentence, though he added the proviso that he must leave the State and never return. He was discharged on June 25, 1883.

It would be kinder to Jack's memory to leave him at this point, and if he had obeyed the Governor's injunction to shake the dust of California from his feet this would round out his story nicely. Unhappily Jack did not leave. In the spring of 1884, the Tehama *Democrat* reported that he had been drunk and disorderly in front of Cone & Kimball's store. Nor was that all. Sheriff Morton had come up to him to suggest that he get off the street, and Jack had drawn his revolver and thrust it into the officer's face. Morton had been too quick for him; he had caught the pistol barrel and forced Jack's arm down until the weapon was reversed, saying coolly, "Pull 'er off now if you want to, Jack!" Under-sheriff Lennon and two police officers had come to the sheriff's assistance when Jack began to struggle; it "took all of them and one or two citizens" said the *Democrat*, to get him to the jail. Once more, Sheet-Iron Jack's longing for company had been his undoing. For while Jack was sleeping it off in the lockup of the town he should have stayed away from, Detective Coffee of the San Francisco police force arrived. He was pleased to hear that Jack was where he could lay hands on him easily; in fact, it was Jack he was looking for. A horse was involved, a fine animal worth a good five hundred dollars; it had been stolen in the city and sold to a pair of Frenchmen for seventy-five. The Frenchmen had got as far as Stockton and were trying to sell the horse there for two hundred and fifty dollars when the police found them. They had a bill-of-sale covering their purchase, which left them in the clear. It was plainly signed "John Allen." The little ex-barber had not added his nickname, Sheet-Iron Jack, but he might as well have put it all down. Sheriff Morton assured Detective Coffee that his man would be where he could find him in the morning. He was. By that time they wanted Jack on yet another count. When the two officers were at breakfast an agitated station-agent rushed in to report that his safe had been robbed the night before. Now they understood how Jack happened to have seven hundred dollars on him when, a day or two earlier, he had been so hard up that he had sold a five-hundred-dollar horse for seventy-five dollars.

This time they put Sheet-Iron Jack in Folsom Prison; the record says that it was done at the prisoner's own instance, though why he preferred Folsom is not explained. Perhaps the speech in which he made the request was a final flicker of Jack's irresistible urge to focus attention on himself. The Judge did not discuss his reasons for granting Jack's request, and apparently nobody ever asked Jack. This was Sheet-Iron Jack's last official brush with the law. He served his term, was discharged, and may have taken Governor Perkins' advice to leave the State. A writer of fifty years ago, romancing in an old magazine about early-day outlaws, hints that Jack made his way from Folsom up to the rugged country of the lava beds and hid out there with "his friends, the Modoc Indians." Maybe he did.

# TIBURCIO VASQUEZ

**T**HE SEVENTIES AND EARLY Eighties saw the last of the long line of California's stage-robbers. Gold shipments were fewer and smaller. (The reader will recall that Black Bart's last haul was under five thousand dollars.) In many regions the railroad had made the coach obsolete, and even where it hung on, the increasingly well-organized express system with its armed guards, its able detectives, and its tenacity in pursuit had proved that holding up stages no longer paid. The stage-robber had had his day. But while he had been fading from the picture—and all banditry in California with him, for that matter—one man had held out. This was Vasquez, whose band, operating much in the manner of the Joaquins of the early gold-rush time, had managed to continue in existence through the Sixties and on into the Seventies, even while organized outlawry was being wiped out every-where else. Just as Black Bart was the last of the great stage-robbers, Vasquez and his followers constituted the last of the gangs. With his capture, trial, and legal execu-tion, and with the consequent break-up of his band. broad-scale lawlessness in California came to an end.

Tiburcio Vasquez, last of the Mexican bandits that infested California from the earliest gold-rush years well into the Seventies, was finally run to earth in the spring of 1874. Never one to give in quietly, he had made a run for it when the Los Angeles sheriff's posse surprised him in his hideout in the Cahuenga hills, and not until several shots were fired—including a blast from a shotgun in the hands of a reporter representing the San Francisco *Chronicle*—did he surrender. Later that day, when he was safely in the Los Angeles jail, the editor of the *Herald* managed to get an interview with him. At first Vasquez refused; he was weak from loss of blood. Buckshot from the reporter's gun had caught him in the left arm, the left leg, the left side of the head, and high in the chest, passing out under the arm. But he had been bandaged and fed, and when they told him that the interview would be printed also in the San Francisco papers and doubtless in the big journals of the East, he consented to talk. He understood English well, but preferred to reply through an interpreter, and Sheriff Rowland undertook the chore. Mr. Bassett of the *Herald* asked him, among other things, how he happened to start on his career of crime, and Vasquez told him much the same story that was later found to be a matter of record in Monterey County. It involved a brawl with the police in which Vasquez may or may not have been guilty of attacking an officer, but with a record of previous scrapes against him he had felt that his only hope lay in leaving Monterey. Editor Bassett's account quotes Vasquez as saying, "I got my mother's blessing and told her I was going out into the world to suffer and take my chances." Bassett seems to have felt that something more specific was indicated, for he writes, "I asked him what he meant by that, and he replied, 'That I should live off the world and perhaps suffer at its hands!'"

For more than twenty years Tiburcio lived off the world. Eventually, as might have been expected considering the methods he chose, he suffered at its hands; he was hanged by the neck until he was dead, in San José, California, and with a good deal more in the way of ceremony, sob-sistering, and outside interference from publicity-seekers, including a minister of the gospel, than his case warranted. For those two-decades-and-a-bit he and his band had robbed and killed pretty much as they pleased, making themselves one of the major headaches among many that afflicted peace officers everywhere in the State in those days. Black Bart was still to come; he had not even dreamed up his nickname when Vasquez was swung off. And there was Dick Fellows, of course, though the career of that singular horseman and would-be holdup expert came nearer to comedy than to tragedy. These men, however, were of a gentler kidney; as the reader will recall, Bart never so much as fired a single shot in his eight-year career, and Fellows seemed content to hope that his fierce and bearded aspect would be as effective as powder and ball. But Vasquez and his gang were real trouble; death followed in their wake as well as fire and robbery. No one after the Joaquins had such a reputation. And no other California bandit dodged the law as long and as successfully as Vasquez. It is not surprising that his name has become something of a legend, nor that the legend had begun to burgeon almost as soon as he was hanged. Only four year after his death, Robert Louis Stevenson in Monterey, writing his piece, *The Old Pacific Capital*, spoke of Vasquez to prove the clannishness of Monterey's Mexican population; his point was that "Vasquez, the bandit" had been able to come back to Monterey and walk the streets fearing no man. Stevenson's casual reference seems to indicate that he assumed his readers might easily have heard of Vasquez, and very likely they had.

But a legend is one thing, and fact rather frequently is something else. Because he came later, Vasquez was somewhat less fictionized than Joaquin Murieta for example. Yet the sentimental folk-pattern may be detected in far too much that has been written about him. Since the record is detailed and exact, though the romanticizers have carefully avoided referring to it, perhaps it is as well to tell his story as historians, reporters, editors, sheriffs, and State and county records of the time reflect it. If his life and career were not according to the Robin Hood formula, as too many have tried to make them seem, there is still a story in them, and one fully as interesting in another way.

Tiburcio Vasquez may or may not have been descended from a man of the same name who came colonizing from Mexico in 1777, settled near the San Francisco Mission, and removed to San José in 1783. H. H. Bancroft cautiously says the bandit "may have been" the grandson of the original Tiburcio, but lets it go at that. A man of the same name was major-domo at the Mission Dolores in 1840, according to Hittell's history, and he could have been identical with the Tiburcio Vasquez who appeared as witness in a San Francisco land case with which the Vigilance Committee of 1856 improperly concerned itself, though whether he was a son of the original Tiburcio or father of the later one, or both, has not been proved.

At any rate, the boy Tiburcio, who grew up to terrorize Californians for so many years, was born in Monterey County, perhaps in the town of Monterey, and probably in August, 1837. (Vasquez himself is authority for this date, though various "biographers" have spread his birth all the way from 1835 to 1839.)

The boy was eleven when the news of gold first excited Californians, and when he was fifteen and got into his first serious trouble it was still only 1852 and the gold rush was at its peak. The prejudice against "foreigners" in the mines still raged unabated; the Joaquins were taking toll of the miners' lives and purses; Californians of Mexican descent found themselves a minority group and the objects of active discrimination. It was wholly logical that when young Tiburcio was suddenly at outs with the law he should conclude, first, that he had little hope of a fair hearing, and then that he would emulate the exploits of the Joaquins who had the State by the ears. Wherefore, when the hotheaded youngster found himself in the middle of a dance-hall quarrel in which a man was knifed, and officers came to arrest him, he skipped, making his way north to Mendocino County. He had word there from friends that the stabbing had been forgotten and that he might safely come back to Monterey, but before he could settle into any peaceful routine the police came looking for him once more. This time, apparently, they intended only to question him, but the boy had little confidence in such justice as the police might dispense to a Mexican and there was a short, brisk fight—later Vasquez steadfastly denied that anyone was killed—and young Tiburcio escaped again. This time he concluded, as he afterward told Editor Bassett, to "live off the world."

His apprenticeship was thorough. One writer has said that Vasquez became a member of Murieta's gang, but there is no evidence, and the dates do not correspond well. By the time he had made up his mind to live the life of an outlaw, the Joaquins had only a few months to go; Captain Love was close on their trail and soon caught up with them. If the Joaquins had wanted a fifteen-year-old boy along, and if Tiburcio had made his way to where they were hiding and had been accepted, it is possible he raided and robbed in their company for a month or two, but since the suggestion is made by only one of the many who have told Vasquez' story in one form or another, and since no proof is offered, the likelihood that he was a member of the gang is slight. In any event, Tiburcio learned fast enough under the tutor he chose, one García whose rascally career in the Monterey region was abruptly and unofficially ended by a rope while he was still teaching the young man the tricks of his trade. His master's taking-off convinced young Vasquez that for the moment this part of the State was too touchy about cattle-stealing, and he made himself scarce. For two or three years his name was mentioned now and then as an associate of several more notable thieves who preyed on the cattlemen of the Coast Range hills, but official records do not pick him up until 1857, when he was just twenty years old. In August of that year he was sentenced to five years in State's Prison for horse-stealing. He appears on the prison books as Number 1217, his name spelled "Basquez." This phonetically excusable error on the part of a Yankee prison secretary almost enabled Tiburcio to fool the authorities a few

years later. For he had served not quite two years of his
sentence when, in the general prison break of 1859, he
made his escape. Why he then chose to move up into the
mining country was never explained, but he found the
people of that region coldly inhospitable to thieves and
exceptionally good at catching them. Seven weeks from the
date he escaped from San Quentin he was back again, sentenced to one year for larceny in Amador County. This
time he was entered on the records as "Tebuzzo Baskes"
and nothing was said about his having been in San Quentin
before. Some sharp-eyed clerk discovered the mistake—or
perhaps a fellow-prisoner mentioned the matter in return
for an extra tobacco ration—and Tiburcio's record bears
an added footnote: "Same as Tiburcio Basquez who escaped June 25, 1859." He served his year plus the three
left over from the earlier sentence. He was discharged
August 13, 1863.

A writer of the period says that Vasquez next "behaved
himself, so to speak, by going into the more honest and
less dangerous profession of gambling." The New Almaden
quicksilver mines near San José were operating then on
forced production schedules; Chancellorsville and Gettys-
burg had just been fought and wars jump the demand for
mercury. Oddly, Vasquez seems to have got into no trouble
over his gambling directly; perhaps profit was easy enough,
what with the large payrolls at the mines, and anyhow
the percentage of Spanish and Mexican miners was high
and they were the ones least likely to bring any little dif-
ficulties to the attention of the law. Just the same, the
evidence is that though his gambling may have gone well
enough, Vasquez still needed money. The next year an
Italian butcher near the workings was found dead in his

bed; he had been both stabbed and shot. The sum of four hundred dollars, known to have been in his possession, was missing. Here, if the story is true, Vasquez showed remarkable coolness under pressure. An inquest was held, and for the purpose an interpreter was needed. Vasquez knew a little English, whereas none of the witnesses did and neither the coroner nor his jury knew any Spanish to speak of. Tiburcio, therefore, was pressed into service. Sheriff Adams and Coroner J. A. Cory heard what testimony they could drag out of those most likely to have any to give, but no arrests were made. The next day Vasquez disappeared. A short time afterward, the sheriff became convinced from what he called "information received" (the phrase has a Scotland Yard ring), that Vasquez and a local bad character musically named Faustino Lorenzo were concerned in the murder, but there was not enough evidence, and neither man was charged.

For a year or two Vasquez kept on the move. Still operating in a fairly small way, he roamed Contra Costa, Sonoma, and Mendocino counties, turning up occasionally in the newspapers in connection with a horse-stealing here, a cattle theft there. No officer laid a hand on him. There is a story, told by two of those who have written about him, that Vasquez ran away with the daughter of a rancher near Mount Diablo, but details are confused. In one version, the father caught up with the pair near Livermore, shot Vasquez in the arm, and inflicted a flesh wound on his daughter in the excitement. According to this story, Tiburcio galloped off nursing his injured arm and never saw his inamorata again. The other story has Vasquez breaking an arm when his horse fell, recovering under the tender ministrations of the rancher's daughter, and then

eloping with her. This version agrees with the first in the
particulars about the encounter in Livermore Valley, and
the father's recovery of his daughter, though there is no
mention of the girl's being injured and the reporter does
not specify whether the parental bullet lodged in Vasquez'
broken arm or the other one.

The tale may have some foundation; at least it de-
velops one side of Tiburcio's character—his talents as a
lady-killer. For this aspect of the man is mentioned too
often to be ignored. It got him into one fight after another,
often with his own friends, as in the case of his abduction
of the young and handsome wife of an otherwise respectable citizen named Salazar who frequently sheltered the
outlaw in his house. Vasquez ran off with her too, and was
shot through the neck for his pains by his indignant host,
who then went to the length of swearing out a complaint
against Tiburcio for intent to murder, on the ground
that when he had charged him with stealing his wife the
outlaw had drawn his pistol. The Grand Jury found a true
bill, but Vasquez kept hidden. And there is a long and circumstantial tale that Vasquez coolly took the wife of one
of his own men, a Chileño named Leiva who had been a
blacksmith at the New Idria cinnabar mines before turning bandit. As King David had done some three thousand
years earlier, Tiburcio began his campaign by sending a
husband on a dangerous mission. Unlike Uriah the injured Leiva returned safe and sound and, when he saw
what was going on, calmly took care of it in his own way.
He surrendered immediately to the sheriff and turned
state's evidence. On his information one of the gang was
captured and given a life sentence, but Vasquez could not
be found. The story goes that he kept Leiva's wife with

him until she was well along in pregnancy and then callously abandoned her in the hills where she was accidentally found and rescued. Leiva may or may not have taken her back; contemporary reporters disagree on that detail.

What next happened to Tiburcio, though, is clear enough. He left Monterey County for a time and near Sonoma, north of San Francisco Bay, he attempted to run off a sizeable herd of cattle. But again he was in a part of the State he did not know so well, and the hills did not afford the cover he was used to in his own range. A posse hastily assembled and found his trail easy to follow. For this offense he served three years and six months in San Quentin. Given a third try at it, the warden got his name about right; he appears on the records as "Vasques" though his first name is spelled "Teburcio." He was discharged on June 4, 1870. Now, experienced in crime, his prestige among his fellows enhanced by his three terms in State's Prison, Vasquez was ready to launch upon the four years of organized and sustained villainy that made his name a byword throughout the whole of California. What he did not know was that Alameda County's sheriff, Harry Morse, had begun to take a special interest in him, in his companions, and in his misdeeds.

Vasquez' first effort to get together an effective band of outlaws was something less than successful.

With an ex-convict, Francisco Barcenas, whom he had known in prison, he assembled several notorious characters including a Garciá Rodriguez and the handsome Procopio whom the reader has already encountered at the moment when Sheriff Harry Morse took him by the throat in a San Francisco dance hall. With these men, Tiburcio held up his first stage near Soap Lake, about twelve miles north of Hollister. The robbery went well. The driver was taken by surprise and stopped when he was told. The bandits ordered the passengers out, lined them up, and robbed them, then compelled them to lie prone while their hands were tied behind their backs and their ankles were secured. This method was to become the Vasquez trademark in all cases when victims submitted quietly. A few hours later he and his friends met Thomas McMahon, a storekeeper from Hollister who had the misfortune to be carrying some seven hundred and fifty dollars in cash with him. Vasquez and his men got that too, leaving McMahon tied and face down in the dust. As it happened he was released sooner than the stage passengers; a passer-by found him within half an hour. McMahon, who had recognized Vasquez, went straight to the authorities with the information. By pure chance Sheriff Harry Morse of Alameda County was in Monterey and when the local sheriff got the news Morse set out with him on Vasquez' trail. It was neither of the sheriffs that found the bandits, but the constable of Santa Cruz. There was a short exchange of fire. Barcenas was killed outright. Rodriguez escaped. Vasquez succeeded in wounding the constable seriously but not before receiving a bullet himself, full in the right side of the chest. Injured as he was, he managed to ride some sixty miles to the same Arroyo Cantua where the Joaquins had hidden two decades earlier, and stayed there until his wound healed. Rodriguez was captured a few days afterward and went to prison, where he died from the effects of drinking straight alcohol stolen from the dispensary. Procopio had not been in on the robbery; he was in San Francisco where Sheriff Morse found him dancing and sent him up for the nine-year term that put an end to his outlawry.

Tiburcio's injury kept him relatively quiet for some months. From his hiding place he conducted occasional raids, sometimes alone, sometimes with one or another of the new band he was beginning to gather around him. Friendly Mexican settlers once brought him news that three officers had traced him to the neighborhood of the New Idria mines. Vasquez slipped out of the little valley, coming up from the opposite direction as far as the inn where his pursuers were spending the night. In the morning the officers' horses were gone. Vasquez had them. He grew bolder in other ways, too, frequently appearing in Hollister to visit one or another of the various women for whom he appeared to have such an attraction. More than once the news that he was in town would be brought to the constable, but as always the Mexican population politely befooled the *gringo* and Tiburcio would slip quietly away. Once during this period of recovery he and the new gang he was building robbed a stage, managing it with the connivance of a friend, José Castro, ostensibly a rancher down on the San Benito. Again a group of armed deputies went out to find him, and again they were deceived and misled. They found Castro, though, and strung him up without the formality of a trial.

Then, in the early spring of 1873, Vasquez began a fresh series of organized robberies. This time he had a better organized gang and a right-hand man of some talent named Chavez. Their first crime went smoothly— the robbery of a general store at Firebaugh's Ferry. It was on this occasion that a story got about which persuaded many credulous people of Vasquez' inherent kindness. The trouble with it is that it is a little too familiar; sooner or later it has been told of every highwayman who ever took the road. Readers will recognize the familiar pattern in the tale of the woman who begged so prettily for her watch to be returned because her husband had given it to her during their courtship. Every reader who has ever listened to anecdotes of robbery will know ahead of time that the woman, charmed by the gallantry of the gentlemanly bandit who wiped a tear from his eye and handed back the watch with a deep bow, produces another watch and presents it with warm thanks to the bandit whose heart had melted at her romantic plea. (At least, in this case, the story does not require one to suppose that the lady was a kind of traveling showcase of watches; here she is allowed to run to a room behind the store to get the second one.) It is solely on this fantasy, common to every tongue in which tales of banditry are told, that the sentimentalists have based their notions of Tiburcio's essential humanity. The reader who has heard it before will judge for himself its worth as evidence.

The robbery at Firebaugh's was no more than a trial run. During the spring and summer of that year the gang worked on its technique. Stores and lonely roadside inns were robbed; horsemen were held up all through the region from San José south to Gilroy. Always the victims were tied and left face down where they had been robbed. Vasquez grew more reckless, too, appearing quite openly among the miners at New Idria who protected him at every turn; some of them said later that they had Vasquez' promise never to molest them so long as they helped him when he needed information or concealment. However this may have been, though he and his gang stole horses and robbed throughout the area, the miners were left alone. Then, in the late summer of 1873, the gang worked out its most ambitious plan to date. It was no less than a scheme to stick up a payroll car on the Southern Pacific Railroad. The planning may have been good, but the robbery never occurred. One writer says the bandits failed because they had not allowed enough time to block the track, and that the train passed safely over what was to have been an obstacle sufficient to derail it; another suggests that the Southern Pacific agent had been warned, though there is no explanation of what action he took to forestall the robbers. Since nothing came of the plan, perhaps it does not make much difference. But on the evening of the same day, August 26, 1873, Vasquez and his men were involved in what they had doubtless intended to make one more of their routine store robberies, but which turned out to be something very like a massacre. Labeled "The Tres Pinos Tragedy," this crime was what brought Sheriff Harry Morse, now widely known for his special talent at tracking criminals, all the way down from Alameda County to take charge of what was at last a seriously organized effort to wipe out Vasquez and his entire band.

The incident began like many others in which Vasquez was concerned. Two of the gang rode up to Andrew Snyder's store in Tres Pinos, dismounted, entered the building, and engaged Snyder's clerk in conversation. In a few moments five more arrived. Two tied their horses outside and went into the store, leveling pistols and ordering all present to lie on the floor. Three, one of whom was Vasquez himself, remained on watch with the horses.

Snyder's clerk, several customers, and one small boy were tied up in the usual fashion and the store was ransacked. The four members of the gang were ready to leave with the cash from the till, several bundles of clothing, tobacco, food, and liquor, and the money and watches of the customers, when there was a sudden burst of firing outside the door. When the stories of witnesses were pieced together it became clear what had happened.

At the moment when the robbers inside were about to go, a Portuguese sheepherder had come along the street and turned to enter the store. Vasquez, on guard with his two companions, ordered him to stop. The man failed to hear or was confused; whichever it was, he did not obey, and either Vasquez or one of the others shot him twice, the second bullet killing him. There were two other men, both teamsters, busy about their wagons in front of the store; they had noticed nothing out of the way until the firing and had been left unmolested. Now something had to be done. Vasquez ordered them both to lie down in the road and when one hesitated, knocked him unconscious with his revolver. The other, George Redford, was deaf and probably did not hear the order, but he realized something was wrong and ran for it. Vasquez shot him through the heart just as he reached the corner of the building. After this, events moved more rapidly. Another local man who was walking past saw and heard what was happening and headed back toward the nearby hotel, calling out to warn a Mr. and Mrs. Davidson who were just inside the door. One of the outlaws fired after him but missed and, as the man gained the hotel entrance, shouted to him and the Davidsons to close the door and stay inside and they would not be harmed. By this time Vasquez had snatched his rifle from the saddle where it hung. He ignored his companion's promise and fired through the hotel door, killing Davidson who toppled against his wife, knocking her down as he fell. Meantime a small boy, brother of the one who had been tied up, ran from the back door of the store into the stable yard. Chavez, who had been one of the four inside the store, followed him and brutally knocked him over the head with his pistol-butt.

Perhaps the old adage about the sheep and the lamb occurred to the outlaws then. At any rate they took their time, released Snyder long enough so that he might show them where he had some money hidden in his house, secured him again, and chose seven of the best horses they could find in the hotel stables. These they loaded with their plunder, and the grim procession rode out of town leaving three dead, and the teamster and small boy still unconscious.

The news of the Tres Pinos tragedy horrified the public, and fresh efforts were made to capture Vasquez. For a month or two there was a great amateur riding up and down in the Coast Range and the San Joaquin Valley. All that the posses found was a dead campfire here or an abandoned horse and some clothing in another place. Vasquez had been seen; he had just left; he was reported somewhere else. One of his men, Moreno, was caught; it was during this period that Vasquez had stolen Leiva's wife, and the injured husband had told deputies what he knew. But Vasquez remained at large. In December, he and eleven of his men swooped down on the little town of Kingston in Fresno County. Here no less than thirty-five men were tied hand and foot and laid on their faces while the bandits plundered two stores and the hotel, riding off with two thousand dollars in coin besides watches and other jewelry. Now there were rewards posted; by January of 1874 Governor Newton Booth had issued a proclamation offering three thousand dollars for Vasquez' arrest. Later, the amount was jumped to eight thousand. But the depredations continued. Late in February Vasquez and his lieutenant, Chavez, descended on Coyote Hole station and held up the Los Angeles and Owens River stage when it arrived. Next day the two stopped another stage and robbed the passengers of three hundred dollars. Then, for a few weeks, no more was heard of any of them.

This lull gave rise to one of the oddest rumors connected with the entire Vasquez story. The San Francisco *Chronicle* published the yarn, in which a reporter wrote that he had found in the city an old-clothes dealer who declared that on the day before the steamer sailed for Mexico—this was early in March—Vasquez had come to his shop, bought an assortment of women's clothing, warned him to say nothing, and left. The old-clothes man added, though he did not say how he knew, that the bandit had taken the steamer next day, arrayed in the feminine garments he had bought. There was a follow-up, a report that Vasquez had been seen in Guaymas, though the *Chronicle* did not explain how the steamer had made the trip so fast. One man knew better. But he kept quiet. He was Sheriff Harry N. Morse. He had his sources of information and was well aware that Vasquez was still in California. He even had a fairly good idea where he was hiding. More to the point, Governor Booth had got a special appropriation from the Legislature enabling him to supply Morse with funds to organize an expedition.

Those who knew Morse and how he worked were sure that it was only a matter of time.

The reader has learned something of Morse's methodical style. On this new manhunt the sheriff followed his usual careful tactics. From what his sources told him, he was sure that Vasquez had moved into the southern part of the State, but he led his party on a cautious combing of the mountains and valleys all the way down. Later he reported conscientiously that he had kept track of the actual miles covered; between March 12 and the first week of May, Morse and his men had traversed more than twenty-seven hundred miles altogether, searching thoroughly some of the wildest and most difficult country in California.

For almost all that time Vasquez remained quiet. He did make one raid near San Gabriel Mission, tying to a tree a well-to-do sheepman named Repetto and demanding eight hundred dollars in ransom. The incident has special interest because it bears on the much-discussed matter of Vasquez' literacy. Repetto persuaded Tiburcio that he had no money in the house, and offered to write a check. When the bandit looked skeptical, Repetto explained to him that he had money in the bank and offered to read the entries in his bank book. Vasquez interrupted him angrily to say that he was able to read figures, and took the bank book from him, looked at it for a time, and handed it back. In view of the fact that various writers have gone so far as to say that Vasquez, among his more practical accomplishments, possessed talent as a poet, it is worth calling attention to his eagerness to make it clear that he had learned to read numbers. Vasquez was able to write; samples of his careful schoolboy-hand have survived. But it is wholly unlikely that he could compose verse. The story undoubtedly springs from an often-reprinted facsimile of some writing-practice with which Tiburcio whiled away the long months in jail after he was caught. This particular sample of his effort to learn to write a better hand happens to be a copy of a poem. But a man whose pride bristles to the point where he takes time during a robbery to say indignantly that he can read written figures does not seem quite the man to compose the poem Vasquez so painstakingly copied in the San José jail. At all events, Repetto sent his young nephew into Los Angeles with the check. At the bank the boy's evident agitation aroused suspicion. He was questioned and let out the whole story. Once more a posse went out after Vasquez. They came close enough to see him and his men ride furiously up the valley, but that was the end of it. As they were about to give up the chase, they met a well-known Angeleño, Charley Miles, and three of his friends in a buggy. Yes, the four had seen the bandits. In fact they had been stopped by them and relieved of their watches and all the cash they had on them.

Morse did not learn about this until afterward, but he was closing in. His careful, slow progress had assured him that Vasquez was still to the southward, and in the Tehachapis, almost over the ridge into the general region of Los Angeles, the break came. He found a Mexican from whom, "for a consideration" as he put it, he got the information he needed. Vasquez was hiding in Alison Canyon in the Cahuengas, in the adobe house of an unsavory character named George Allen and known as "Greek George." It was his plain, old-fashioned courtesy that robbed Harry Morse of his chance to capture Vasquez right then. For it seemed to him that since he was in the territory of the sheriff of Los Angeles County it would be proper to put the facts before him and make a joint enterprise of it. Leaving his men in the Tejon Pass, Morse rode down into Los Angeles and told Sheriff Rowland what he knew.

It is plain that the sheriff had different notions of courtesy from those entertained by Harry Morse. First he said flatly that he did not believe a word of what Morse told him. Then he appeared to be irritated by Morse's presence in Los Angeles County and gave him to understand that he, Rowland, was competent to handle affairs thereabouts, that he had certain knowledge that Vasquez was not south of the Tehachapi at all but was holed up in the hills whence Morse had just come, and finally that he would be happy if Sheriff Morse would take himself and his men out of Los Angeles County northward again into those same hills where there might be some likelihood of finding the man they were after. There was nothing for Morse to do but assent. He rode back to the Tejon, gathered his party, and went back the way he had come. Sheriff Rowland immediately picked a group of deputies, took care that the press knew what was happening (which accounts for the presence of the San Francisco *Chronicle's* man at the capture), and set out for the house of Greek George. Before they came into sight of the adobe, the party stopped a teamster and arranged with him to drive them, hidden in his wagon, directly up to the house. As they arrived, the deputies jumped from the wagon and surrounded the adobe, and Under-sheriff Johnson went to the door. It was opened by a woman who called a warning and tried to block his way. Johnson thrust her aside in time to see Vasquez leap from a window and run for his horse. Several shots were fired by the men posted outside, but it was Reporter Beers' shotgun blast that stopped Tiburcio. In less than an hour he was snugly lodged in the Los Angeles jail. The criminal career of California's last Mexican bandit-leader had come to its end. A few weeks later the Sacramento papers carried a brief item which informed the public that the State Controller had drawn a warrant for eight thousand dollars in favor of Sheriff Rowland of Los Angeles County for his service in capturing Tiburcio Vasquez.

Because adequate jail facilities were lacking in the area in which Vasquez should have been tried for the murder of Redford and Davidson, a change of venue was obtained to Santa Clara County, and the bandit was remanded to the San José jail, his trial finally being set for January 5, 1875.

San José suited Vasquez very well. Through the press he issued an appeal for funds, urging all his countrymen especially to contribute. A purse was made up, and two excellent lawyers were engaged for the defense. In the months before the trial, his cell was constantly visited by all sorts of people, chiefly women, and he was never without fresh flowers, delicate viands, fine wines, and other tokens; even the most vicious thief and murderer can always find some segment of the population to sympathize with him. In prison he conducted himself circumspectly, diligently practiced his handwriting, held pleasant conversations with his jailers, made gallant remarks to the feminine sensation-seekers who fluttered on the other side of the bars. The day the trial opened, the newspapers reported that the gallery was "filled with ladies representing the elite and respectability of the city," and that Tiburcio "unblushingly directed his glances upon them." Today's student will wonder what the good ladies of San José saw in the little man (he stood barely five feet seven in his boots), with his retreating forehead, his sullen look, and thick mane of coarse black hair. Perhaps his dress impressed them, for during his prison stay he had acquired a soberly elegant outfit. Major Ben Truman described him as "neatly and well garbed, in a black sack coat, white shirt, and narrow-rimmed 'nobby' hat." Truman added, "He has small and well shaped feet, which he encases in fine boots. Perhaps 130 pounds is as much as he weighs." Before the trial he had given newspapermen a statement which he hoped might help him. "I am not as bad a man as I am represented," he said. "I have robbed men, and I have tied them up, but I never shed human blood, and have always advised those with me not to kill or wound those we robbed. I have been persecuted and driven from point to point from year to year. The Americans heaped wrongs upon me in Monterey, and the officers of the law hounded me." The statement is so nearly routine that newspaper readers, even in that less sophisticated time, must have wondered if they had not heard it somewhere before. It failed to affect the jury. A former Judge named Collins, who presented the closing argument for the defense, did his all-out best in the florid oratorical style of the period. He made much of the fact that witnesses are sometimes unreliable, and that at least some of those called by the prosecution had cause for private grudges against his client. Before he was finished, he had brought in Ulysses and Penelope, had referred somewhat cloudily to Blennerhasset and Aaron Burr, and had reminded the jury that the

Lord did not smite Cain dead but had merely set a mark
upon his forehead. (One wonders about this reference to
Biblical murder when the defense had all along been
claiming that their client had murdered no one anywhere
at any time.) Somehow, too, the pearly gates got into
the speech, along with the snow-clad Sierra and the orange-
groves of Los Angeles, and Collins quoted Whittier at
considerable length. In closing, he sketched a clear if
grisly picture of the District Attorney, "howling for revenge . . . standing under a great black cloud of prejudice . . . a law officer of the State who, not content
with justice, holds before you a cup and says, 'Fill it with
blood! Fill it with blood! Here is the Golden Bowl, break
it! Here is the Silver Pitcher, crush it!'" One reporter
who chose to watch Vasquez instead of listening to the
lawyer's poetic flights, wrote acidly, "The prisoner appeared as pleased as a monkey at the present of a tin
trumpet!"

The jury's deliberations were brief. They returned a
verdict of guilty and Foreman Reynolds added that they
assigned the death penalty. On January 23, two weeks
after the verdict, Judge Belden told Tiburcio Vasquez
that his life had been "one unbroken record of lawlessness and outrage, a career of pillage and murder," and
that his name was "a synonym for all that was wicked
and infamous," and sentenced him to hang on March 19.
In view of the Judge's remarks, it is interesting to note
the deliberate invention of a later sentimental writer to
the effect that "Even the judge who sentenced Vasquez
stated that he did not believe him guilty."

The two months intervening were enlivened by one
episode that gave the citizens of Hollister something to

think about. Vasquez' lieutenant, Chavez, dropped a message into the Wells, Fargo Express letter-box there. It was a rambling, pompous communication, the gist of which was that Chavez himself had been in command at the time of the Tres Pinos murders and that therefore Vasquez was not responsible, and that "if Vasquez is hanged by his enemies, I will show you I know how to avenge the death of my captain." The letter concluded, "You will have to suffer as in the time of Joaquin Murieta; the just and the unjust alike will be reached by my revenge." Some, at the time, thought the letter a fraud, and it may have been.

As a matter of fact, an appeal had been taken; Vasquez' lawyers did their honest best. When the Supreme Court of the State denied it, certain soft-hearted persons took the opportunity to deplore, in letters to the papers, the absence of the quality of mercy in the Justices' hearts. The editor of the San José *Mercury* had his own opinion on that point and expressed it forcibly. He wrote, "As long as Vasquez, the ordinary, cowardly highway assassin and robber, was at large, the cry was 'Down with him!' Now a vulgar sentiment discloses itself, commiserating the robber, and 'Oh-poor-fellowing' him for a sort of bloody, bold and resolute hero of a delightful romance. This sentiment, we believe, will tend to dissipate toward the region of Tres Pinos."

It was March 12 when the news came that the appeal had been denied, and Sheriff Adams of Santa Clara County began his preparations. San José had no gallows; the sheriff borrowed one from the Sacramento authorities. Three robbers and murderers had already been hanged on it. He had his invitations printed, too:

Sheriff's Office
County of Santa Clara
San José, March 16, 1875

To ——;

Sir:—Pursuant to the statute in such cases, you are hereby invited to be present at the execution of Tiburcio Vasquez at the jail of said county, in San José, on the 19th day of March, A.D. 1875, at 1 :30 p.m.

J. H. ADAMS, Sheriff

*Present at Jail Entrance*          *Not Transferable*

There were rumors of a last-minute rescue, but these died down; perhaps the citizens of San José liked the momentary thrill of imagining such a thing might happen, but it is doubtful if anyone took the whispers seriously and in fact no attempt at rescue was made.

The gallows was set up in the yard of the jail. For some time Vasquez had refused to talk to a local priest, Father Serda. Now, aware that he was doomed, Tiburcio permitted the priest to visit him, and they held quiet conversations each day. On March 18, Vasquez dictated two messages. (Sheriff Adams is authority for the fact that these were dictated and not written by the bandit.) One began with an admonition "To the Fathers and Mothers of Children," urging them to keep their offspring "aloof, as far as is in the nature of things possible, from the degrading companionship of the immoral and the vicious." (The reader will detect in this phrasing the influence of Father Serda.) It went on to ask pardon "from each and every one whom I have in any way injured," and to solicit the "prayers of all good Christian people." Vasquez then thanked the lawyers who had defended him, expressed gratitude to all the prison officials (here the sheriff un-

doubtedly had a hand in things), added a word of affection
for his sisters, and finished with what may very well have
been the bandit's only actual contribution in words: "Farewell! The end has come!"

The second message was addressed to his former associates and sounds a good deal more like Vasquez himself.
It reminds them that even under pressure their leader had
not turned state's evidence against any of them, suggests
that they forget the threats of revenge some of them had
made, and concludes by advising them all to take warning
from his fate and change their course while they may.
Both letters were witnessed by eight persons, including the
sheriff, Vasquez' lawyers, and George A. Beers, the ubiquitous *Chronicle* reporter. Beers added a final dash of
grue to his picture of this last group-scene in the condemned man's cell. Wrote the reporter, who understood
the titillating details his readers liked, "Vasquez then
asked to see his coffin, and it was brought to the jail by the
undertakers. Vasquez examined the satin lining, pressed
the cushions, and remarked, 'I can sleep here forever very
well!'"

The reader is at liberty to consider this a feature-writer's
fiction if he likes. But Beers did not invent the telegram
that was delivered as the coffin was being carried away.
It came from a man described by the newspapers as "the
sensational revivalist, the Rev. E. P. Hammond, now
'starring it' in San Francisco," and it read: "Dear Vasquez:
God bless you. Trust in Jesus. He will be with you and
love you. I shall continue to pray for you. Yours, E. P.
Hammond." When it was read to him, Vasquez smiled,
pointed upward, and said, "Yes, I know." Then he told
Sheriff Adams' son who remained with him as guard that

he was not sleepy, and talked for twenty-five minutes or
so. It was apparently to young Adams that he made a
remark widely repeated at the time—the reply, when
asked if he believed in a life after death, "I hope so, for
in that case tomorrow I shall see all my old sweethearts
together!" About midnight he fell into a sound slumber.
He woke again at two in the morning, drank a glass of
wine, and smoked a cigar and then, according to his guard,
slept soundly for the rest of the night.

Father Serda was with him early next morning, and
no visitors excepting relatives were permitted. Outside,
the crowd began to gather early, and by one in the afternoon the streets on all sides were jammed, reporters noting
that bets were made on whether the outlaw would "die
game."

At twenty minutes past one, Sheriff Adams read the
death warrant to Vasquez in his cell; the process was too
long for the scaffold since the text was translated, sentence
by sentence, as the sheriff read. Tiburcio showed no emotion, and when he had finished the sheriff said "Vasquez,
the time has come!" The procession began, two deputies
leading, and then the condemned man, Adams on one side
and Father Serda on the other holding him by the arms.
Vasquez carried a small crucifix before him and looked
fixedly at it all the way, even as he mounted the steps to the
gallows. As he stood on the drop, a white robe was thrown
over his shoulders and those who were close said that
Tiburcio made his responses to the priest's words in a
calm, distinct tone, showing no agitation. Earlier he had
asked if he might make a speech from the scaffold, but
this had been refused, and some thought he might attempt
to speak at the last minute. He remained silent, removing

the robe and then his coat at the sheriff's order, and taking off his collar so that the rope might be adjusted. A deputy pinioned him rapidly, arms behind him with a strap at the elbows and another at the wrists, the latter buckled to three more tight bands of leather at hips, knees, and ankles. When the last buckle was fastened, Tiburcio had one word to say—"*Pronto!*" It was his last. The trap was sprung at 1:35 P.M., and Doctors Todd of San Francisco and Coney, Brown, and Thorne of San José noted that the heart stopped in six and a half minutes, and that life was extinct at 1:47. The body was allowed to hang for twenty-five minutes longer and was then cut down and delivered to the relatives. Until March 23, the remains of the bandit lay at Santa Clara near by, the editor of the San José *Patriot* noting that the face "was whitened up by some process, and looked very natural." On the morning of the 23rd, the corpse was taken to the Catholic church and a solemn High Mass was said for the repose of the dead. It was then returned to a cousin's house where it remained until two in the afternoon, when a brief burial service was held in the Catholic cemetery at Santa Clara. Presumably the *Patriot's* editor had no objections to Vasquez' interment, but he made very plain his views concerning the curious observers who streamed in and out of the house where the outlaw's body had lain. "The corpse," he wrote indignantly, "lay in state as though it had been the remains of a noble martyr!"

But by the time the funeral took place vulgar curiosity had apparently been satisfied. The writer sent down by the San Francisco *Alta* to cover the event found no excitement among the people; citizens went about their everyday affairs as usual. He watched the interment, observing that few except immediate relatives accompanied the coffin to the graveyard. And he wrote Tiburcio Vasquez off, finally and completely, in the sentence with which he ended his story on the burial of the man who had terrorized the State for twenty years. He could not have foreseen that there would arise a cult of romantics whose semi-fictions would substitute for the small, swarthy, shock-headed, lady-killing murderer and thief a Gallant Bandit-Captain, smiling and debonair, kind to the poor and hard on the rich, just in his dealings and a champion of justice, unfairly executed, and followed by weeping thousands to his grave. Lacking a crystal ball which would tell him these things, the reporter closed his story with a plain, simple statement of fact as he had seen it. "Never before," he wrote, "in the annals of criminal jurisprudence among our people, has such a feeling of utter indifference prevailed."

# NOTES ON SOURCES

In a book of this kind, in which the chief effort is to straighten out confusions that have found their way into print, and to make plain in what respects long-credited legends have deviated from the facts as these can be ascertained, the author must decide which of two courses to take when it comes to providing bibliographical notes. One way would be to set down, as in the notes for a doctoral dissertation for example, the exact and detailed record of every source examined. The other is to note briefly the general nature of those sources and let it go at that. Since this is a book for the general reader, to record all sources consulted would be aside from the purpose. To do this would run to dozens of pages in small type and would constitute a parade of scholarly apparatus to no good end. It is enough, I believe, to indicate the nature of the material in a general way, so that those interested in pursuing the subject further may have some idea of how best to go at it.

Primary sources are the records of San Quentin and Folsom Prisons in California, the carefully preserved files of Wells, Fargo & Company, the scrapbooks and printed memoirs of such important peace officers as the late James B. Hume and Harry N. Morse, and documents, diaries, and letters by the hundreds which are available in such collections as those of the Bancroft Library at the University of California in Berkeley, the Huntington Library in San Marino, the California Historical Society, the Society of California Pioneers, and the Native Sons of the Golden West, all in San Francisco, and the California State Library in Sacramento.

Next in importance are the newspaper files for the period concerned—the San Francisco and Los Angeles papers for their detailed coverage of the better known cases and criminals, and especially the papers of the smaller California cities, from 1850 to the late 1880s, for their intimate, informal reporting of what came under their editors' jurisdiction. Along with such papers as the San Francisco *Alta, Chronicle, Bulletin, Call,* and *Examiner,* go a few other newspapers of statewide importance in their time—the Sacramento *Union,* for example, the Santa Barbara *Press,* and the San José *Mercury.* Even more useful for their close attention to crimes that occurred in their territory and especially for the free-and-easy editorializing their reporters were encouraged to do in news stories—a practice now frowned upon for good reasons, perhaps, but one which is extraordinarily helpful at from fifty to a hundred years' distance—are such papers as the Amador *Sentinel,* the Marysville *Express,* the San Joaquin *Republican,* the Calaveras *Chronicle* and *Weekly Citizen,* the Stockton *Argus* the San Andreas *Independent,* the Sonora *Union-Democrat,* the Santa Cruz *Daily Echo,* the Shasta *Courier,* the Tehama *Democrat,* and dozens more, ranging from Redding in the north down through Grass Valley and Nevada City, Auburn, Placerville, Jackson, Angels Camp, Columbia, Sonora, Mariposa, and Merced in the southern mines, and also those of many valley cities and towns, especially in the time of such latter-day outlaws as Black Bart and Tiburcio Vasquez.

In addition to newspapers many magazines have contributed their bit to this piecing-together of facts, though in general the old magazines—almost all now out of existence—have been useful mainly for their perpetuation and encouragement of legend as opposed to fact. The California *Police Gazette* is mentioned in the text of the Murieta chapter. Western magazines which, doubtless with the best of intentions, printed almost entirely the inventions of rewrite experts and sensational feature-writers were *The Overland Monthly, The Argonaut, Land of Sunshine, Sunset Magazine* (long since become quite another kind of periodical), Hutchings *California Magazine, Out West,* and others. While these magazines printed little in the way of verifiable fact and a great deal in the way of romantic nonsense, they are invaluable in the step-by-step tracing of the development of such legends as those about Murieta and Black Bart particularly.

Beyond the sources mentioned, the various California county histories, many published in the 1880s by Thompson & West of Oakland, contributed greatly to the task of digging out the truth and comparing fact with fiction. In most cases the county historians—often anonymous—were content to repeat whatever stories happened to come their way, but now and then the writer of one of those volumes was a careful and conscientious worker with enough sense of history to consider the romancing that had already been done and painstakingly deny it, chapter and verse, sometimes even providing useful contrary proofs. Even those who were content with repeating the old stories, however, were of some help, for such repetitions are often clues to the age and the degree of distribution of this or that portion of the built-up fairy-tale.

As for books consulted for general background, to list these would be to list most of the outstanding works on California's history. A search such as this can and does lead almost anywhere. It would not appear at first glance, for example, that a volume on the California Missions would be a likely reference work for a study of this character. Yet the story that Joaquin Murieta's portrait had been painted by "a young priest at the Mission in Carmel in the spring of 1853" made it necessary to refer to Fr. Zephyrin Englehardt's *Mission San Carlos Borromeo* in order to find, in his painstakingly exact record, the names of the priests in residence there at the time. One can think of few more unlikely books than the Dale-Littleton *Cherokee Cavaliers* as a reference in an examination into the subject of California bandits, yet it was in that compilation of papers relating to the Cherokee Nation that I discovered the letter of part-Cherokee John Rollin Ridge to his Indian cousin, and turned up the long-missing clue to why Ridge's first *Life of Murieta* is so scarce today. H. H. Bancroft's *History of California* and Theodore Hittell's work on the same subject are, naturally, standard reference books in the field; both were of value here, Bancroft's because it gave currency to the Murieta legend by repeating Ridge's fiction quite uncritically, Hittell's because the author noted the unreliability of all the Murieta stories and quoted Ridge by name and with due warning. On the question of the methods used by American miners to make it uncomfortable for foreigners, Charles Howard Shinn's *Mining Camps; A Study in Frontier Government* and Josiah Royce's *California* were valuable, as were Rodman Paul's recent *California Gold* and, on the origins of the Murieta legend, Franklin Walker's *San Francisco's Literary Frontier,* my indebtedness to which I have acknowledged elsewhere in this book.

Actually, moreover, aside from material in the newspapers of the time, in Express Company records and the prison-books, very little that is trustworthy has been printed. And both magazine and newspaper articles of the last quarter-century or thereabouts are almost wholly useless excepting to provide clues which will send the student to the reports of the time itself. For instance, almost nothing that has been written since 1900 about Black Bart, that most delightful—and most incredibly successful—of highwaymen, contains more than a bare speck or two of truth. To get at the facts it was necessary to start from scratch with the Wells, Fargo reports, circulars, reward-posters, and, finally, Hume's and Morse's memoirs. A newspaper article printed in 1935 provided a tantalizing glimpse of Sheet-Iron Jack, but neglected to mention his true name or even the decade of his career in crime; it was only after a careful search through Wells, Fargo's Robber's Record that he was pinned down as John Allen. After that, the San Quentin Prison record showed the dates of the terms he served and the county from which he was committed. With those clues it was possible to dig out his story, piece by piece, in the files of the newspapers which reported his crimes as they were committed. And so on.

What it comes down to, then, is that you find the truth about men like Murieta and Bart, Tom Bell and Rattlesnake Dick, Jack Powers, Tiburcio Vasquez and the rest, only by going to original sources and then exercising your wits as nearly in the manner of Mr. Sherlock Holmes as you are able. When you have done all you can, you are still painfully aware that there are holes in your account. Who fired the shot that wounded Rattlesnake Dick's horse? Some day someone may find out. Did Dick Fellows actually attend Harvard, and if he did under what name? Maybe some student of the future will come up with the answer. Most fascinating puzzle of all, because it concerns the greatest of the California stage-robbers, a man about whom it has been possible to verify so much, what really became of Black Bart, the PO8? Possibly one day that question will be answered too. Meantime the pursuit of the truth and the legends about these once-famous men of the road—and distinguishing between the two as far as possible—has been a pleasant and often absorbing task.

# APPENDIX I

Apropos the Murieta legend and the way in which the original fiction by John Rollin Ridge, published in 1854, was copied, pirated, rewritten, and imitated—such piratings for years having been taken by the innocent reader as new and "authentic" histories of the shadowy Murieta's career—it may be instructive to examine a few parallel accounts of Murieta's beginnings here reprinted from some of the different accounts of his life, each in its time, of course, put forward as an original and reliable work.

First, Ridge's own description of Joaquin Murieta, the boy, before he came to California:

"Joaquin Murieta was a Mexican of good blood, born in the province of Sonora, of respectable parents, and educated to a degree sufficient for the common purposes of life in the schools of his native country. While growing up, he was remarkable for a very mild and peaceable disposition, and gave no sign of that indomitable and daring spirit which afterward characterized him. Those who knew him in his school-boy days speak affectionately of his generous and noble nature at that period of his life, and can scarcely credit the fact that the renowned and bloody bandit of California was one and the same being."

Now the description of Murieta as a boy, as it appears in the San Francisco *Police Gazette's* version, published in 1859 without credit to Ridge, as an original *Life* of the bandit:

"Joaquin was born of respectable parents in Sonora, Mexico, where he received a good education, and while growing up was remarkable for a very mild and peaceful disposition, giving no sign of that daring and indomitable spirit which subsequently characterized him. Those who knew him in his school-boy days, speak affectionately of his noble and generous nature, at that period of his life, and can scarcely credit the fact that the renowned and bloody bandit of California was one and the same being."

In 1865, in De Witt's Fifteen Cent Library, there was published *Joaquin: The Claude Duval of California* (later issued by the Echo Series as *Joaquin: The Marauder of the Mines*), declared to be a "faithful narrative" of the deeds of Murieta. Here is the De Witt idea, considerably condensed (note the gratuitous phrase of anti-Catholic bias), of Joaquin's youth:

"He was born in Sonora's capital, in Mexico, of a family respectable enough, and sufficiently well off to give him a good education, as education went in that priest-ridden country. He was noticeable during his youth for the gentlest and most placid of natures; everybody who knew him in those days speaking rapturously of his then noble and generous spirit."

In the 1920s and 1930s (there are several editions and evidently more than one publisher used the same plates) there was published in Chicago a *Life and Adventures of the Celebrated Bandit, Joaquin Murieta,* translated from the Spanish of one Ireneo Paz by Francis P. Belle. The translator evidently had no knowledge of earlier sources or of the stages through which the Paz version had passed, but the reader here will be interested to see how closely the passage below, after undergoing translation and re-translation, corresponds to the original:

"Joaquin Murieta was born in the Republic of the United States of Mexico. His family, highly respectable people of Sonora, brought him up in his native town where he received a finished education. During his childhood he was remarkable for his sweet and gentle disposition. There was nothing in him then to indicate that daring, unconquerable disposition which made him so celebrated later. All who knew him in his youth spoke affectionately of his good, noble and generous nature. They were hardly able to believe that the terrible adventurer of California whom we are going to portray could be the same kind, pleasant, Joaquin Murieta whom they knew."

These brief examples might be multiplied into hundreds, all showing the same thing—that wherever and however one finds an account of Murieta's "life," the "facts" in it may be traced to their source in John Rollin Ridge's story of 1854, a yarn filled with such obviously demonstrable fictions as the recording of private conversations between the leader and his men, the bandit's own meditations, and so on.

For further knowledge of Ridge himself, and for some highly interesting speculations concerning his hidden motives for writing the Murieta story as he did, the interested reader is referred to Franklin Walker's *San Francisco's Literary Frontier* (New York: 1939), in which will also be found some observations about Ridge's story of the public whipping of Murieta and an account of a similar occurrence in the *Shirley Letters* (San Francisco, 1933). Mr. Walker drops the matter there, but it is worth noting, I believe, that Ridge could easily have read the Shirley material in proof in the office of Ferdinand Ewer, whose *Pioneer* was publishing the *Letters* serially at precisely the time when Ridge was at work on his *Life* of Murieta. It is my own view that Ridge did indeed see the Shirley material, and that he appropriated the whipping incident in the *Letters* as ideal for the purpose of showing why his Joaquin's "mild and peaceable disposition" was so signally and so suddenly changed. A final parallel will show one reason why I believe this.

Here is Dame Shirley's young "Spaniard" after the lashing he received in Rich Bar:

"He swore a most solemn oath that he would murder every American that he should chance to meet alone."

And here is Ridge's Joaquin Murieta after he was, according to Ridge's story, publicly whipped in Murphy's Diggings:

"He swore an oath of the most awful solemnity that his soul should never know peace until his hands were dyed deep in the blood of his enemies!"

# APPENDIX II

The following list of Black Bart's stage-robberies is taken from Wells, Fargo's confidential circular, issued in the fall of 1888 after Bart had served his San Quentin term, had been discharged, and had disappeared. Two lone-bandit holdups led James B. Hume, Wells, Fargo's Special Officer, to suspect that Bart might be involved, and he brought out a circular containing a full description of Bart, his picture, and the list of stage-robberies he had acknowledged as his. Agents were instructed not to post the circular publicly but simply to keep an eye out for Bart, and if they identified him to report immediately to Hume. The fact that this circular was issued, by the way, is the best evidence that there is no truth in the legend that Wells, Fargo & Company paid Black Bart a "subsidy" to refrain from robbing their stages after he was discharged from State's Prison. If Bart had been collecting such a subsidy or wage, it would hardly have been necessary to print a circular of this kind; the Company would have had to know the whereabouts of a man to whom it was paying out regular sums of money.

(Note: It was not until the fourth holdup listed below that "Black Bart," as such, actually came into existence. It was after this robbery of the stage between Point Arenas and Duncan's Mills that the first piece of doggerel signed "Black Bart, the PO-8" was left in the ransacked treasure-chest.)

### Complete List of Stage Robberies
### Committed by Black Bart

*1.* Stage from Sonora to Milton, July 26th, 1875, 4 miles from Copperopolis.—John Shine, driver.

*2.* Stage from San Juan to Marysville, December 28th, 1875, 10 miles from San Juan.—Mike Hogan, driver.

*3.* Stage from Roseburg to Yreka, June 2d, 1876, 5 miles from Cottonwood.—A. C. Adams, driver.

*4.* Stage from Point Arenas to Duncan's Mills, August 3d, 1877, between Fort Ross and Russian River.

5. Stage from Quincy to Oroville, July 25th, 1878, 1 mile from Berry Creek.

6. Stage from Laporte to Oroville, July 30th, 1878, 5 miles from Laporte. —D. E. Barry, driver.

7. Stage from Cahto to Ukiah, October 2d, 1878, 12 miles from Ukiah.

8. Stage from Covelo to Ukiah, October 3d, 1878, 10 miles from Potter Valley.

9. Stage from Laporte to Oroville, June 21st, 1879, 3 miles from Forbestown.—Dave Quadlin, driver.

10. Stage from Roseburg to Redding, October 25th, 1879, 2 miles from Bass Station.

11. Stage from Alturas to Redding, October 27th, 1879, 12 miles above Millville.

12. Stage from Point Arenas to Duncan's Mills, July 22d, 1880, 2½ miles from Henry's Station. M. K. McLennan, driver. Mr. W. J. Turner and wife, of San Francisco, passengers.

13. Stage from Weaverville to Redding, September 1st, 1880, 1 mile from Last Chance.—Charles Cramer, driver. Took breakfast next morning at Mr. Adkinson's on Eagle Creek.

14. Stage from Roseburg to Yreka, September 16th, 1880, 1 mile from Oregon State Line.—Nort Eddings, driver.

15. Stage from Redding to Roseburg, November 20th, 1880, 1 mile from Oregon State Line. Joe Mason, driver.

16. Stage from Roseburg to Yreka, August 31st, 1881, 9½ miles from Yreka.—John Lulloway, driver.

17. Stage from Yreka to Redding, October 8th, 1881, 3 miles from Bass Station.—Horace Williams, driver.

18. Stage from Lakeview to Redding, October 11th, 1881, 2 miles from Round Mountain Post-office. Louis Brewster, driver.

19. Stage from Downieville to Marysville, December 15th, 1881, 4 miles from Dobbin's Ranch. George Sharpe, driver.

20. Stage from North San Juan to Smartesville, December 27th, 1881.

21. Stage from Ukiah to Cloverdale, January 26th, 1882, 6 miles from Cloverdale.—Harry Forse, driver.

22. Stage from Little Lake to Ukiah, June 14th, 1882, 3 miles from Little Lake.—Thomas B. Forse, driver.

23. Attempt to rob stage from Laporte to Oroville, July 13th, 1882, 9 miles from Strawberry. George Helms, driver. Geo. W. Hackett, Wells, Fargo & Co's messenger, fired at robber and put him to flight.

24. Stage from Yreka to Redding, September 17th, 1882, 14 miles from Redding.—Horace Williams, driver.

25. Stage from Lakeport to Cloverdale, November 24th, 1882, 6 miles from Cloverdale.—Ed. Crawford, driver.

26. Stage from Lakeport to Cloverdale, April 12th, 1883, 5 miles from Cloverdale.—Connibeck, driver.

27. Stage from Jackson to Ione City, June 23d, 1883, 4 miles from Jackson.—Clint Radcliffe, driver.

[*In all the above mentioned robberies, he also robbed the U. S. Mail.*]

28. Stage from Sonora to Milton, November 3d, 1883, 3 miles from Copperopolis.—R. E. McConnell, driver.

# INDEX